Richard Price

Two Tracts on Civil Liberty

The war with America, and the debts and finances of the kingdom; with a general

introduction and supplement

Richard Price

Two Tracts on Civil Liberty
*The war with America, and the debts and finances of the kingdom; with a general
introduction and supplement*

ISBN/EAN: 9783337245528

Printed in Europe, USA, Canada, Australia, Japan

Cover: Foto ©ninafisch / pixelio.de

More available books at **www.hansebooks.com**

TWO TRACTS

ON

CIVIL LIBERTY,

THE

WAR WITH AMERICA,

AND

THE DEBTS AND FINANCES OF
THE KINGDOM:

WITH

A GENERAL INTRODUCTION and
SUPPLEMENT.

By RICHARD PRICE, D.D. F.R.S.

LONDON:
Printed for T. CADELL, in the STRAND.
MDCCLXXVIII.

GENERAL INTRODUCTION.

THE first of the following tracts was published in the beginning of the year 1776;
and the second in the beginning of last year.
They are now offered to the public in one volume,
with corrections and additions. All the calculations, in the *Appendix* to the first tract, have been
transferred to the *second* and *fourth* sections, in the
third part of the second tract.

The section on PUBLIC LOANS, in the second
tract, has been revised with care; and a *supplement* to it, containing additional proposals and
some necessary explanations, has been given at the
end of the whole.——This is a subject to which
I have applied (perhaps too unprofitably) much
of my attention. I have now done with it; and
the whole is referred to the candid examination
of those who may be better informed, hoping
for their indulgence should they find that, in any
instance, I have been mistaken. I have not meant,
in any thing I have said on this subject, to censure
any persons. That accumulation of artificial debt
which I have pointed out, and by which the danger of the kingdom from its growing burdens

A .   has

has been fo needlefsly increafed, has, I doubt not, been the effect of inattention in our minifters; and the fcheme, by which the loan of laft year has been procured, gives reafon to hope that better plans of borrowing will be adopted for the future.

The principal defign of the firft part of the fecond tract was (as I have obferved in the introduction to it) to remove the mifapprehenfions of my fentiments on CIVIL LIBERTY AND GOVERNMENT into which fome had fallen. It gives me concern to find that it has not anfwered that end in the degree I wifhed. I am ftill charged with maintaining opinions which tend to fubvert all civil authority. I paid little regard to this charge, while it was confined to the advocates for the principles which have produced the prefent war; but as it feems lately to have been given the public from the authority of a writer of the firft character, (a) it is impoffible I fhould not be impreffed by it; and I find myfelf under a neceffity of taking farther notice of it.

There are two accounts, directly oppofite to one another, which have been given of the origin of civil government. One of them is, that " civil government is an expedient contrived by

(a) See Mr. *Burke's* Letter to the Sheriffs of *Briftol*, page 53, 54.

4

" human

" human prudence for gaining fecurity againft
" oppreffion ; and that, confequently, the power
" of civil governors is a delegation or truft from
" the people for accomplifhing this end."

The other account is, that " civil government
" is an ordinance of the Deity, by which the
" body of mankind are given up to the will of a
" few ; and, confequently, that it is a truft from
" the Deity, in the exercife of which civil go-
" vernors are accountable only to him."

The queftion " which of thefe accounts we ought
" to receive," is important in the higheft degree.
There is no queftion which more deeply affects
the happinefs and dignity of man as a citizen of this world.——If the former account is
right, the people (that is, the body of independent agents) in every community are their
own legiflators. All civil authority is properly
their authority. Civil governors are only public
fervants ; and their power, being *delegated*, is by
its nature *limited*.——On the contrary. If the latter account is right, the people have nothing to
do with their own government. They are placed
by their maker in the fituation of cattle on an
eftate, which the owner has a right to difpofe of
as he pleafes. Civil Governors are a body of
mafters ; and their power is a commiffion from
·Heaven held by divine right, and unbounded in
its extent.

A 2   I have

I have efpoufed, with fome zeal, the firft of thefe accounts ; and in the following tracts, endeavoured to explain and defend it. And this is *all* I have done to give countenance to the charge I have mentioned.——Even the mafterly writer who, after a croud of writers infinitely his inferiors, feems to have taken up this accufation againft me, often expreffes himfelf as if he had adopted the fame idea of government (*a*). Such indeed is my opinion of his good fenfe, and fuch has been the zeal which he has difcovered for the rights of mankind, that I think it fcarcely poffible his ideas and mine on this fubject fhould be very different. His language, however, fometimes puzzles me; and, particularly, when he intimates that government is an inftitution of divine authority ; (*b*) when he fcouts all difcuffions of the nature of civil liberty, the foundation of civil rights, and the principles of free government; and when he afferts the *competence* of our legiflature to revive the *High-Commiffion Court* and *Star-Chamber*, and its BOUNDLESS

AUTHO-

(*a*) " To follow, not to force the public inclination ; to " give a direction, a form, a technical drefs and a fpecific " fanction to the general fenfe of the community, is the " true end of legiflature. When it goes beyond this, its " authority will be precarious, let its rights be what they " will." Letter to the Sheriffs of Briftol, p. 49.

(*b*) Ibid. p. 55. Thoughts on the caufes of the prefent difcontents, p. 67, " Government certainly, is an inftitution

AUTHORITY not only over the people of *Britain*, but over diftant communities who have no voice in it.

But

" of divine authority ; though its *forms* and the *perfons* who " adminifter it, all originate from the people." It is probable that Mr. *Burke* means only that government is a divine inftitution, in the fame fenfe in which any other expedient of human prudence for gaining protection againft injury, may be called a Divine inftitution. All that we owe *immediately* to our own forefight and induftry, muft *ultimately* be afcribed to God the giver of all our powers, and the caufe of all caufes. It is in this fenfe that St. Paul in Rom. xiii. 1, 2. calls civil magiftracy the *ordinance of God*, and fays that *there is no power but of God*. If any one wants to be convinced of this, he fhould read the excellent bifhop HOADLY's Sermon entitled *The Meafures of Submiffion to the civil Magiftrate*, and the defences of it.

It is further probable, that when Mr. *Burke* afferts the *omnipotence* of Parliaments, or their *competence* to eftablifh any oppreffions (Letter, p. 46, 49) he means mere *power* abftracted from *right*, or the fame fort of *power* and *competence* that truftees have to betray their truft, or that armed ruffians have to rob and murder. Nor fhould I doubt whether this is his meaning, were it not for the paffage I have quoted from him in the laft page, the latter part of which feems to imply, that a legiflature may contradict its *end*, and yet retain its *rights*.——Some of the jufteft remarks on this fubject may be found in the Earl of ABINGDON's thoughts on Mr. *Burke*'s letter, a pamphlet which (on account of the excellent public principles it maintains, and the fpirit of liberty it breathes, as well as the rank of the writer) muft give to every friend to the true interefts of this country particular pleafure.

In

But whatever may be Mr. BURKE's sentiments on this subject, he cannot possibly think of the-

In p. 46, Mr. *Burke* says, that " if there is one man in " the world more zealous than another for the supremacy of " parliament and the rights of this imperial crown, it is " himself; though many may be more knowing in the ex- " tent and the foundation of these rights." He adds, that " he has constantly declined such disquisitions, not " being qualified for the chair of a professor in metaphysics, " and not chusing to put the solid interests of the kingdom " on speculative grounds."———*The less knowledge, the more zeal,* is a maxim which experience has dreadfully veri- fied in *religion.* But he that, in the present case, should apply this maxim to Mr. *Burke,* would, whatever he may say of him- self, greatly injure him. Though he chuses to decry enquiries into the nature of liberty, there are, I am persuaded, few in the world whose zeal for it is more united to extensive knowledge and an exalted understanding.———He calls it, p. 55. " the vital spring and energy of a state, and a blessing " of the first order." He cannot, therefore, think that too much pains may be taken to UNDERSTAND it. He must know, that nothing but usurpation and error can suffer by enquiry and discussion.

Mr. WILKES, in an excellent speech which he lately made in moving for the repeal of the declaratory law, observed, that this law was a *compromise* to which the great men, under whose administration it was passed, were forced in order to obtain the repeal of the *Stamp-act.* I think so highly of that administration and of the service it did the public, that I have little doubt of the truth of this observation. But, at the same time, I cannot help wishing Mr. *Burke* had given no reason for doubt by defending the *principle* of that act; a *principle* which, unquestionably, he and his friends would never have acted upon; but which others have since acted upon, with a violence which has brought us to the brink of ruin.

former

former account of government that " it is a " fpeculation which deſtroys all authority."—Both accounts eſtabliſh an authority. The difference is, that one derives it from the *people*, and makes it a *limited* authority; and the other derives it from *Heaven*; and makes it *unlimited*.——I have repeatedly declared my admiration of ſuch a conſtitution of government as our own would be, were the Houſe of Commons a fair repreſenta-tion of the kingdom, and under no undue influ-ence.——The ſum of all I have meant to main-tain is, " that LEGITIMATE ·GOVERNMENT, as " oppoſed to OPPRESSION and TYRANNY, con-" fiſts in the dominion of equal laws made with " common conſent, or of men over *themſelves*; " and not in the dominion of communities over " communities, or of any men over other men." Introduction to the ſecond Tract, p. 9.——How then can it be pretended, that I have aimed at deſtroying all authority? Does our own conſti-tution deſtroy all authority? Is the authority of equal laws made with common conſent no autho-rity? Muſt there be no government in a ſtate that governs itſelf? Or, muſt an inſtitution, con-trived by the united counſels of the members of a community, for reſtraining licentiouſneſs and gaining ſecurity againſt injury and violence, *en-courage* licentiouſneſs, and give to every one a power to commit what outrages he pleaſes?

The

The Archbifhop of York, (in a fermon preached before the fociety for propagating the gofpel in foreign parts, Feb. 21, 1777,) has taken notice of fome loofe opinions, as he calls them, which have been lately current on civil liberty ; fome who mean delinquency having given accounts of it " by " which every man's humour is made to be the " rule of his obedience, all the bad paffions are " let loofe, and thofe dear interefts abandoned " to outrage for the protection of which we truft " in law," 4to edit. p. 15 and 16. It is not difficult to guefs at one of the delinquents intended in thefe words. In oppofition to the horrid fentiments of liberty which they defcribe, but which in reality no man in his fenfes ever entertained, the Archbifhop defines it to be fimply, the fupremacy of law, or GOVERNMENT by LAW, without adding to *law*, as I had done, the words *equal* and *made with common confent* ; (*a*) and without oppofing a GOVERNMENT by LAW to a GOVERNMENT BY MEN, as others had done.——Ac-

(*a*) In p. 19. he calls liberty " a freedom from all re-" ftraints except fuch as eftablifhed law impofes for THE " GOOD OF THE COMMUNITY." But this addition can make no difference of any confequence, as long as it is not fpecified *where* the power is lodged of judging what laws are for the good of the community. In countries where the *laws* are the *edicts* of abfolute princes, the end profeffed is always the good of the Community.

cording

cording to him, therefore, the supremacy of law must be liberty, whatever the law is, or whoever makes it.——In despotic countries government by law is the same with government by the will of one man, which HOOKER has called *the misery of all men*; but, according to this definition, it is liberty.——In ENGLAND *formerly*, the law consigned to the flames all who denied certain established points of faith. Even *now*, it subjects to fines, imprisonment and banishment all teachers of religion who have not subscribed the doctrinal articles of the church of England; and the good Archbishop, not thinking the law in this case sufficiently rigorous, has proposed putting Protestant Dissenters under the same restraints with the Papists. (*a*) And should this be done,

---

(*a*) " The laws against Papists have been extremely severe. " New dangers may arise; and if at any time ANOTHER " DENOMINATION of men should be equally dangerous to " our civil interests, it would be justifiable to lay them " under similar restraints." Page 17.——In another part of this sermon the great men in opposition (some of the first in the kingdom in respect of rank, ability, and virtue) are described as a body of men void of principle, who, without regarding the relation in which they stand to the community, have entered into a league for advancing their private interest; and " who " are held together by the same bond that keeps together " the lowest and wickedest combinations."——Was there ever such a censure delivered from a pulpit? What wonder is

done, if done by *law*, it will be the eftablifhment of *liberty*.

The truth is, that a government by law is or
is not liberty, juft as the laws are juft or unjuft;
and as the body of the people do or do not participate in the power of making them. The
learned Prelate feems to have thought otherwife, and therefore has given a definition of liberty, which might as well have been given of
flavery.

At the conclufion of his fermon, the Archbifhop adds words which he calls comfortable,
addreffed

is it that the Diffenters fhould come in for a fhare in his
Grace's abufe?——Their political principles, he fays, are
growing dangerous.——On what does he ground this infinua-
tion? He is miftaken if he imagines that they are all fuch
delinquents as the author of the following tracts, or that they
think univerfally as he does of the war with America. On
this fubject they are, like other bodies of men in the kingdom, of different opinions.——But I will tell him in what
they agree.——They agree in deteiling the doctrines of
paffive obedience and non-refiftance. They are all WHIGS,
enemies to arbitrary power, and firmly attached to thofe
principles of civil and religious liberty which produced the
GLORIOUS REVOLUTION and the HANOVERIAN SUCCES-
SION.——Such principles are the nation's beft defence; and
Proteftant Diffenters have hitherto reckoned it their glory
to be diftinguifhed by zeal for them, and an adherence to
them. ONCE thefe principles were *approved* by men in
power. No good can be expected, if they are now reckoned
dangerous.

addreſſed to thoſe who had been *patient in tribu-*
lation,(a) and intimating that they might *rejoice*
in hope, " a ray of brightneſs then appearing
" after a proſpect which had been long dark."
And in an account which follows the ſermon,
from one of the miſſionaries in the province of
New-York, it is ſaid, that " the rebellion would
" undoubtedly be cruſhed, and that THEN will
" be the time for taking ſteps for the increaſe of
" the church in America, by granting it an epiſ-
" copate." In conformity to the ſentiments of

(*a*) That is, the miſſionaries of the ſociety in America.—
The charter of the ſociety declares the end of its incorpora-
tion to be " propagating the goſpel in foreign parts,
" and making proviſion for the worſhip of God in thoſe
" plantations which wanted the adminiſtration of God's
" word and ſacraments, and were abandoned to atheiſm
" and infidelity." The chief buſineſs, on the contrary, of
the ſociety has been to provide for the ſupport of *epiſcopa-*
lianiſm in the northern colonies, and particularly NEW-
ENGLAND, where the ſacraments are more regularly admi-
niſtered, and the people leſs abandoned to infidelity, than
perhaps in any country under heaven. The miſſionaries employed and paid by the ſociety for this purpoſe, have generally been clergymen of the higheſt principles in church and
ſtate. *America,* having been for ſome time very hoſtile to men
of ſuch principles, moſt of them have been obliged to take
refuge in this country; and here they have, I am afraid,
been too ſucceſsful in propagating their own reſentments,
in miſleading our rulers, and widening the breach which
has produced the preſent war.

this

this miſſionary, the Archbiſhop alſo expreſſes his
hope, that the opportunity which ſuch an event
will give, for eſtabliſhing epiſcopacy among the
coloniſts, will not be loſt ; and adviſes, that meaſures ſhould be thought of for that purpoſe,
and for thereby reſcuing the church from the
perſecution it has long ſuffered in *America.*

This is a ſubject ſo important, and it has been
ſo much miſrepreſented, that I cannot help going
out of my way to give a brief account of it.

It does not appear that the lay members themſelves of the church in *America* have ever wiſhed
for Biſhops. On the contrary, the aſſembly of *Vir-
ginia* (the firſt epiſcopal colony) ſome years ago returned thanks to two clergymen in that colony,
who had proteſted againſt a reſolution of the other
clergy to petition for Biſhops. The church *here*
cannot have a right to *impoſe* Biſhops on the
church in another country ; and therefore, while
churchmen in *America* are averſe to Biſhops, it
muſt be perſecution to ſend Biſhops among them.
The *Preſbyterians,* and other religious ſects there,
are willing, from a ſenſe of the reaſonableneſs
of toleration, to admit Biſhops whenever the body
of epiſcopalian laity ſhall deſire them, provided
ſecurity is given that they ſhall be officers merely
ſpiritual, poſſeſſed of no other powers than thoſe
which are neceſſary to the full exerciſe of that
mode

mode of religious worſhip. It is not Biſhops, as *ſpiritual* officers, they have oppoſed; but Biſhops on a ſtate-eſtabliſhment; Biſhops with *civil* powers; Biſhops at the head of eccleſiaſtical courts, maintained by taxing other ſects, and poſſeſſed of a PRE-EMINENCE which would be incompatible with the equality which has long ſubſiſted among all religious ſects in *America*. In this laſt reſpect, the colonies have hitherto enjoyed a happineſs which is unparalleled, but which the introduction of ſuch Biſhops as would be ſent from hence would deſtroy. In *Penſilvania* (one of the happieſt countries under heaven before we carried into it deſolation and carnage) all ſects of chriſtians have been always perfectly on a level, the legiſlature taking no part with any one ſect againſt others, but protecting all equally as far as they are peaceable. The ſtate of the colonies north of *Penſilvania* is much the ſame; and, in the province of *Maſſachuſett's-Bay* in particular, civil authority interpoſes no farther in religion than by impoſing a tax for ſupporting public worſhip, leaving to all the power of applying the tax to the ſupport of that mode of public worſhip which they like beſt. This tax the epiſcopalians were, at one time, obliged to pay in common with others; but ſo far did the province carry its indulgence to them, that an act was paſſed on purpoſe to excuſe them.

them.—With this let the state of Protestant Dissenters in this country be compared. Not only
are they obliged to pay tithes for the support of
the established church, but their worship is not
even tolerated, unless their ministers will sub-
scribe the articles of the church. In consequence
of having long scrupled this subscription, they
have lost all legal right to protection, and are ex-
posed to the cruellest penalties. Uneasy in such
a situation, they not long ago applied twice to
parliament for the repeal of the penal laws
against them. Bills for that purpose were brought
into the *House of Commons*, and passed that
House. But, in the House of Lords, they were
rejected in consequence of the opposition of the
Bishops.—There are few I reverence so much as
some on the sacred bench; but such conduct
(and may I not add the alacrity with which most
of them support the present measures?) must
leave an indelible stain upon them, and w llpro-
bably exclude them for ever from *America*.

On this occasion, I cannot help thinking with
concern of the learned Prelate's feelings. After
a prospect long dark, he had discovered a ray of
brightness shewing him *America* reduced, and
the church triumphant: But lately, that ray of
brightness has vanished, and defeat has taken
place of victory and conquest.—And what do we
now see?—What a different prospect, mortifying

to

to the learned Prelate, prefents itfelf?—A great people likely to be formed, in fpite of all our efforts, into free communities, under governments which have (*a*) no religious tefts and eftablifhments!—A new æra in future annals, and a new

(*a*) I am forry to mention one exception to the fact here intimated. The new conftitution for *Penfilvania* (in other refpects wife and liberal) is difhonoured by a religious teft. It requires an acknowledgment of the divine infpiration of the Old and New Teftament, as a condition of being admitted to a feat in the Houfe of Reprefentatives; directing however, at the fame time, that no other religious teft fhall *for ever* hereafter be required of any civil officer.——This has been, probably, an accommodation to the prejudices of fome of the narrower fects in the province, to which the more liberal part have for the prefent thought fit to yield; and, therefore, it may be expected that it will not be of long continuance.

Religious tefts and fubfcriptions in general, and all eftablifhments of particular fyftems of faith, with civil emoluments annexed, do inconceivable mifchief, by turning religion into a trade, by engendering ftrife and perfecution, by forming hypocrites, by obftructing the progrefs of truth, and fettering and perverting the human mind; nor will the world ever grow much *wifer*, or *better*, or *happier*, till, by the abolition of them, truth can gain fair play, and reafon free fcope for exertion. The Archbifhop, page 11, fpeaks of chriftianity as " infufficient to rely on its own energies; and " of the affiftances which it is the bufinefs of civil authority " to provide for gofpel truths."——A worfe flander was never thrown on gofpel truths. Chriftianity difdains fuch affiftances as the corrupted governments of this world are capable of giving it. Politicians and ftatefmen know little of it. Their *enmity* has fometimes done it good; but their *friendfhip*, by fupporting corruptions carrying its name, has been almoft fatal to it.

opening

opening in human affairs beginning, among the descendants of *Englishmen*, in a new world;—A rising empire, extended over an immense continent, without Bishops,—without Nobles,—and without Kings.

O the depth of the riches of the wisdom of God! How unsearchable are his judgments!

But to proceed to another subject.

In the second of the following tracts, page 48. I have observed, that in former times it was the custom of parliament to pass bills for appointing commissioners to take, state, and examine the public accounts. I have lately had it in my power to inform myself more particularly on this subject; and I shall here beg leave to give a brief recital of some of the principal facts relating to it.

The first bill for the purpose I have mentioned was passed in the times of the commonwealth, and in the year 1653. It was called an " act for accounts, and for clearing of public " debts, and discovering frauds and conceal- " ments." Seven commissioners were named in it, and the necessary powers given them. In 1667, another act was passed for the same purpose; after which I find no account of any such acts till the beginning of the reign of King William.

William. At this time complaints of mifma-
nagement and embezzlements in the difpofition
of public money were become fo prevalent, that
the *Houfe of Commons* thought it neceffary to enter
into meafures for effectually preventing them, by
obliging all revenue officers to make up their
accounts, and bringing defaulters to juftice.

With thefe views, fix of the acts I have mentioned were paffed between the years 1690 and
1701. Another was paffed in the firft of Queen
Anne; and *three* more in her four laft years.
In King *William*'s reign they were always paffed by
the *Houfe of Commons* without a divifion. In *Queen
Anne's reign*, not *one* paffed without a divifion. In
1717, a motion for fuch an act was *rejected* without
a divifion; and fince 1717, only one motion (*a*)
has been made for fuch a bill, and it was rejected by a majority of 136 to 66.

The preamble to thefe acts declares the reafon of them to be, that " the kingdom may be
" fatisfied and truly informed, whether all the
" monies granted by parliament have been faith-
" fully iffued and applied to the end for which
" they had been given; and that all loyal fubjects
" may be thereby encouraged more chearfully to
" bear the burthens laid upon them." The
number of commiffioners named in them was
generally nine or feven, all members of the *Houfe*

(*a*) In 1742, after the refignation of Sir *Robert Walpole.*

of

of Commons. It was particularly ordered, that they should take an account of all the revenues brought into the receipt of the Exchequer, and all arrears thereof; of all monies in the hands of the receivers general of the land-tax, customs and excise; of all the public stores, provisions, &c. as well for land as sea service; of all ships of war, and the sums of money provided or paid for the use of the forces by sea and land, and the number of them respectively; and of any briberies or corruptions in any persons concerned in the receiving or disposing of the national treasure. And, for these purposes, they were impowered to call before them, and to examine upon oath the officers of the exchequer, the secretary at war, paymaster of the forces, commissioners of the navy and ordnance, and all persons whatever employed as commissioners, or otherwise, in or about the *Treasury.*

The reports, which the commissioners thus appointed delivered from time to time to parliament, contain accounts of a waste of public money, arising from the rapacity of contractors, and many scandalous abuses and frauds in every part of the public service, which must shock every person not grown callous to all the feelings of honesty and honour. In consequence of these reports, the *House of Commons* addressed the throne, and remonstrated; several great men

3   were

were accufed, and brought to fhame; fome were difmiffed from their places, and ordered to be prosecuted; fome expelled, and fome committed to the Tower. Thus did our reprefentatives in thofe times difcharge their duty as guardians of the public property; and it is, in my opinion, only by fuch means that they are capable of doing this properly and effectually. It muft, however, be acknowledged, that thefe commiffions of enquiry did not produce all the good effects which might have been expected from them. The influence of the crown, and the intereft in parliament of many great men entrufted with the difpofition of public money, rendered the proper execution of them extremely difficult. This led fome even of the Tories, at the time of the great change of miniftry in 1710, to propofe, that the receiving and iffuing of the public money fhould be taken from the crown; and, in defence of this propofal, it was urged, that the iffuingof public money, being in fome of the moft defpotic countries left in the hands of the people, it was by no means a neceffary part of the royal prerogative. This would indeed have provided a complete remedy; and it might have perpetuated the conftitution. But, even in thefe times, it was a reformation too great and too impracticable to engage much attention.

Ever

Ever fince thofe times the public accounts have
been growing more complicated ; and the temptations to profufion and embezzlement have been
increafing with increafing luxury and diffipation.
How aftonifhing then is it that every idea of fuch
commiffions fhould be now loft ; and that, at a time
when the nation is labouring under expences almoft too heavy to be borne, the paffing of accounts by the *Houfe of Commons* is become little
more than a matter of form ; our reprefentatives
fcarcely thinking it worth their while to attend
on fuch occafions, and MILLIONS of the public
treafure being fometimes given away, in a few
hours, juft as propofed by the *Treafury*, without
debate or enquiry.

I muft not forget to mention particularly on this
fubject, that the commiffioners named in the acts
I have defcribed, were always declared incapable
of holding any place or office of profit under the
crown ; and directed to take an account " of all
" penfions, falaries, and fums of money paid
" or payable to members of parliament out of
" the revenue or otherwife."———Not long before this time, the *Houfe of Commons* would not
fuffer even the *Attorney-general* (a) to fit and vote in
the

(a) Sir FRANCIS BACON was the *fecond* ATTORNEY-
GENERAL who fat in the *Houfe of Commons* ; but, to prevent
its being drawn into a precedent, the Houfe would not admit him, till they had made an order, that no Attorney-

General

the houfe becaufe he was the king's fervant; and in 1678, a member, as Mr. *Trenchard* fays, was committed to the Tower, for only faying in the houfe that the king might keep guards for his defence, if he could pay them.———Such *once* was the Houfe of Commons———So jealous of the power of the crown, and fo chafte.———Since the reign of Queen *Ann* and the pafling of the *Septennial Act,* a great change has taken place. (*a*)

A change

General fhould for the future be allowed to fit and vote in that Houfe.———In conformity to this order, whenever afterwards a member was appointed Attorney-General, his place was vacated, and a new writ iffued. This continued to be the practice till the year 1670, when Sir HENEAGE FINCH (afterwards EARL OF NOTTINGHAM) being appointed Attorney-General, he was allowed by connivance to preferve his feat, which connivance has been continued ever fince.— I give thefe facts not from any enquiry or knowledge of my own, but from the authority of a friend, who is perhaps better informed than any perfon in the kingdom on every fubject of this kind.

(*a*) The following facts will fhew, in fome degree, how this change has been brought about.———For ten years ending Aug. 1, 1717 (a period comprehending in it a general war abroad; and the demife of the crown, the eftablifhment of a new family, and an open rebellion at home) the money expended in fecret fervices amounted only to 279,444 l.——— For TEN YEARS ending Feb. 11, 1742, it amounted to no lefs a fum than 1.384,600; of which 50,077 l. was paid to printers of News-papers and writers for government; and a greater fum expended, in the laft *fix weeks* of thefe ten years, than had been fpent in *three years* before Aug. 1710.———See

the

A change which is little lefs than the total
ruin of the conftitution, and which may end in
a tyranny the moft oppreffive and infupportable.
It is, therefore, the greateft evil, which could have
happened to us ; and the men, by whofe abomin-
able

the Report of the COMMITTEE appointed March 23, 1742,
to enquire into the conduct of ROBERT EARL OF ORFORD,
printed in the Journals of the Houfe of Commons, vol. 24, p.
295, 296, 300.—One paffage, in this report, contains remarks,
fo much to my prefent purpofe and fo important, that I cannot help copying it.————" There are no laws particularly
" adapted to the cafe of a minifter who clandeftinely em-
" ploys the money of the public, and the whole power and
" profitable employments that attend the collecting and dif-
" pofing of it, *againft* the people : And, by this profufion
" and criminal diftribution of offices, in fome meafure juf-
" tifies the expence that particular perfons are obliged to be
" at, by making it neceffary to the prefervation of all that
" is valuable to a free nation.   For in that cafe, the conteft
" is plain and vifible. It is, whether the Commons fhall
" retain the *third* ftate in their own hands ; while this
" whole difpute is carried on at the expence of the people,
" and, on the fide of the minifter, out of the money granted
" to fupport and fecure the conftitutional independence of
" the three branches of the legiflature.————This method of
" corruption is as fure, and, therefore, as criminal a way of
" fubverting the conftitution as by an armed force.   It is a
" crime, productive of a total deftruction of the very being
" of this government ; and is fo *high* and *unnatural*, that no-
" thing but the powers of parliament can reach it ; and, as
" it never can meet with parliamentary animadverfion but
" when it is unfuccefsful, it muft feek for its *fecurity* in the
" extent

'able policy it has been accomplifhed, ought to be followed with the everlafting execrations of every friend to public virtue and liberty.

I now withdraw to the fituation of an anxious fpectator of public events ; but before I do this, I muft leave with the public, at this threatening period, the following fentiments.

Not long ago, the colonies might have been kept, without bloodfhed or trouble, by repealing the *acts* which have made us the aggreffors in the prefent war; but *now* it would be great folly to expect this.—At the fame time I think it certain, that they may be rendered more ufeful to us by a pacification on liberal terms, which fhall bind them to us as Friends, than by any victories or flaughters (were they poffible) which can force them to fubmit to us as Subjects.—I think it alfo certain, that fhould the offer of fuch terms be delayed till they have formed an alliance with *France*, this country is undone.——Such an alliance, we may hope, is not yet fettled.——Our rulers, therefore, may *poffibly*

"" extent and efficacy of the mifchief it produces." P. 395. The obftructions which this committee met with in their enquiry proved that the crime they here defcribe in fuch emphatical language, had *even then* obtained that very fecurity, in the extent of the mifchief it produced, which, they obferve, it was under a neceffity of feeking.

have

have ftill a moment for paufing and retreat-
ing; and every dictate of prudence and feeling of humanity requires them to be fpeedy and
earneft in improving it.—But what am I faying?
I know this muft not be expected. Too full of
ideas of our own dignity; too proud to retract;
and too tenacious of dominion, we feem determined to perfift: And the confequence muft be,
that the colonies will become the allies of *France*;
that a general war will be kindled; and, perhaps,
this once happy country be made, in juft re-
tribution, the feat of that defolation and mifery
which it has produced in other countries.

January 19, 1778.

SINCE the publication of the preceding
Introduction, the event referred to at the end of
it has been announced to the public. A memorial from the *French* court has been delivered to
our court, declaring, that the former has con-
cluded a treaty of commerce and friendfhip with
the colonies as INDEPENDENT STATES; and ac-
quainting us that, IN CONCERT WITH THEM, the
King of France is determined and prepared to
defend his commerce againft any interruption we
may give it.——A new turn, therefore, is now
given to our affairs of a nature the moft critical
and alarming. Would to God there were any

concefſions

conceffions by which we could extricate ourfelves.
But the opportunities for this have been fhame-
fully loft, and cannot be now recovered.——With
a judicial blindnefs in our councils which has hitherto carried us uniformly from *bad* to *worfe*——
With near half our ftrength torn from us, and
our vaunted dignity in the duft——With our
refources failing; our credit tottering; and a
debt threatening to overwhelm us of more than a
HUNDRED AND FIFTY MILLIONS——In thefe circumftances, we feem to be entering on a war
with the united powers of *France*, *Spain*, and
America.——This, fhould it happen, will complete the meafure of our troubles, and foon
bring on that *cataftrophe* which there has been
all along reafon to expect and dread.

April 24, 1778.

ACCOUNT

Account of the Customs for the Last Six Years.

IN the following tracts I have reckoned, among the destructive consequences of the war with *America*, the loss of a considerable part of our trade. In consequence of several accidental causes, particularly the demand created by the war, this effect has not yet been so much felt as was generally expected. The truth, however, is, that the war has operated in this way to a degree that is alarming, as will appear from the following account of the Customs for the last six years.

	Gross Receipt.	Debentures.	Net Receipt.	Payments into the Exchequer.
1772	5.134,503	2.214,508	2.441,038	2.525,515
1773	5.159,800	2.463,767	2.221,460	2.431,071
1774	5.068,000	2.132,600	2.455,500	2.547,717
1775	5.146,900	1.904,900	2.709,340	2.476,302
1776	3.726,970	1.544,300	1.633,380	2.460,402
1777	3.293,200	932,860	1.846,390	2.199,105

It should be observed, that though, in 1776, there had been no importation of *tobacco*, yet the duties on *tobacco* brought into the *Exchequer* as much as ever, these duties having been paid for old stock taken out of the warehouses for *home consumption*, instead of *exportation*. This is one of the causes which kept up the payments into the *Exchequer* in 1776, notwithstanding a sudden fall of near a MILLION AND A HALF in the gross receipt, and a MILLION in the net receipt. ——In the last year, or 1777, the duties on tobacco fell very short; and this contributed to diminish the payments into the *Exchequer* near a *quarter of a million.* But what seems of more

3. importance

importance is, that the debentures (or duties returned at exportation) which had fallen in 1775
and 1776 above a *fourth*, continued to fall in
1777; and did not then amount to more than *two-
fifths* of the ufual fum.

I have examined the cuftoms from the Revolution to the prefent time; but cannot find that
any thing like fuch a fall in them has ever happened before.

FIRST ADVERTISEMENT.

THE prefent ftate of the public funds makes it neceffary for me to acquaint the reader, that when
the *Supplement* to the following Tracts was written, the
3 *per cent.* annuities were at the price which the calculations in it fuppofe, or nearly at 78. They have fince
fallen to 72, and once even below 69, which is a lower
price than they were ever at during the whole laft war,
except juft at the pinch of the loan of twelve millions in
1762.—The difference of price alfo between them and
the new 4 *per cents.* is fallen, (for no reafon that I can
difcover) from 14 to about 10½.—I find, likewife, that
in confequence of a diftreffing fcarcity of money, the
fubfcribers to the laft loan of *five millions* have not yet been
able to complete their payments.—Thefe facts afford a
dark profpect; and make it doubtful whether, if things
don't mend, it will be poffible, by any fchemes, to procure the money neceffary to bear the expence of another
campaign.——Should it happen, for thefe reafons, that
what I have written on loans can be of no ufe; or,
though capable of being of ufe, fhould it be neglected;
I fhall ftill reflect with fatisfaction, that I have now
given what I wifhed to offer on this fubject with more
correctnefs; and proved, beyond a doubt, that a great
part of the National Debt is an *artificial* debt, for which
no money has been received, and which might have been
eafily avoided.

Jan. 19, 1778.

SECOND

SECOND ADVERTISEMENT.

SINCE the foregoing Advertisement in January last, the price of the 3 *per cent.* annuities has fallen from 72 to 60½. But the difference of price between them and the 4 *per cent.* annuities created in 1777, has risen to near 18l. agreeably to the true comparative value of these annuities, as computed in page 14 of the Supplement.—— It is necessary I should farther mention, that there has been a new loan of six millions for the service of the present year; but that, contrary to my hopes, the managers of our finances have returned to the old modes of borrowing——The consolidated 3 *per cent.* annuities being, when the loan was settled on the 6th of February, at 66½; one hundred 3 *per cent. stock* estimated at this price, was given for every 100l. in *money*, with FOUR-FIFTHS of the profits of a lottery ticket reckoned at 2½l. and an ANNUITY of 2½l. for 30 years, reckoned worth 14 years purchase (or 135l.) but really worth above 15 years purchase. This made a profit of 4l. on every 100l. advanced. But the 3 *per cent.* annuities falling immediately to 64, and in a few days to 60½; and the short annuity also happening to sell for no more than 13 years purchase, this loan has been constantly at a discount, which has fluctuated between 2 and 4½ *per cent.*

The scheme of this loan is the first of the old schemes described in the following Supplement, page 2d; and it is apparent that by including the value of the *douceurs* in the capital, it brings on the public an artificial debt, for which nothing will be received, of above two millions.——The sum to be lent, should it be ever paid, might have been as well obtained, without making any material addition to the annual charge, by selling separately the two *douceurs* worth 2.244,000l. and offering for the remaining sum necessary to make up six millions, an interest of five *per cent.* subject to the regulations proposed in the Second Tract, page 98, or in the Supplement, page 24.

April 24, 1778.

THE

THE following accounts have been laid before the House of Commons since January
last.

Account of the Gold Coin brought into the Mint from Great Britain and Ireland by the Proclamations in 1773, 1774, and 1776.

	£.	s.	d.
First Proclamation brought in	3.806,435	7	2 deficient more than 6 grains in a guinea.
2d Proclamation brought in	4.876,171	18	3 deficient between 3 and 6 grains.
3d Proclamation brought in	6.880,986	5	3 deficient between 1 and 3 grains.

Total   15.563,593   10 8

Compare Second Tract from page 56 to 64.

Account of the Expence of calling in and recoining all the Gold Coin deficient more than a grain in a guinea.

	£.	s.	d.
Expence to the BANK for melting	16,786	14	6
Deficiency in melting —	317,314	6	11
Interest of money advanced to the holders of gold coin —	231,982	17	7
To master of the Mint for the charge of recoining and other charges — — — —	115,459	12	9
To several persons who were appointed in the several counties to take in and exchange the gold coin, and for other charges and expences — — —	72,476	8	0

Total   754,019 19 9

Towards

Towards defraying this expence there have been applied the following fums :

		£.	s.	d.
Out of the fupplies in	1774	250,000	0	0
in	1775	69,671	8	3
in	1776	92,421	14	11¼
Out of the million vote of credit in ———	1776	30,000	0	0
Out of the million vote of credit in ———	1777	206,699	8	3¾
Provided for in —	1778	105,227	8	3
		754,019	19	9

Thefe accounts fhew, that in the note, p. 63 of the Second Tract, the words 16 *millions and a half* fhould have been 15 *millions and a half* ; and that in p. 69, 2d line, 650,000l. fhould have been 754,019l. 19s. 9d.

N. B. The lofs attending the deficiency in the coin brought in by the firft proclamation amounted nearly to 300,000l. but having been thrown on the holders of the coin, it could not be brought to account.

OBSERVATIONS

ON THE NATURE OF

CIVIL LIBERTY,

THE PRINCIPLES OF

GOVERNMENT,

AND THE

JUSTICE AND POLICY

OF THE

WAR WITH AMERICA.

Quis furor iste novus? quo nunc, quo tenditis ——
Heu! miseri cives? non Hostem, inimicaque castra,
—— Vestras Spes uritis. VIRG.

By RICHARD PRICE, D.D. F.R.S.

THE EIGHTH EDITION,
With CORRECTIONS and ADDITIONS.

LONDON:
Printed for T. CADELL, in the STRAND.
M.DCC.LXXVIII.

THE FIRST EDITION.

IN the following Observations, I have taken that liberty of examining public measures, which, happily for this kingdom, every person in it enjoys. They contain the sentiments of a private and unconnected man; for which, should there be any thing wrong in them, he alone is answerable.

After all that has been written on the dispute with America, no reader can expect to be informed, in this publication, of much that he has not before known. Perhaps, however, he may find in it some new matter; and if he should, it will be chiefly in the Observations on the Nature of Civil Liberty, and the Policy of the War with America.

February 8th, 1776.

P R E-

PREFACE

TO

THE FIFTH EDITION.

THE favourable reception which the following Tract has met with, makes me abundant amends for the abuse it has brought upon me. I should be ill employed were I to take much notice of this abuse: But there is one circumstance attending it, which I cannot help just mentioning.—The principles on which I have argued form the foundation of every state as far as it is free; and are the same with those taught by Mr. Locke, and all the writers on Civil Liberty who have been hitherto most admired in this country. But I find with concern, that our Governors chuse to decline trying by them their present measures: For, in a Pamphlet which has been circulated by government with great industry, these principles are pronounced to be " unnatural and wild, in-
" compatible with practice, and the off-
" spring

" spring of the diftempered imagination of
" a man who is biaffed by party, and who
" writes to deceive."

I muft take this opportunity to add, that
I love quiet too well to think of entering
into a controverfy with any writers; particularly, NAMELESS ones. Confcious of
good intentions, and unconnected with any
party, I have endeavoured to plead the caufe
of general liberty and juftice: And happy
in knowing this, I fhall, in filence, commit
myfelf to that candour of the public of
which I have had fo much experience.

March 12th, 1776.

CON-

CONTENTS.

PART I.

PART II.

OBSER-

OBSERVATIONS, &c.

OUR Colonies in NORTH AMERICA appear to be now determined to rifk and fuffer every thing, under the perfuafion, that GREAT BRITAIN is attempting to rob them of that Liberty to which every member of fociety, and all civil communities, have a natural and unalienable title. The queftion, therefore, whether this is a right perfuafion, is highly interefting, and deferves the careful attention of every *Englifhman* who values Liberty, and wifhes to avoid ftaining himfelf with the guilt of invading it. But it is impoffible to judge properly of this queftion without juft ideas of Liberty *in general*; and of the nature, limits, and principles of Civil Liberty *in particular*.—The following obfervations on this fubject appear to me of fome importance; and I cannot make myfelf eafy without offering them to the public at the prefent period, big with events of the laft confequence to this kingdom. I do this, with reluctance and pain, urged by ftrong feelings, but at the fame

time

[2]

time checked by the confcioufnefs that I am likely to deliver fentiments not favourable to the prefent meafures of that government, under which I live, and to which I am a conftant and zealous well-wifher. Such, however, are my prefent fentiments and views, that this is a confideration of inferior moment with me; and, as I hope never to go beyond the bounds of decent difcuffion and expoftulation, I flatter myfelf, that I fhall be able to avoid giving any perfon reafon for offence.

The obfervations with which I fhall begin, are of a more general and abftracted nature; but being neceffary to introduce what I have principally in view, I hope they will be patiently read and confidered.

SECT. I.

Of the Nature of Liberty in General.

IN order to obtain a more diftinct view of the nature of Liberty as fuch, it will be ufeful to confider it under the four following general divifions.

Firft, *Phyfical* Liberty.——Secondly, *Moral* Liberty. —— Thirdly, *Religious* Liberty. —— And Fourthly, *Civil* Liberty.——Thefe heads comprehend all the different kinds of Liberty. And I have placed *Civil* Liberty laft, because

cause I mean to apply to it all I shall say of the other kinds of Liberty.

By PHYSICAL LIBERTY I mean that principle of *Spontaneity*, or *Self-determination*, which constitutes us *Agents*; or which gives us a command over our actions, rendering them properly *ours*, and not effects of the operation of any foreign cause.——— MORAL LIBERTY is the power of following, in all circumstances, our sense of right and wrong; or of acting in conformity to our reflecting and moral principles, without being controuled by any contrary principles.———RELIGIOUS LIBERTY signifies the power of exercising, without molestation, that mode of religion which we think best; or of making the decisions of our own consciences respecting religious truth, the rule of our conduct, and not any of the decisions of our fellow-men. —In like manner; CIVIL LIBERTY is the power of a *Civil Society* or *State* to govern itself by its own discretion, or by laws of its own making, without being subject to the impositions of *any* power, in appointing and directing which the collective body of the people have no concern, and over which they have no controul.

It should be observed, that, according to these definitions of the different kinds of liberty, there is one general idea, that runs through them all; I mean, the idea of *Self-direction*, or *Self-government*.—Did our volitions originate not with *our-*

selves, but with some cause over which we have no power; or were we under a necessity of always following some will different from our own, we should want PHYSICAL LIBERTY.

In like manner; he whose perceptions of moral obligation are controuled by his passions has lost his *Moral Liberty*; and the most common language applied to him is, that he wants *Self-government*.

He likewise who, in religion, cannot govern himself by his convictions of religious duty, but is obliged to receive formularies of faith, and to practise modes of worship imposed upon him by others, wants *Religious Liberty*.——And the Community also that is governed, not by itself, but by some will independent of it, wants *Civil Liberty*.

In all these cases there is a force which stands opposed to the agent's *own* will; and which, as far as it operates, produces *Servitude*.——In the *first* case, this force is incompatible with the very idea of voluntary motion; and the subject of it is a mere passive instrument which never *acts*, but is always *acted upon*.——In the *second* case; this force is the influence of passion getting the better of reason; or the *brute* overpowering and conquering the will of the *man*.——In the *third* case; it is *Human Authority* in religion requiring conformity to particular modes of faith and worship, and superseding *private judgment*.——And in the last case,

cafe, it is any will diftinct from that of the Majority of a Community, which claims a power
of making laws for it, and difpofing of its property.

This it is, I think, that marks the limit
between *Liberty* and *Slavery*. As far as, in
any inftance, the operation of any caufe comes
in to reftrain the power of Self-government,
fo far Slavery is introduced : Nor do I think that
a precifer idea than this of Liberty and Slavery
can be formed.

. I cannot help wifhing I could here fix my reader's attention, and engage him to confider carefully the dignity of that bleffing to which we give
the name of LIBERTY, according to the reprefentation now made of it. There is not a word in the
whole compafs of language which expreffes fo
much of what is important and excellent. It is,
in every view of it, a bleffing truly facred and in-
valuable.——Without *Phyfical Liberty*, man would
be a machine acted upon by mechanical fprings,
having no principle of motion in himfelf, or command over events ; and, therefore, incapable of all
merit and demerit.——Without *Moral Liberty*, he
is a wicked and deteftable being, fubject to the
tyranny of bafe lufts, and the fport of every vile
appetite.——And without *Religious* and *Civil Liberty* he is a poor and abject animal, without rights,
without property, and without a confcience, bend-

B 3

ing

ing his neck to the yoke, and crouching to the will of every filly creature who has the infolence to pretend to authority over him.——Nothing, therefore, can be of fo much confequence to us as *Liberty*. It is the foundation of all honour, and the chief privilege and glory of our natures.

In fixing our ideas on the fubject of Liberty, it is of particular ufe to take fuch an enlarged view of it as I have now given. But the immediate object of the prefent enquiry being *Civil Liberty*, I will confine to it all the fubfequent obfervations.

S E C T. II.

Of Civil Liberty and the Principles of Government.

FROM what has been faid it is obvious, that all civil government, as far as it can be denominated *free*, is the creature of the people. It originates with them. It is conducted under their direction; and has in view nothing but their happinefs. All it, different forms are no more than fo many different modes in which they chufe to direct their affairs, and to fecure the quiet enjoyment of their rights.——In every free ftate every man is his own Legiflator. (*a*)——All *taxes* are free-gifts for public fervices.——All *laws* are particular provifions or regulations eftablifhed by COMMON

(*a*) See a particular explanation of this affertion in the Second Tract, Page 9.

CONSENT

CONSENT for gaining protection and fafety.——
And all *Magiſtrates* are Truſtees or Deputies for
carrying thefe regulations into execution.

Liberty, therefore, is too imperfectly defined
when it is faid to be " a Government by Laws,
and not by Men." If the laws are made by one
man, or a junto of men in a ſtate, and not by COM-
MON CONSENT, a government by them does not differ from Slavery. In this cafe it would be a contradiction in terms to fay that the ſtate governs itfelf.

From hence it is obvious that *Civil Liberty*, in
its moſt perfect degree, can be enjoyed only in
ſmall ſtates, where every independent agent is capable of giving his ſuffrage in perſon, and of being
chofen into public offices. When a ſtate becomes fo
numerous, or when the different parts of it are removed to fuch diftances from one another, as to
render this impracticable, a diminution of Liberty
neceffarily arifes. There are, however, in thefe
circumſtances, methods by which fuch near ap-
proaches may be made to perfect Liberty as fhall
anfwer all the purpofes of government, and at the
fame time fecure every right of human nature.

Tho' all the members of a ſtate fhould not be
capable of giving their ſuffrages on public meafures, *individually* and *perfonally*, they may do this
by the appointment of *Subſtitutes* or *Reprefentatives*. They may entruſt the powers of legiſlation,

fubject

subject to such restrictions as they shall think necessary, with any number of *Delegates*; and whatever can be done by such delegates within the limits of their trust, may be considered as done by the united voice and counsel of the Community. ——In this method a free government may be established in the largest state; and it is conceivable that by regulations of this kind, any number of states might be subjected to a scheme of government,—that would exclude the desolations of war, and produce universal peace and order.

Let us think here of what may be practicable in this way with respect to *Europe* in particular. ——While it continues divided, as it is at present, into a great number of independent kingdoms whose interests are continually clashing, it is impossible but that disputes will often arise which must end in war and carnage. It would be no remedy to this evil to make one of these states supreme over the rest; and to give it an absolute plenitude of power to superintend and controul them. This would be to subject all the states to the arbitrary discretion of one, and to establish an ignominious slavery not possible to be long endured. It would, therefore, be a remedy worse than the disease; nor is it possible it should be approved by any mind that has not lost every idea of Civil Liberty. On the contrary.—Let every state, with respect to all its internal concerns, be continued

tinued independent of all the reft; and let a general confederacy be formed by the appointment of
a SENATE confifting of Reprefentatives from all
the different ftates. Let this SENATE poffefs the
power of managing all the *common* concerns of the
united ftates, and of judging and deciding between them, as a common *Arbiter* or *Umpire*, in all
difputes; having, at the fame time, under its direction, the common force of the ftates to fupport its
decifions.——In thefe circumftances, each feparate
ftate would be fecure againft the interference of foreign power in its private concerns, and, therefore,
would poffefs *Liberty*; and at the fame time it
would be fecure againft all oppreffion and infult
from every neighbouring ftate.——Thus might
the fcattered force and abilities of a whole continent
be gathered into one point; all litigations fettled
as they rofe; univerfal peace preferved; and nation prevented *from any more lifting up a fword
againft nation.*

I have obferved, that tho', in a great ftate, all
the individuals that compofe it cannot be admitted to an immediate participation in the powers of
legiflation and government, yet they may participate
pate in thefe powers by a delegation of them to a
body of reprefentatives.——In this cafe it is evident that the ftate will be ftill *free* or *felf-governed*;
and that it will be more or lefs fo in proportion

as

as it is more or lefs fairly and adequately reprefented. If the perfons to whom the truft of government is committed hold their places for fhort
terms ; if they are chofen by the unbiaffed voices
of a majority of the ftate, and fubject to their inftructions ; Liberty will be enjoyed in its higheft
degree. But if they are chofen for long terms by
a part only of the ftate ; and if during that term
they are fubject to no controul from their conftituents ; the very idea of Liberty will be loft, and the
power of chufing reprefentatives becomes nothing
but a power, lodged in a *few*, to chufe at certain
periods, a body of *Mafters* for themfelves and for
the reft of the Community. And if a ftate is fo
funk that the majority of its reprefentatives are
elected by a handful of the meaneft *(a)* perfons in
it, whofe votes are always paid for; and if alfo,
there is a higher will on which even thefe mock reprefentatives themfelves depend, and that directs
their voices : In thefe circumftances, it will be an
abufe of language to fay that the ftate poffeffes Liberty. Private men, indeed, might be allowed the
exercife of Liberty ; as they might alfo under the
moft defpotic government ; but it would be an *indul-*

(*a*) In *Great Britain*, confifting of near fix *millions* of inhabitants, 5723 perfons, moft of them the loweft of the people,
elect one half of the *Houfe of Commons*; and 364 votes chufe a
ninth part. This may be feen diftinctly made out in the *Political Difquifitions*, Vol. 1. Book 2. C. 4. a work full of important and ufeful inftruction.

gence,

gence or *connivance* derived from the fpirit of the times, or from an accidental mildnefs in the adminiftration. And, rather than be governed in fuch a manner, it would perhaps be better to be governed by the will of one man without any reprefentation: For a reprefentation fo degenerated could anfwer no other end than to miflead and deceive, by difguifing flavery, and keeping up a *form* of Liberty when the *reality* was loft.

Within the limits now mentioned, Liberty may be enjoyed in every poffible degree; from that which is complete and perfect, to that which is merely nominal; according as the people have more or lefs of a fhare in government, and of a controuling power over the perfons by whom it is adminiftered.

In general, to be *free* is to be guided by one's own will; and to be guided by the will of another is the characteriftic of *Servitude*. This is particularly applicable to Political Liberty. That ftate, I have obferved, is *free*, which is guided by its own will; or, (which comes to the fame) by the will of an affembly of reprefentatives appointed by itfelf and accountable to itfelf. And every ftate that is not fo governed; or in which a body of men reprefenting the people make not an effential part of the Legiflature, is in *flavery*.——In order to form the moft perfect conftitution of government,

ment, there may be the beſt reaſons for joining to
ſuch a body of repreſentatives, an *Hereditary Council* conſiſting of men of the firſt rank in the ſtate,
with a *Supreme executive Magiſtrate* at the head of
all. This will form uſeful checks in a legiſlature ;
and contribute to give it vigour, union, and diſ-
patch, without infringing liberty : for, as long aa
that part of a government which repreſents the
people is a *fair repreſentation* ; and alſo has a negative on all public meaſures, together with the
ſole power of impoſing taxes and originating ſupplies ; the eſſentials of liberty will be preſerved.
———We make it our boaſt in this country, that
this is our own conſtitution. I will not ſay with
how much reaſon.

Of ſuch Liberty as I have now deſcribed, it
is impoſſible there ſhould be an exceſs. Government is an inſtitution for the benefit of the
people governed, which they have power to model as they pleaſe ; and to ſay, that they can have
too much of this power, is to ſay, that there ought
to be a power in the ſtate ſuperior to that which
gives it being, and from which all juriſdiction in
it is derived.———Licentiouſneſs, which has been
commonly mentioned, as an extreme of liberty, is
indeed its oppoſite. It is government by the will
of rapacious individuals, in oppoſition to the will
of

of the community, made known and declared in the laws. A free ſtate, at the ſame time that it is free itſelf, makes all its members free, by excluding licentiouſneſs, and guarding their perſons and pr operty and good name againſt inſult. It is the end of all juſt government, at the ſame time that it ſecures the liberty of the public againſt *foreign* injury, to ſecure the liberty of the individual againſt *private* injury. I do not, therefore, think it ſtrictly juſt to ſay, that it belongs to the nature of government to entrench on private liberty. It ought never to do this, except as far as the exerciſe of private liberty encroaches on the liberties of others. That is; it is licentiouſneſs it reſtrains, and liberty itſelf only when uſed to deſtroy liberty.

It appears from hence, that licentiouſneſs and deſpotiſm are more nearly allied than is commonly imagined. They are both alike inconſiſtent with liberty, and the true end of government; nor is there any other difference between them, than that the one is the licentiouſneſs of *great* men, and the other the licentiouſneſs of *little* men ; or that, by the one, the perſons and property of a people are ſubject to outrage and invaſion from a King, or a lawleſs body of *Grandees* ; and that, by the other, they are ſubject to the like outrage from a *lawleſs mob.*——In avoiding one of theſe evils, mankind have often run into the other. But all well conſtituted governments guard equally againſt both.

7   Indeed

Indeed of the two, the laſt is, on ſeveral accounts, the leaſt to be dreaded, and has done the leaſt miſchief. It may be truly ſaid, that if licentiouſ- neſs has deſtroyed its thouſands, deſpotiſm has de- ſtroyed its millions. The former, having little power, and no ſyſtem to ſupport it, neceſſarily finds its own remedy; and a people ſoon get out of the tumult and anarchy attending it. But a deſpotiſm, wearing the form of government, and being armed with its force, is an evil not to be conquered without dreadful ſtruggles. It goes on from age to age, debaſing the human faculties, le- velling all diſtinctions, and preying on the rights and bleſſings of ſociety.——It deſerves to be add- ed, that in a ſtate diſturbed by licentiouſneſs, there is an animation which is favourable to the human mind, and which puts it upon exerting its powers. But in a ſtate habituated to a deſpotiſm, all is ſtill and torpid. A dark and ſavage tyranny ſtifles every effort of genius; and the mind loſes all its ſpirit and dignity.

Before I proceed to what I have farther in view, I will obſerve, that the account now given of the principles of public Liberty, and the nature of an equal and free government, ſhews what judgment we ſhould form of that OMNIPOTENCE, which, it has been ſaid, muſt belong to every government as ſuch. Great ſtreſs has been laid on this, but

most

moſt unreaſonably.——Government, as has been before obſerved, is, in the very nature of it, a TRUST; and all its powers a DELEGATION for gaining particular ends. This *truſt* may be miſ-applied and abuſed. It may be employed to de-feat the very ends for which it was inſtituted; and to ſubvert the very rights which it ought to pro-tect.——A PARLIAMENT, for inſtance, conſiſting of a body of repreſentatives, choſen for a limited period, to make laws, and to grant money for pub-lic ſervices, would forfeit its authority by making itſelf perpetual, or even prolonging its own dura-tion; by nominating its own members; by accept-ing bribes; or ſubjecting itſelf to any kind of fo-reign influence. This would convert a *Parlia-ment* into a *conclave* or *junto* of ſelf-created tools; and a ſtate that has loſt its regard to its own rights, ſo far as to ſubmit to ſuch a breach of truſt in its rulers, is enſlaved.——Nothing, therefore, can be more abſurd than the doctrine which ſome have taught, with reſpect to the omnipotence of parlia-ments. They poſſeſs no power beyond the limits of the truſt for the execution of which they were formed. If they contradict this truſt, they betray their conſtituents, and diſſolve themſelves. All de-legated power muſt be ſubordinate and limited.—— If omnipotence can, with any ſenſe, be aſcribed to a legiſlature, it muſt be lodged where all legiſlative authority originates; that is, in the PEOPLE. For

their

their fakes government is inftituted ; and their's is the only real omnipotence.

I am fenfible, that all I have been faying would be very abfurd, were the opinions juft which fome have maintained concerning the origin of government. According to thefe opinions, government is not the creature of the people, or the refult of a convention between them and their rulers : But there are certain men who poffefs in themfelves, independently of the will of the people, a right of governing them, which they derive from the Deity. This doctrine has been abundantly refuted by many *(a)* excellent writers. It is a doctrine which avowedly fubverts Civil Liberty ; and which reprefents mankind as a body of vaffals, formed to defcend like cattle from one fet of owners to another, who have an abfolute dominion over them. It is a wonder, that thofe who view their fpecies in a light fo humiliating, fhould ever be able to think of themfelves without regret and fhame. The intention of thefe obfervations is not to oppofe fuch fentiments ; but, taking for granted the reafonablenefs of Civil Liberty, to fhew wherein it confifts, and what diftinguifhes it from its con-

(a) See among others Mr. Locke on Government, and Dr. Prieftley's Effay on the firft Principles of Government.

trary.

trary.——And, in confidering this fubject, as it has been now treated, it is unavoidable to reflect on the excellency of a free government, and its tendency to exalt the nature of man.——Every member of a free ftate, having his property fecure, and knowing himfelf his own governor, poffeffes a confcioufnefs of dignity in himfelf, and feels incitements to emulation and improvement, to which the miferable flaves of arbitrary power muft be utter ftrangers. In fuch a ftate all the fprings of action have room to operate, and the mind is ftimulated to the nobleft exertions (*a*).——But to be obliged, from our birth, to look up to a creature no better than ourfelves as the mafter of our fortunes; and to receive his will as our law—What can be more humiliating ? What elevated ideas can enter a mind in fuch a fituation ?——Agreeably to this remark; the fubjects of free ftates have, in all ages, been moft diftinguifhed for genius and knowledge. Liberty is the foil where the arts and fciences have flourifhed; and the more free a ftate has been, the more have the powers of the human mind been drawn forth into action, and the greater number of brave men has it produced. With what luftre do the antient free ftates of *Greece* fhine in the annals of the world? How different is that country now, under the Great *Turk* ? The differ-

(*a*) See Dr. Prieftley on Government, page 63, 69, &c.

C   ence

ence between a country inhabited by men and by brutes is not greater.

These are reflexions which should be constantly present to every mind in this country.——As *Moral* Liberty is the prime blessing of man in his *private* capacity, so is *Civil* liberty in his *public* capacity. There is nothing that requires more to be *watched* than power. There is nothing that ought to be opposed with a more determined resolution than its encroachments. Sleep in a state, as *Montesquieu* says, is always followed by slavery.

The people of this kingdom were once warmed by such sentiments as these. Many a sycophant of power have they sacrificed. Often have they fought and bled in the cause of Liberty. But that time seems to be going. The fair inheritance of Liberty left us by our ancestors many of us are willing to resign. An abandoned venality, the inseparable companion of dissipation and extravagance, has poisoned the springs of public virtue among us: And should any events ever arise that should render the same opposition necessary that took place in the times of King *Charles* the First, and *James* the Second, I am afraid all that is valuable to us would be lost. The terror of the standing army, the danger of the public funds, and the all-corrupting influence of the treasury, would deaden all zeal, and produce general acquiescence and servility.

SECT.

S E C T. III.

Of the Authority of one Country over another.

FROM the nature and principles of Civil Liberty, as they have been now explained, it is an immediate and neceſſary inference that no one community can have any power over the property or legiſlation of another community, which is not incorporated with it by a juſt and adequate repreſentation.——Then only, it has been ſhewn, is a ſtate *free*, when it is governed by its own will. But a country that is ſubject to the legiſlature of another country, in which it has no voice, and over which it has no controul, cannot be ſaid to be governed by its own will. Such a country, therefore, is in a ſtate of ſlavery. And it deſerves to be particularly conſidered, that ſuch a ſlavery is worſe, on ſeveral accounts, than any ſlavery of private men to one another, or of kingdoms to deſpots within themſelves.—Between one ſtate and another, there is none of that fellow-feeeling that takes place between perſons in private life. Being detached bodies that never ſee one another, and reſiding perhaps in different quarters of the globe, the ſtate that governs cannot be a witneſs to the ſufferings occaſioned by its oppreſſions ; or a competent judge of the circumſtances and abilities

of

of the people who are governed. They muſt alſo have in a great degree ſeparate intereſts; and the more the one is loaded, the more the other may be eaſed. The infamy likewiſe of oppreſſion, being in ſuch circumſtances ſhared among a multitude, is not likely to be much felt or regarded.——On all theſe accounts there is, in the caſe of one country ſubjugated to another, little or nothing to check rapacity; and the moſt flagrant injuſtice and cruelty may be practiſed without remorſe or pity.——I will add, that it is particularly difficult to ſhake off a tyranny of this kind. A ſingle deſpot, if a people are unanimous and reſolute, may be ſoon ſubdued. But a deſpotic ſtate is not eaſily ſubdued; and a people ſubject to it cannot emancipate themſelves without entering into a dreadful, and, perhaps, very unequal conteſt.

I cannot help obſerving farther, that the ſlavery of a people to internal deſpots may be qualified and limited; but I don't ſee what can limit the authority of one ſtate over another. The exerciſe of power in this caſe can have no other meaſure than diſcretion; and, therefore, muſt be indefinite and abſolute.

Once more. It ſhould be conſidered that the government of one country by another, can only be ſupported by a military force; and, without
ſuch

such a support, must be destitute of all weight and efficiency.

This will be best explained by putting the following case.——There is, let us suppose, in a province subject to the sovereignty of a distant state, a subordinate legislature consisting of an Assembly chosen by the people; a Council chosen by that Assembly; and a Governor *appointed* by the Sovereign state, and paid by the Province. There are, likewise, judges and other officers, appointed and paid in the same manner, for administering *justice* agreeably to the laws, by the verdicts of juries fairly chosen.——This forms a constitution seemingly free, by giving the people a share in their own government, and some check on their rulers. But, while there is a higher legislative power, to the controul of which such a constitution is subject, it does not itself possess Liberty, and therefore cannot be of any use as a security to Liberty; nor is it possible that it should be of long duration. Laws offensive to the Province will be enacted by the Sovereign State. The legislature of the Province will remonstrate against them. The magistrates will not execute them. Juries will not convict upon them; and consequently, like the Pope's Bulls which once governed *Europe*, they will become nothing but forms and empty sounds, to which no regard will be shewn.——In order to remedy this evil, and

to

to give efficiency to its government, the supreme
state will naturally be led to withdraw the *Governor*,
the *Council*, and the *Judges* (a) from the controul

(a) The independency of the Judges we esteem in this country one of our greatest privileges.——Before the revolution
they generally, I believe, held their places *during pleasure.*
King William gave them their places *during good behaviour.*
At the accession of the present Royal Family their places were
given them *during good behaviour*, in consequence of the Act
of Settlement, 12 and 13 W. III. C. 2. But an opinion having
been entertained by some, that though their commissions were
made under the Act of Settlement to continue, during good behaviour, yet that they determined on the demise of the Crown;
it was enacted by a statute made in the first year of his present
Majesty. Chap. 23. " That the commissions of Judges for
" the time being shall be, continue, and remain in full force,
" during their good behaviour, notwithstanding the demise
" of his Majesty, or of any of his Heirs and Successors;"
with a proviso, " that it may be lawful for his Majesty, his
" Heirs and Successors, to remove any Judge upon the address
" of both Houses of Parliament." And by the same Statute
their salaries are secured to them during the continuance of
their commissions: His Majesty, according to the preamble of
the Statute, having been pleased to declare from the Throne
to both Houses of Parliament, " That he looked upon the
" independency and uprightness of Judges as essential to the
" impartial administration of Justice, as one of the best secu-
" rities to the Rights and Liberties of his loving Subjects, and
" as most conducive to the honour of his Crown."

A worthy friend and able Lawyer has supplied me with this
note. It affords, when contrasted with that *dependence* of the
Judges which has been thought reasonable in *America*, a sad
specimen of the different manner in which a kingdom may
think proper to govern itself, and the provinces subject to it.

of the Province, by making them entirely depen-
dant on itſelf for their *pay* and *continuance in office*,
as well as for their appointment. It will alſo alter
the mode of chuſing Juries on purpoſe to bring
them more under its influence : And in ſome caſes,
under the pretence of the impoſſibility of gaining
an impartial trial where government is reſiſted, it
will perhaps ordain, that offenders ſhall be removed
from the Province to be tried within its own territories : And it may even go ſo far in this kind of
policy, as to endeavour to prevent the effects of
diſcontents, by forbidding all meetings and aſſo-
ciations of the people, except at ſuch times, and
for ſuch particular purpoſes, as ſhall be permitted
them.

Thus will ſuch a Province be exactly in the
ſame ſtate that *Britain* would be in, were our firſt
executive magiſtrate, our Houſe of Lords, and
our Judges, nothing but the inſtruments of a foreign democratical power; were our Juries no-
minated by that power ; or were we liable to be
tranſported to a diſtant country to be tried for
offences committed here, and reſtrained from calling any meetings, conſulting about any grievances, or aſſociating for any purpoſes, except
when leave ſhould be given us by a *Lord Lieu-
tenant* or *Viceroy.*

It is certain that this is a ſtate of oppreſſion
which no country could endure, and to which it

C 4   would

would be vain to expect, that any people should submit an hour without an armed force to compel them.

The late transactions in *Massachuset's Bay* are a perfect exemplification of what I have now said. The government of *Great Britain* in that Province has gone on exactly in the train I have described; till at last it became necessary to station troops there, not amenable to the civil power; and all terminated in a government by the SWORD. And such, if a people are not sunk below the character of men, will be the issue of all government in similar circumstances.

It ma be asked——" Are there not causes by " which one state may acquire a *rightful* authority " over another, though not consolidated by an ade- " quate Representation ?"——I answer, that there are no such causes.——All the causes to which such an effect *can* be ascribed are CONQUEST, COMPACT, or OBLIGATIONS CONFERRED.

Much has been said of the right of *conquest*; and history contains little more than accounts of kingdoms reduced by it under the dominion of other kingdoms, and of the havock it has made among mankind. But the authority derived from hence, being founded on violence, is never *rightful*. The *Roman Republic* was nothing but a faction against the general liberties of the world; and

had

had no more right to give law to the Provinces
fubject to it, than thieves have to the property
they feize, or to the houfes into which they break.
———Even in the cafe of a juft war undertaken by
one people to defend itfelf againft the oppreffions
of another people, conqueft gives only a right to
an indemnification for the injury which occafioned
the war, and a reafonable fecurity againft future
injury.

Neither can any ftate acquire fuch an authority
over other ftates in virtue of any *compacts* or *ceffions.* This is a cafe in which compacts are not
binding. *Civil* Liberty is, in this refpect, on the
fame footing with *Religious* Liberty. As no people can lawfully furrender their *Religious* Liberty,
by giving up their right of judging for themfelves
in religion, or by allowing any human beings to
prefcribe to them what faith they fhall embrace,
or what mode of worfhip they fhall practife; fo
neither can any civil focieties lawfully furrender
their *Civil* Liberty, by giving up to any extraneous jurifdiction their power of legiflating for themfelves and difpofing their property. Such a ceffion, being inconfiftent with the unalienable rights
of human nature, would either not bind at all;
or bind only the individuals who made it. This
is a bleffing which no one generation of men can
give up for another; and which, when loft, a people have always a right to refume.———Had our
anceftors

anceftors in this country been fo mad as to have fubjected themfelves to any foreign Community, we could not have been under any obligation to continue in fuch a ftate. And all the nations now in the world who, in confequence of the tamenefs and folly of their predeceffors, are fubject to arbitrary power, have a right to emancipate themfelves as foon as they can.

If neither *conqueft* nor *compact* can give fuch an authority, much lefs can any favours received, or any fervices performed by one ftate for another. ——Let the favour received be what it will, Liberty is too dear a price for it. A ftate that has been *obliged* is not, therefore, bound to be *enflaved.* It ought, if poffible, to make an adequate return for the fervices done to it ; but to fuppofe that it ought to give up the power of governing itfelf, and the difpofal of its property, would be to fuppofe, that, in order to fhew its gratitude, it ought to part with the power of ever afterwards exercifing gratitude.——How much has been done by this kingdom for *Hanover ?* But no one will fay that on this account, we have a right to make the laws of *Hanover* ; or even to draw a fingle penny from it without its own confent.

After what has been faid it will, I am afraid, be trifling to apply the preceding arguments to the cafe of different communities, which are confidered

fidered as different parts of the fame *Empire*. But there are reafons which render it neceffary for me to be explicit in making this application.

What I mean here is juft to point out the dif-ference of fituation between communities forming an *Empire*; and particular bodies or claffes of men forming different parts of a *Kingdom*. Different communities forming an *Empire* have no con-nexions, which produce a neceffary reciprocation of interefts between them. They inhabit different diftricts, and are governed by different legiflatures. ——On the contrary. The different claffes of men *within* a *kingdom* are all placed on the fame ground. Their concerns and interefts are the fame; and what is done to one part muft affect all. ——Thefe are fituations totally different; and a conftitution of government that may be confiftent with Liberty in one of them, may be entirely in-confiftent with it in the other. It is, however, certain that, even in the laft of thefe fituations, no one part ought to govern the reft. In order to a fair and equal government, there ought to be a fair and equal reprefentation of all that are govern-ed; and as far as this is wanting in any govern-ment, it deviates from the principles of Liberty, and becomes unjuft and oppreffive.——But in the circumftances of different communities, all this holds with unfpeakably more force. The govern-ment of a part in this cafe becomes complete tyranny;

ranny; and fubjection to it becomes complete flavery.

But ought there not, it is afked, to exift fomewhere in an *Empire* a fupreme legiflative authority over the whole; or a power to controul and bind all the different ftates of which it confifts? — This enquiry has been already anfwered. The truth is, that fuch a fupreme controuling power ought to exift no-where except in fuch a SENATE or body of delegates as that defcribed in page 8; and that the authority or fupremacy of even this fenate ought to be limited to the common concerns of the *Empire*.——I think I have proved that the fundamental principles of Liberty neceffarily require this.

In a word. An *Empire* is a collection of ftates or communities united by fome common bond or tye. If thefe ftates have each of them free conftitutions of government, and, with refpect to taxation and internal legiflation, are independent of the other ftates, but united by compacts, or alliances, or fubjection to a Great *Council*, reprefenting the whole, or to one monarch entrufted with the fupreme executive power: In thefe circumftances, the Empire will be an Empire of Freemen.—If, on the contrary, like the different provinces fubject to the *Grand Seignior*, none of the ftates poffefs any independent legiflative authority; but are all

4

fubject

subject to an absolute monarch, whose will is their law ; then is the Empire an Empire of Slaves.——— If one of the states is free, but governs by its will all the other states ; then is the Empire, like that of the Romans in the times of the republic, an Empire confisting of one state free, and the rest in flavery : Nor does it make any more difference in this case, that the governing state is itself free, than it does, in the case of a kingdom subject to a *despot*, that this despot is himself free. I have before observed, that this only makes the flavery worse. There is, in the one case, a chance, that, in the quick succession of despots, a good one will sometimes arise. But bodies of men continue the same ; and have generally proved the most unrelenting of all tyrants.

A great writer before (*a*) quoted, observes of the *Roman Empire*, that while Liberty was at the center, tyranny prevailed in the distant provinces ; that such as were free under it were extremely so, while those who were flaves groaned under the extremity of flavery ; and that the same events that *destroyed* the liberty of the former, *gave* liberty to the latter.

The Liberty of the *Romans*, therefore, was only an additional calamity to the provinces governed by them ; and though it might have been said of the *citizens* of *Rome*, that they were the " freest

(*a*) Montesquieu's Spirit of Laws, Vol. I. Book 11. C. xix.

" members

" members of any civil fociety in the known
" world ;" yet of the *fubjects* of *Rome*, it muft
have been faid, that they were the completeft
flaves in the known world.——How remarkable
is it, that this very people, once the freeft of
mankind, but at the fame time the moft proud and
tyrannical, fhould become at laft the moft contemptible and abject flaves that ever exifted ?

PART

IN the foregoing difquifitions, I have, from one leading principle, deduced a number of confequences, that feem to me incapable of being difputed. I have meant that they fhould be applied to the great queftion between this kingdom and the Colonies which has occafioned the prefent war with them.

It is impoffible, but my readers muft have been all along making this application; and if they ftill think, that the claims of this kingdom are reconcileable to the principles of true liberty and legitimate government, I am afraid, that nothing I fhall farther fay will have any effect on their judgments. I wifh, however, they would have the patience and candour to go with me, and grant me a hearing fome time longer.

Though clearly decided in my own judgment on this fubject, I am inclined to make great allowances for the different judgments of others. We have been fo ufed to fpeak of the Colonies as *our*

Colonies

Colonies, and to think of them as in a ſtate of ſub-
ordination to us, and as holding their exiſtence in
America only for our uſe, that it is no wonder the
prejudices of many are alarmed, when they find a
different doctrine maintained.   The meaneſt perſon among us is diſpoſed to look upon himſelf as
having a body of ſubjects in *America*; and to be
offended at the denial of his right to make laws
for them, though perhaps he does not know what
colour they are of, or what language they talk.
——Such are the natural prejudices of this country.——But the time is coming, I hope, when the
unreaſonableneſs of them will be ſeen ; and more
juſt ſentiments prevail.

Before I proceed, I beg it may be attended to,
that I have choſen to try this queſtion by the general principles of Civil Liberty ; and not by the
practice of former times ; or by the *Charters* granted the colonies.——The arguments *for* them,
drawn from theſe laſt topics, appear to me greatly
to outweigh the arguments *againſt* them.   But I
wiſh to have this queſtion brought to a higher teſt,
and ſurer iſſue.   The queſtion with all liberal en-
quirers ought to be, not what juriſdiction over
them *Precedents*, *Statutes*, and *Charters* give, but
what reaſon and equity, and the rights of humanity
give.——This is, in truth, a queſtion which no
kingdom has ever before had occaſion to agitate.
The

The cafe of a free country branching itfelf out in the manner *Britain* has done, and fending to a diftant world colonies which have there, from fmall beginnings, and under free legiflatures of their own, increafed, and formed a body of powerful ftates, likely foon to become fuperior to the parent ftate—This is a cafe which is new in the hiftory of mankind; and it is extremely improper to judge of it by the rules of any narrow and partial policy; or to confider it on any other ground than the general one of reafon and juftice.——Thofe who will be candid enough to judge on this ground, and who can diveft themfelves of national prejudices, will not, I fancy, remain long unfatisfied.——But alas! Matters are gone too far. The difpute probably muft be fettled another way; and the fword alone, I am afraid, is now to determine what the rights of *Britain* and *America* are.——Shocking fituation!—Detefted be the meafures which have brought us into it: And, if we are endeavouring to enforce injuftice, curfed will be the war.——A retreat, however, is not yet impracticable. The duty we owe our gracious fovereign obliges us to rely on his difpofition to ftay the fword, and to promote the happinefs of all the different parts of the Empire at the head of which he is placed. With fome hopes, therefore, that it may not be too late to reafon on this fubject, I will, in the fol-

lowing

lowing Sections, enquire what the war with *America* is in the following respects.

1. In respect of Justice.
2. The Principles of the Constitution.
3. In respect of Policy and Humanity.
4. The Honour of the Kingdom.

And lastly, The Probability of succeeding in it.

SECT. I.

Of the Justice of the War with America.

THE enquiry, whether the war with the Colonies is a *just* war, will be best determined by stating the power over them, which it is the end of the war to maintain: And this cannot be better done, than in the words of an act of parliament, made on purpose to define it. That act, it is well known, declares, " That this kingdom has " power, and of right ought to have power to " make laws and statutes to bind the Colonies, " and people of *America*, in all cases whatever." ——Dreadful power indeed! I defy any one to express slavery in stronger language. It is the same with declaring " that we have a right to do with them what we please."——I will not waste my time by applying to such a claim any of the preceding arguments. If my reader does not feel

more

more in this cafe, than words can exprefs, all reafoning muft be vain.

But, probably, moft perfons will be for ufing
milder language ; and for faying no more than,
that the united legiflatures of *England* and *Scotland* have of right power to tax the Colonies, and
a *fupremacy* of legiflation over *America*.——But
this comes to the fame. If it means any thing, it
means, that the property and the legiflations of
the Colonies, are fubject to the abfolute difcretion
of *Great Britain*, and ought of right to be fo. The
nature of the thing admits of no limitation. The
Colonies can never be admitted to be judges, how
far the authority over them in thefe cafes fhall extend. This would be to deftroy it entirely.——
If *any* part of their property is fubject to our difcretion, the *whole* muft be fo. If we have a right
to interfere at all in their internal legiflations, we
have a right to interfere as far as we think proper.
——It is felf-evident, that this leaves them nothing
they can call *their own*.——And what is it that
can give to any people fuch a fupremacy over
another people? ——I have already examined
the principal anfwers which have been given to
this enquiry. But it will not be amifs in this place
to go over fome of them again.

It has been urged, that fuch a right muft be
lodged fomewhere, " in order to preferve the
" UNITY of the Britifh Empire."

Pleas

Pleas of this fort have, in all ages, been ufed to juftify tyranny.———They have in RELIGION given rife to numberlefs oppreffive claims, and flavifh Hierarchies. And in the *Romifh Communion* particularly, it is well known, that the POPE claims the title and powers of the fupreme head on earth of the Chriftian church, in order to pre-ferve its UNITY.———With refpect to the *Britifh Empire*, nothing can be more prepofterous than to endeavour to maintain its unity, by fetting up fuch a claim. This is a method of eftablifhing unity, which, like the fimilar method in religion, can produce nothing but difcord and mifchief.——— The truth is, that a common relation to one fu-preme executive head; an exchange of kind of-fices; tyes of intereft and affection, and *compacts*, are fufficient to give the Britifh Empire all the unity that is neceffary. But if not———If, in or-der to preferve its *Unity*, one half of it muft be en-flaved to the other half, let it, in the name of God, want Unity.

Much has been faid of " the *Superiority* of the " Britifh State." But what gives us our fuperiori-ty?—Is it our *Wealth*?—This never confers real dignity. On the contrary: Its effect is always to debafe, intoxicate, and corrupt.———Is it the *num-ber of our people*? The colonies will foon be equal to us in number.—Is it our *Knowledge* and *Virtue*? They are probably *equally* knowing, and *more* virtuous.

virtuous. There are names among them that will not ftoop to any names among the philofophers and politicians of this ifland.

But we are the PARENT STATE."——Thefe are the magic words which have fafcinated and mifled us.————The Englifh came from *Germany*. Does that give the *German* ftates a right to tax us?—— Children, having no property, and being incapable of guiding themfelves, the author of nature has committed the care of them to their parents, and fubjeéted them to their abfolute authority. But there is a period when, having acquired property, and a capacity of judging for themfelves, they become independent agents; and when, for this reafon, the authority of their parents ceafes, and becomes nothing but the refpeét and influence due to benefaétors. Suppofing, therefore, that the order of nature in eftablifhing the relation between parents and children, ought to have been the rule of our conduét to the Colonies, we fhould have been gradually relaxing our authority as they grew up. But, like mad parents, we have done the contrary; and, at the very time when our authority fhould have been moft relaxed, we have carried it to the greateft extent, and exercifed it with the greateft rigour. No wonder then, that they have turned upon us; and obliged us to remember, that they are not Children.

D 3 " But

" But we have, it is said, protected them, and
" run deeply in debt on their account."—The full
answer to this has been already given, (page 26.)
Will any one say, that all we have done for them
has not been more on our *own* account, (*a*) than
on *theirs* ?——But suppose the contrary. Have
they done nothing for us? Have they made no
compensation for the protection they have received? Have they not helped us to pay our *taxes*, to
support our poor, and to bear the burthen of our
debts, by taking from us, at our own price, all the
commodities with which we can supply them?—
Have they not, for our advantage, submitted to

(*a*) This is particularly true of the *bounties* granted on some
American commodities (as pitch, tar, indigo, &c.) when imported into *Britain*; for it is well known, that the end of
granting them was, to get those commodities cheaper from the
Colonies, and in return for our manufactures, which we used
to get from *Russia* and other foreign countries. And this is
expressed in the preambles of the laws which grant these bounties. See the Appeal to the Justice, &c. page 21; third edition.
It is, therefore, strange that Doctor TUCKER and others, should
have insisted so much upon these bounties as favours and indul-
gencies to the Colonies.—But it is still more strange, that the
same representation should have been made of the compensa-
tions granted them for doing more during the last war in assist-
ing us than could have been reasonably expected; and also
of the sums we have spent in maintaining troops among them
without their consent; and in opposition to their wishes.——
See a pamphlet, entitled " The rights of Great Britain af-
serted against the claims of America."

many

many reftraints in acquiring property ? Muft they likewife refign to us the difpofal of that property ? —Has not their exclufive trade with us been for many years one of the chief fources of our wealth and power ?—In all our wars have they not fought by our fide, and contributed much to our fuccefs ? In the laft war, particularly, it is well known, that they ran themfelves deeply in debt; and that the parliament thought it neceffary to grant them confiderable fums annually as compenfations for going beyond their abilities in affifting us. And in this courfe would they have continued for many future years; perhaps, for ever.—In fhort; were an accurate account ftated, it is by no means certain which fide would appear to be moft indebted. When afked as *freemen*, they have hitherto feldom difcovered any reluctance in giving. But, in obedience to a demand, and with the bayonet at their breafts, they will give us nothing but blood.

It is farther faid, " that the land on which they " fettled was ours."—But how came it to be ours ? If failing along a coaft can give a right to a country, then might the people of *Japan* become, as foon as they pleafe, the proprietors of *Britain*. Nothing can be more chimerical than property founded on fuch a reafon. If the land on which the Colonies firft fettled had any proprietors, they were the natives. The greateft part of it they

bought

bought of the natives. They have since cleared
and cultivated it; and, without any help from us,
converted a wilderneſs into fruitful and pleaſant
fields. It is, therefore, now on a double account
their property; and no power on earth can have
any right to diſturb them in the poſſeſſion of it, or
to take from them, without their conſent, any part
of its produce.

But let it be granted, that the land was ours.
Did they not ſettle upon it under the faith of charters, which promiſed them the enjoyment of all
the rights of *Engliſhmen*; and allowed them to tax
themſelves, and to be governed by legiſlatures of
their own, ſimilar to ours? Theſe charters were
given them by an authority, which at the time was
thought competent; and they have been rendered
ſacred by an acquieſcence on our part for near
a century. Can it then be wondered at, that
the Colonies ſhould revolt, when they found their
charters violated; and an attempt made to force
INNOVATIONS upon them by famine and the ſword;
——But I lay no ſtreſs on charters. They derive
their rights from a higher ſource. It is inconſiſtent with common ſenſe to imagine, that any people
would ever think of ſettling in a diſtant country,
on any ſuch condition, as that the people from
whom they withdrew, ſhould for ever be maſters of
their property, and have power to ſubject them to
any modes of government they pleaſed. And had
there

there been exprefs ftipulations to this purpofe in all
the charters of the colonies, they would, in my
opinion, be no more bound by them, than if it
had been ftipulated with them, that they fhould go
naked, or expofe themfelves to the incurfions of
wolves and tigers.

The defective ftate of the reprefentation of this
kingdom has been farther pleaded to prove our
right to tax *America*. We fubmit to a parliament
that does not reprefent us, and therefore they
ought.——How ftrange an argument is this? It
is faying we want liberty; and therefore, they
ought to want it.——Suppofe it true, that they
are indeed contending for a better conftitution of
government, and more liberty than we enjoy:
Ought this to make us angry?——Who is there
that does not fee the danger to which this country
is expofed?——Is it generous, becaufe we are in
a fink, to endeavour to draw them into it? Ought
we not rather to wifh earneftly, that there may at
leaft be ONE FREE COUNTRY left upon earth, to
which we may fly, when venality, luxury, and vice
have completed the ruin of liberty here?

It is, however, by no means true, that *America*
has no more right to be exempted from taxation
by the *Britifh* parliament, than *Britain* itfelf.——
Here, all freeholders, and burgeffes in boroughs,
are reprefented. *There*, not one *Freeholder*, or any
other perfon, is reprefented.——*Here*, the *aids*
granted

granted by the reprefented part of the kingdom muft be proportionably *paid* by themfelves; and the laws they make for *others*, they at the fame time make for *themfelves*. *There*, the aids they would grant would not be *paid*, but *received*, by themfelves; and the laws they made would be made for *others only*.—In fhort. The relation of one country to another country, whofe reprefentatives have the power of taxing it (and of appropriating the money raifed by the taxes) is much the fame with the relation of a country to a fingle defpot, or a body of defpots, within itfelf, invefted with the like power. In both cafes, the people taxed and thofe who tax have feparate interefts; nor can there be any thing to check oppreffion, befides either the abilities of the people taxed, or the humanity of the *taxers*.—But indeed I can never hope to convince that perfon of any thing, who does not fee an effential difference (*a*) between the two cafes now

(*a*) It is remarkable that even the author of the *Remarks on the Principal Acts of the* 13*th Parliament of Great Britain*, &c. finds himfelf obliged to acknowledge this difference.——— There cannot be more deteftable principles of government, than thofe which are maintained by this writer. According to him, the *properties* and *rights* of a people are only a kind of *alms* given them by their civil governors. Taxes, therefore, he afferts, are not the *gifts* of the people. See page 58, and 191.

mentioned;

mentioned; or between the circumftances of individuals, and claffes of men, making parts of a community imperfectly reprefented in the legiflature that governs it; and the circumftances of a whole community, in a diftant world, not at all reprefented.

But enough has been faid by others on this point; nor is it poffible for me to throw any new light upon it. To finifh, therefore, what I meant to offer under this head, I muft beg that the following confiderations may be particularly attended to.

The queftion now between us and the Colonies is, Whether, in refpect of taxation and internal legiflation, they are bound to be fubject to the jurifdiction of this kingdom : Or, in other words, Whether the *Britifh* parliament has or has not of right, a power to difpofe of their property, and to model as it pleafes their governments?——To this fupremacy over them, we fay, we are entitled ; and in order to maintain it, we have begun the prefent war.——Let me here enquire,

1ft, Whether, if we have now this fupremacy, we fhall not be equally entitled to it in any future time?——They are now but little fhort of half our number. To this number they have grown, from a fmall body of original fettlers, by a very rapid increafe. The probability is, that they will

go

go on to increafe ; and that, in 50 or 60 years, they will be *double* our number ; (*a*) and form a mighty Empire, confifting of a variety of ftates, all equal or fuperior to ourfelves in all the arts and accomplifhments, which give dignity and happinefs to human life. In that period, will they be ftill bound to acknowledge that fupremacy over them which we now claim ? Can there be any perfon who will affert this ; or whofe mind does not revolt at the idea of a vaft continent, holding all that is valuable to it, at the difcretion of a handful of people on the other fide the *Atlantic* ?——— But if, at *that* period, this would be unreafonable ; what makes it otherwife *now* ?—Draw the line, if you can.—But there is a ftill greater difficulty.

Britain is now, I will fuppofe, the feat of Liberty and Virtue ; and its legiflature confifts of a body of able and independent men, who govern with wifdom and juftice. The time may come when all will be reverfed : When its excellent conftitution of government will be fubverted : When, preffed by debts and taxes, it will be greedy to draw to itfelf an increafe of revenue from every diftant Province, in order to eafe its own burdens : When the influence of the crown, ftrengthened by luxury and an univerfal profligacy of manners, will have tainted every heart, broken down every fence

(*a*) See Obfervations on Reverfionary Payments, page 207, &c.

of

of Liberty, and rendered us a nation of tame and contented vaffals : When a General *Election* will be nothing but a general *Auction* of Boroughs : And when the PARLIAMENT, the Grand Council of the nation, and once the faithful guardian of the ftate, and a terror to evil minifters, will be degenerated into a body of *Sycophants*, dependent and venal, always ready to confirm *any* meafures ; and little more than a public court for regiftering royal edicts.——Such, it is poffible, may, fome time or other, be the ftate of *Great Britain.*——What will, at that period, be the duty of the Colonies ? Will they be ftill bound to unconditional fub-miffion ? Muft they always continue an appendage to our government ; and follow it implicitly through every change that can happen to it ?—— Wretched condition, indeed, of millions of free-men as good as ourfelves.——Will you fay that we now govern equitably ; and that there is no danger of any fuch revolution ?—Would to God this were true.——But will you not always fay the fame ? Who fhall judge whether we govern equi-tably or not ? Can you give the Colonies any *fecurity* that fuch a period will never come ? Once more.

If we have indeed that power which we claim over the legiflations, and internal rights of the Colonies, may we not, whenever we pleafe, fub-ject them to the arbitrary power of the crown ? —— I do not mean, that this would be a difad-

vantageous

vantageous, change: For I have before obferved;
that if a people are to be fubject to an external
power over which they have no command, it is
better that power fhould be lodged in the hands of
one man than of a multitude. But many perfons
think otherwife; and fuch ought to confider that;
if this would be a calamity, the condition of the
Colonies muft be deplorable.———" A government by King, Lords, and Commons, (it has
been faid) is the perfection of government;" and
fo it is, when the Commons are a juft reprefentation of the people; and when alfo, it is not
extended to any diftant people, or communities,
not reprefented. But if this is the *beft*, a government by a king only muft be the *worft*; and
every claim implying a right to eftablifh fuch
a government among any people muft be unjuft
and cruel.———It is felf-evident, that by claiming
a right to alter the conftitutions of the Colonies,
according to our difcretion, we claim this power:
And it is a power that we have thought fit to exercife in *one* of our Colonies; and that we have attempted to exercife in *another*.———*Canada*, according to the late extenfion of its limits, is a
country almoft as large as half *Europe*; and it may
poffibly come in time to be filled with Britifh fubjects. The *Quebec* act makes the king of *Great
Britain* a defpot over all that country.———In the
Province of *Maffachufet's Bay* the fame thing has
been attempted and begun.

The

The act for BETTER *regulating their government*, passed at the same time with the *Quebec* act, gives the king the right of appointing, and removing at his pleasure, the members of one part of the legislature; alters the mode of chusing juries, on purpose to bring it more under the influence of the king; and takes away from the province the power of calling any meetings of the people without the king's consent. (*a*) ——The judges, likewise, have been made dependent on the king, for their nomination and pay, and continuance in office.—If all this is no more than we have a right to do; may we not go on to abolish the house of representatives, to destroy all trials by juries, and to give up the province absolutely and totally to the will of the king?——May we not even establish popery in the province, as has been lately done in *Canada*, leaving the support of protestantism to the king's discretion?—Can there be any Englishman who, were it his own case, would not sooner lose his heart's blood than yield to claims so pregnant with evils, and destructive to every thing that can distinguish a *Freeman* from a *Slave?*

I will take this opportunity to add, that what I have now said, suggests a consideration that demonstrates, on how different a footing the Colonies are with respect to our government, from particular bodies of men *within* the kingdom, who hap-

(*a*) See page 22.

pen

pen not to be reprefented. Here, it is impoffible
that the reprefented part fhould fubject the unreprefented part to arbitrary power, without including themfelves. But in the Colonies it is *not*
impoffible. We know that it *has* been done.

S E C T. II.

Whether the War with America *is juftified by
the Principles of the Conftitution.*

I Have propofed, in the next place, to examine
the war with the Colonies by the principles of
the conftitution.—I know, that it is common to
fay that we are now maintaining the conftitution in
America. If this means that we are endeavouring
to eftablifh our own conftitution of government
there; it is by no means true; nor, were it true,
would it be right. They have chartered governments of their own, with which they are pleafed;
and which, if any power on earth may change
without their confent, that power may likewife, if
it thinks proper, deliver them over to the *Grand
Seignior.*——Suppofe the Colonies of *France* had,
by compacts, enjoyed for many years, free governments open to all the world, under which they had
grown and flourifhed; what fhould we think of
that kingdom, were it to attempt to deftroy their
governments, and to force upon them its own
mode of government? Should we not applaud
                                                    any

any zeal they difcovered in repelling fuch an in-
juiy?——But the truth is, in the prefent inftance, that we are not maintaining but violating
our own conftitution in *America*. The effence of
our conftitution confifts in its independency.
There is in this cafe no difference between *fubjection* and *annihilation*. Did, therefore, the Colonies
poffefs governments perfectly the fame with ours,
the attempt to fubject them to ours would be an
attempt to ruin them. A free government lofes
its nature from the moment it becomes liable to be
commanded or altered by any fuperior power.

But I intended here principally to make the following obfervation.

The fundamental principle of our government
is, " The right of a people to give and grant their
own money."——It is of no confequence, in
this cafe, whether we enjoy this right in a proper
manner or not. Moft certainly we do not. It is,
however, the *principle* on which our government,
as a *free* government, is founded. The *fpirit* of
the conftitution gives it us; and, however imperfectly enjoyed, we glory in it as our firft and
greateft blefling. It was an attempt to encroach
upon this right, in a trifling inftance, that produced the civil war in the reign of *Charles* the Firft.——
Ought not our brethren in *America* to enjoy this
right as well as ourfelves? Do the principles of
the conftitution give it *us*, but deny it to *them*?

E   Or

Or can we, with any decency, pretend that when we give to the king *their* money, we give him *our own?* (a)———What difference does it make, that in the time of *Charles the First* the attempt to take away this right was made by *one man:* but that, in the case of *America*, it is made by a body of men?

In a word. This is a war undertaken not only against the principles of our own constitution; but on purpose to destroy other similar constitutions in *America*; and to substitute in their room a military force. See page 23, 24.———It is, therefore, a gross and flagrant violation of the constitution.

S E C T. III.

Of the Policy of the War with America.

IN writing the present Section, I enter upon a subject of the last importance, on which much has been said by other writers with great force, and in the ablest manner (b). But I am not

(a) The author of *Taxation no Tyranny* will undoubtedly assert this without hesitation, for in page 69 he compares our present situation with respect to the Colonies to that of the antient *Scythians*, who, upon returning from a war, *found themselves shut out of their* OWN HOUSES *by their* SLAVES.

(b) See particularly, a speech intended to have been spoken on the bill for altering the Charter of the Colony of Massachuset's Bay; the *Considerations on the Measures carrying on with respect to the British Colonies*; the *Two Appeals to the Justice and Interests of the People*; and the *further Examination*, just published, *of our present American Measures*, by the Author of the *Considerations*, &c.

willing

willing to omit any topic which I think of great confequence, merely becaufe it has already been difcuffed: And; with refpect to this in particular, it will, I believe, be found that fome of the obfervations on which I fhall infift, have not been fufficiently attended to.

The object of this war has been often enough declared to be " maintaining the fupremacy of this " country over the colonies. ' I have already enquired how far reafon and juftice, the principles of Liberty, and the rights of humanity, entitle us to this fupremacy. Setting afide, therefore, now all confiderations of this kind, I would obferve, that this fupremacy is to be maintained, either merely *for its own fake*, or for the fake of fome public intereft connected with it and dependent upon it.——If *for its own fake*; the only object of the war is the extenfion of dominion; and its only motive is the luft of power.——All government, even *within* a ftate, becomes tyrannical, as far as it is a needlefs and wanton exercife of power; or is carried farther than is abfolutely neceffary to preferve the peace and to fecure the fafety of the ftate. This is what an excellent writer calls GOVERNING TOO MUCH; and its effect muft always be, weakening government by rendering it contemptible and odious.——Nothing can be of more importance, in governing

E 2

verning diftant provinces and adjufting the clafh-
ing interefts of different focieties, than attention to
this remark. In thefe circumftances it is *particularly* neceffary to make a fparing ufe of power, in
order to preferve power.——Happy would it have
been for *Great Britain*, had this been remembered
by thofe who have lately conducted its affairs.
But our policy has been of another kind. At the
period when our authority fhould have been moft
concealed, it has been brought moft in view;
and by a progreffion of violent meafures, every
one of which has increafed diftrefs, we have given
the world reafon to conclude, that we are acquainted with no other method of governing than *by
force*——What a fhocking miftake!—If our object
is power, we fhould have known better how to ufe
it; and our rulers fhould have confidered, that
freemen will always revolt at the fight of a naked
fword; and that the complicated affairs of a great
kingdom, holding in fubordination to it a multitude of diftant communities, all jealous of their
rights, and warmed with fpirits as high as our own,
require not only the moft fkilful, but the moft cautious and tender management. The confequences
of a different management we are now feeling.
We fee ourfelves driven among rocks, and in danger of being loft.

The following reafons make it too probable,
that the prefent conteft with *America* is a conteft
for

for power only (*a*), abftracted from all the advantages connected with it.

1ſt. There is a love of power inherent in
human nature; and it cannot be uncharit-
able to ſuppofe that the nation in general, and
the cabinet in particular, are too likely to be influenced by it. What can be more flattering than to
look acrofs the *Atlantic*, and to fee in the boundlefs continent of *America*, increafing MILLIONS
whom we have a right to order as we pleafe, who
hold their property at our difpofal, and who have
no other law than our will. With what compla-
cency have we been ufed to talk of them as OUR
fubjects?——Is it not the interruption they now
give to this pleafure; is it not the oppofition they
make to our pride; and not any injury they have
done us, that is the fecret fpring of our prefent ani-
mofity againft them?———I wifh all in this kingdom would examine themfelves carefully on this
point. Perhaps, they might find, that they have
not known what fpirit they are of.—Perhaps, they
would become fenfible, that it was a fpirit of domination, more than a regard to the true intereft of

(*a*) I have heard it faid by a perfon in one of the firſt de-
partments of the ftate, that the prefent conteft is for Do-
MINION on the fide of the Colonies, as well as on ours: And
fo it is indeed; but with this effential difference. *We* are
ftruggling for dominion over OTHERS. *They* are ftruggling
for SELF-dominion: The nobleft of all bleffings.

E 3   this

this country, that lately led ſo many of them, with
ſuch ſavage folly, to addreſs the throne for the
ſlaughter of their brethren in *America*, if they will
not ſubmit to them ; and to make offers of their
lives and fortunes for that purpoſe.——Indeed, I
am perſuaded, that, were pride and the luſt of dominion exterminated from every heart among us,
and the humility of Chriſtians infuſed in their
room, this quarrel would be ſoon ended.

2*dly*. Another reaſon for believing that this is a
conteſt for power only is, that our miniſters have
frequently declared, that their object is not to draw
a revenue from *America* ; and that many of thoſe
who are warmeſt for continuing it, repreſent the
American trade as of no great conſequence.

But what deſerves particular conſideration here
is, that this is a conteſt from which no advantages can poſſibly be derived.——Not a revenue :
For the provinces of America, when deſolated,
will afford no revenue ; or if they ſhould, the expence of ſubduing them and keeping them in ſub-
jection will much exceed that revenue.——Not
any of the advantages of trade : For it is a folly,
next to inſanity, to think trade can be promoted
by impoveriſhing our cuſtomers, and fixing in
their minds an everlaſting abhorrence of us.——
It remains, therefore, that this war can have no
other object than the extenſion of power.——Mi-
ſerable

ferable reflection !——To fheath our fwords in the
bowels of our brethren, and fpread mifery and
ruin among a happy people, for no other end
than to oblige them to acknowledge our fupremacy. How horrid !—This is the curfed ambition
that led a *Cæfar* and an *Alexander*, and many other
mad conquerors, to attack peaceful communities,
and to lay wafte the earth.

But a worfe principle than even this, influences
fome among us. Pride and the love of dominion
are principles hateful enough ; but blind refentment and the defire of revenge are infernal principles : And thefe, I am afraid, have no fmall fhare
at prefent in guiding our public conduct.——
One cannot help indeed being aftonifhed at the
virulence, with which fome fpeak on the prefent
occafion againft the Colonies.——For, what have
they done?—Have they croffed the ocean and
invaded us ? Have they attempted to take from
us the fruits of our labour, and to overturn that
form of government which we hold fo facred ?—
This cannot be pretended.——On the contrary.
This is what we have done to them.——We have
tranfported ourfelves to their peaceful retreats,
and employed our fleets and armies to ftop up
their ports, to deftroy their commerce, to feize
their effects, and to burn their towns. Would we
but let them alone, and fuffer them to enjoy in
fecurity their property and governments, inftead

of

of difturbing us, they would thank and blefs us.
And yet it is WE who imagine ourfelves ill-ufed.
————The truth is, we expected to find them
a cowardly rabble who would lie quietly at our
feet; and they have difappointed us. They have
rifen in their own defence, and repelled force by
force. They deny the plenitude of our power
over them; and infift upon being treated as free
communities.————It is THIS that has provoked
us; and kindled our governors into rage.

I hope I fhall not here be underftood to inti-
mate, that *all* who promote this war are actuated
by thefe principles. Some, I doubt not, are influenced by no other principle, than a regard to
what they think the juft authority of this country
over its colonies, and to the unity and indivifibi-
lity of the Britifh Empire. I wifh fuch could be
engaged to enter thoroughly into the enquiry,
which has been the fubject of the firft part of this
pamphlet; and to confider, particularly, how different a thing maintaining the authority of government *within* a ftate is from maintaining the authority of one people over another, already happy in
the enjoyment of a government of their own. I
wifh farther they would confider, that the defire of
maintaining authority is warrantable, only as far as
it is the means of promoting fome end, and doing
fome good; and that, before we refolve to fpread
famine and fire through a country in order to make

it

it acknowledge our authority, we ought to be affured that great advantages will arife not only to
ourfelves, but to the country we wifh to conquer.
——That from the prefent conteft no advantage
to *ourfelves* can arife, has been already fhewn, and
will prefently be fhewn more at large.——That no
advantage to the Colonies can arife from it, need
not, I hope, be fhewn. It has however been afferted, that even *their* good is intended by this
war. Many of us are perfuaded, that they will be
much happier under our government, than under
any government of their own ; and that their liberties will be fafer when held for them by us,
than when trufted in their own hands.——How
kind is it thus to take upon us the trouble of
judging for them what is moft for their happinefs?
Nothing can be kinder except the refolution we
have formed to exterminate them, if they will not
fubmit to our judgment.——What ftrange language have I fometimes heard? By an armed
force we are now endeavouring to deftroy the laws
and governments of America; and yet I have
heard it faid, that we are endeavouring to fupport
law and government there. We are infifting upon
our right to levy contributions upon them ; and
to maintain this right, we are bringing upon them
all the miferies a people can endure; and yet it is
afferted, that we mean nothing but their fecurity
and happinefs.

3   But

But I have wandered a little from the point I attended principally to infift upon in this fection, which is, " the folly, in refpect of policy, of the " meafures which have brought on this conteft; " and its pernicious and fatal tendency."

The following obfervations will, I believe, abundantly prove this.

1ft. There are points which are likely always to fuffer by difcuffion. Of this kind are moft points of authority and prerogative; and the beft policy is to avoid, as much as poffible, giving any occafion for calling them into queftion.

The colonies were at the beginning of this reign in the habit of acknowledging our authority, and of allowing us as much power over them as our intereft required; and more, in fome inftances, than we could reafonably claim. This habit they would have retained: and had we, inftead of impofing new burdens upon them, and increafing their reftraints, ftudied to promote their commerce, and to grant them new indulgences, they would have been always growing more attached to us. Luxury, and, together with it, their dependence upon us, and our influence (a) in their affemblies, would have increafed, till in time perhaps they would have become as corrupt as our-

(a) This has been our policy with refpect to the people of *Ireland*; and the confequence is, that we now fee their parliament as obedient as we can wifh.

felves;

felves; and we might have fucceeded to our wifhes
in eftablifhing our authority over them.——But,
happily for *them*, we have chofen a different courfe.
By exertions of authority which have alarmed them,
they have been put upon examining into the
grounds of all our claims, and forced to give up
their luxuries, and to feek all their refources within themfelves: And the iffue is likely to prove
the lofs of *all* our authority over them, and of all
the advantages connected with it. So little do
men in power fometimes know how to preferve
power; and fo remarkably does the defire of ex-
tending dominion fometimes deftroy it.——Mankind are naturally difpofed to continue in fubjection to that mode of government, be it what it
will, under which they have been born and educa-
ted. Nothing roufes them into refiftance but grofs
abufes, or fome particular oppreffions out of the
road to which they have been ufed. And he who
will examine the hiftory of the world will find,
there has generally been more reafon for complain-
ing that they have been too patient, than that they
have been turbulent and rebellious.

Our governors, ever fince I can remember, have
been jealous that the Colonies, fome time or other,
would throw off their dependence. This jealoufy
was not founded on any of their acts or declarations. They have always, while at *peace* with
us, difclaimed any fuch defign; and they have
continued to difclaim it fince they have been at

3 *war*

war with us. I have reason, indeed, to believe, that independency is, even at this moment, (*a*) generally dreaded among them as a calamity to which they are in danger of being driven, in order to avoid a greater.——The jealousy I have mentioned, was, however, natural ; and betrayed a secret opinion, that the subjection in which they were held was more than we could expect them always to endure. In such circumstances, all possible care should have been taken to give them no reason for discontent, and to preserve them in subjection, by keeping in that line of conduct to which custom had reconciled them, or at least never deviating from it, except with great caution ; and particularly, by avoiding all direct attacks on their property and legislations. Had we done this, the different interests of so many states scattered over a vast continent, joined to our own prudence and moderation, would have enabled us to maintain them in dependence for ages to come.——But instead of this, how have we acted ?——It is in truth too evident, that our whole conduct, instead of being directed by that sound policy and foresight which in such circumstances were absolutely necessary, has been nothing (to say the best of it) but a series of the blindest rigour followed by re-

(*a*) It should be remembered, that this was written some time before the Declaration of Independence in July 1776. See page 85 of the next Tract.

tractation ;

tractation ; of violence followed by conceffion ; of miftake, weaknefs and inconfiftency.——A re- cital of a few facts, within every body's recol- lection, will fully prove this.

In the 6th of *George the Second*, an act was paffed for impofing certain duties on all foreign fpirits, molaffes and fugars imported into the plan- tations. In this act, the duties impofed are faid to be GIVEN and GRANTED by the Parliament to the King; and this is the firft *American* act in which thefe words have been ufed. But notwithftanding this, as the act had the appearance of being only a regulation of trade, the colonies fubmitted to it ; and a fmall direct revenue was drawn by it from them.——In the 4th of the prefent reign, many alterations were made in this act, with the declared purpofe of making provifion for raifing a revenue in America. This alarmed the Colonies ; and produced difcontents and remon- ftrances, which might have convinced our rulers this was tender ground, on which it became them to tread very gently.——There is, however, no reafon to doubt but in time they would have funk into a quiet fubmiffion to this revenue act, as being at worft only the exercife of a power which then they feem not to have thought much of contefting ; I mean, the power of taxing them EXTERNALLY.——But before they had time to cool, a worfe provocation was given them ; and the STAMP-ACT was paffed. This being an at- tempt

tempt to tax them INTERNALLY; and a direct attack on their property, by a power which would not suffer itself to be questioned; which eased *itself* by loading *them*; and to which it was impossible to fix any bounds; they were thrown at once, from one end of the continent to the other, into resistance and rage.——Government, dreading the consequences, gave way; and the Parliament (upon a change of ministry) repealed the *Stamp-Act*, without requiring from them any recognition of its authority, or doing any more to preserve its dignity, than asserting, by the declaratory law, that it was possessed of full power and authority to make laws to bind them in all cases whatever.——Upon this, peace was restored; and, had no farther attempts of the same kind been made, they would undoubtedly have suffered us (as the people of *Ireland* have done) to enjoy quietly our declaratory law. They would have recovered their former habits of subjection; and our connexion with them might have continued an increasing source of our wealth and glory.——But the spirit of despotism and avarice, always blind and restless, soon broke forth again. The scheme for drawing a revenue from *America*, by parliamentary taxation, was resumed; and in a little more than a year after the repeal of the *Stamp-Act*, when all was peace, a third act was passed, imposing duties payable in *America* on tea, paper, glass, painters colours, &c.
——This,

——This, as might have been expected, revived all the former heats; and the Empire was a second time threatened with the moſt dangerous commotions.——Government receded again; and the Parliament (under another change of miniſtry) repealed all the obnoxious duties, EXCEPT that upon tea. This exception was made in order to maintain a ſhew of dignity. But it was, in reality, ſacrificing ſafety to pride; and leaving a ſplinter in the wound to produce a gangrene. ——For ſome time, however, this relaxation anſwered its intended purpoſes. Our commercial intercourſe with the Colonies was again recovered; and they avoided nothing but that tea which we had excepted in our repeal. In this ſtate would things have remained, and even tea would perhaps in time have been gradually admitted, had not the evil genius of *Britain* ſtepped forth once more to embroil the Empire.

The *Eaſt India* company having fallen under difficulties, partly in conſequence of the loſs of the *American* market for tea, a ſcheme was formed for aſſiſting them by an attempt to recover that market. With this view an act was paſſed to enable them to export their tea to *America* free of all duties here, and ſubject only to 3d. per pound duty, payable in *America*. It was to be offered at a low price; and it was expected the conſequence would prove that the

Colonies

Colonies would be tempted to buy it; a precedent
gained for taxing them; and at the same time the
company relieved. Ships were, therefore, fitted
out; and large cargoes sent. The snare was too
grofs to escape the notice of the Colonies. They
saw it, and spurned at it. They refused to admit
the tea; and at Boston some persons in disguise
threw it into the sea.—Had our governors in this
case satisfied themselves with requiring a compensation from the province for the damage done, there is
no doubt but it would have been granted. Or
had they proceeded no farther in the infliction of
punishment, than stopping up the port and destroying the trade of Boston, till compensation was
made, the province might possibly have submitted, and a sufficient saving would have been gained for the honour of the nation. But having hitherto proceeded without wisdom, they observed
now no bounds in their resentment. To the Bofton port bill was added a bill which destroyed the
chartered government of the province; a bill
which withdrew from the jurisdiction of the province, persons who in particular cases should commit murder; and the *Quebec* bill. At the same
time a strong body of troops was stationed at *Boston*
to enforce obedience to these bills.

All who knew any thing of the temper of the
Colonies saw that the effect of this sudden accumulation

mulation of vengeance, would probably be not intimidating but exafperating them, and driving them into a general revolt. But our minifter had different apprehenfions. They believed that the malecontents in the Colony of *Maffackufett*'s were a fmall party, headed by a few factious men; that the majority of the people would take the fide of government, as foon as they faw a force among them capable of fupporting them; that, at worft, the Colonies in general would never make a common caufe with this province; and that, the iffue would prove, in a few months, order, tranquility and fubmiffion.—Every one of thefe apprehenfions was falfified by the events that followed.

When the bills I have mentioned came to be carried into execution, the whole province was thrown into confufion. The courts of juftice were fhut up, and all government was diffolved. The commander in chief found it neceffary to fortify himfelf in Bofton; and the other Colonies immediately refolved to make a common caufe with this Colony.

Difappointed by thefe confequences, our minifters took fright. Once more they made an effort to retreat; but indeed the moft ungracious one that can well be imagined. A propofal was fent to the Colonies, called Conciliatory; and the fubftance of which was, that if any of them would raife fuch fums as fhould be demanded of them by taxing themfelves, the Parliament would for-

F bear

bear to tax them.——It will be fcarcely believed, hereafter, that fuch a propofal could be thought conciliatory. It was only telling them; " If " you will tax yourfelves BY OUR ORDER, we will " fave ourfelves the trouble of taxing you."—— They received the propofal as an infult; and rejeced it with difdain.

At the time this conceffion was tranfmitted to *America*, open hoftilities were not begun. In the fword our minifters thought they had ftill a refource which would immediately fettle all difputes. They confidered the people of *New-England* as nothing but a mob, who would be foon routed and forced into obedience. It was even believed, that a few thoufands of our army might march through all *America*, and make all quiet whereever they went. Under this conviction our minifters did not dread urging the Province of *Maffachufett's Bay* into rebellion, by ordering the army to feize their ftores, and to take up fome of their leading men.——The attempt was made.—— The people fled immediately to arms, and repelled the attack.——A confiderable part of the flower of the Britifh army has been deftroyed. ——Some of our beft Generals, and the braveft of our troops, are now (*a*) difgracefully and mif-

(*a*) In February 1776.—In a few weeks after this, they were driven from *Bofton*; and took refuge at *Hallifax* in *Nova Scotia*; from whence, after a ftrong reinforcement, they invaded the Province of *New-York*.

erably

erably imprifoned at *Bofton.*——A horrid civil war is commenced ;——And the Empire is diftracted and convulfed.

Can it be poffible to think with patience of the policy that has brought us into thefe circumftances? Did ever Heaven punifh the vices of a people more feverely by darkening their counfels? How great would be our happinefs could we now recal former times, and return to the policy of the laft reigns?—But thofe times are gone. ——I will, however, beg leave for a few moments to look back to them; and to compare the ground we have left with that on which we find ourfelves. This muft be done with deep regret; but it forms a neceffary part of my prefent defign.

In thofe times our Colonies, foregoing every advantage which they might derive from trading with foreign nations, confented to fend only to us whatever it was for our intereft to receive from them; and to receive only from us whatever it was for our intereft to fend to them. They gave up the power of making fumptuary laws, and expofed themfelves to all the evils of an increafing and wafteful luxury, becaufe we were benefited by vending among them the materials of it. The iron with which providence had bleffed their country, they were required by laws, in which they acquiefced, to tranfport hither, that our people might be

maintained

maintained by working it for them into nails, ploughs, axes, &c. And, in several instances, even one Colony was not allowed to supply any neighbouring Colonies with commodities, which could be conveyed to them from hence.——But they yielded much farther. They consented that we should have the appointment of one branch of their legislature. By recognizing as their King, a King resident among us and under our influence, they gave us a negative on all their laws. By allowing an appeal to us in their civil disputes, they gave us likewise the ultimate determination of all civil causes among them. ——In short. They allowed us every power we could desire, except that of taxing them, and interfering in their internal legislations : And they had admitted precedents which, even in these instances, gave us no inconsiderable authority over them. By purchasing our goods they paid our taxes ; and, by allowing us to regulate their trade in any manner we thought most for our advantage, they enriched our merchants, and helped us to bear our growing burdens. They fought our battles with us. They gloried in their relation to us. All their gains centered among us ; and they always spoke of this country and looked to it as their home.

Such was the state of things.——What is it now?

Not

Not contented with a degree of power, fufficient to fatisfy any reafonable ambition, we have attempted to extend it.——Not contented with drawing from them a large revenue *indirectly*, we have endeavoured to procure one *directly* by an authoritative feizure; and, in order to gain a pepper-corn in this way, have chofen to hazard millions, acquired by the peaceable intercourfe of trade.——Vile policy! What a fcourge is government fo conducted?——Had we never deferted our old ground: Had we nourifhed and favoured *America*, with a view to commerce, inftead of confidering it as a country to be governed: Had we, like a liberal and wife people, rejoiced to fee a multitude of free ftates branched forth from ourfelves, all enjoying independent legiflatures fimilar to our own: Had we aimed at binding them to us only by the tyes of affection and intereft; and contented ourfelves with a moderate power rendered durable by being lenient and friendly, an umpire in their differences, an aid to them in improving their own free governments, and their common bulwark againft the affaults of foreign enemies: Had this, I fay, been our policy and temper; there is nothing fo great or happy that we might not have expected. With their increafe our ftrength would have increafed. A growing furplus in the revenue might have been gained, which, invariably applied to the gradual difcharge of the national debt, would have delivered us from the ruin with which it threatens us.

The

The Liberty of *America* might have preferved our
Liberty ; and, under the direction of a patriot king
or wife minifter, proved the means of reftoring to
us our almoft loft conftitution.   Perhaps, in time,
we might alfo have been brought to fee the neceffity of carefully watching and reftricting our paper-
credit : And thus we might have regained fafety ;
and, in union with our Colonies, have been more
than a match for every enemy, and rifen to a fituation of honour and dignity never before known
amongft mankind.——But I am forgetting myfelf.——Our Colonies are likely to be loft for
ever.   Their love is turned into hatred ; and
their refpect for our government into refentment
and abhorrence.——We fhall fee more diftinctly
what a calamity this is, and the obfervations I have
now made will be confirmed, by attending to the
following facts.

Our American Colonies, particularly the Northern ones, have been for fome time in the hap-
pieft ftate of fociety ; or, in that middle ftate of
civilization, between its firft rude and its laft refin-
ed and corrupt ftate.   Old countries confift, generally, of three claffes of people ; a GENTRY ; a
YEOMANRY ; and a PEASANTRY.   The Colonies
confift only of a body of YEOMANRY (*a*) fupported
by

(*a*) Except the *Negroes* in the Southern Colonies, who
probably will now either foon become extinct, or have their
condition

by agriculture, and all independent, and nearly upon a level; in confequence of which, joined to a boundlefs extent of country, the means of fubfiftence are procured without difficulty, and the temptations to wickednefs are fo inconfiderable, that executions (*b*) are feldom known among them. From hence arifes an encouragement to population fo great, that in fome of the Colonies they double their own number in fifteen years; in others, in eighteen years; and in all, taken one with another, in twenty-five years.——Such an increafe was, I believe, never before known. It demonftrates that they muft live at their eafe; and be free from thofe cares, oppreffions, and difeafes which depopulate and ravage luxurious ftates.

With the population of the Colonies has increafed their trade; but much fafter, on account of the gradual introduction of luxury among them.—— In 1723 the exports to *Penfylvania* were 16,000l. ——In 1742 they were 75,295l.——In 1757 they

condition changed into that of *Freemen*.——It is not the fault of the Colonies that they have among them fo many of thefe unhappy people. They have made laws to prohibit the importation of them; but thefe laws have always had a negative put upon them here, becaufe of their tendency to hurt our Negro trade.

(*b*) In the county of Suffolk, where Bofton is, there has not been, I am informed, more than one execution thefe 18 years.

were

were increafed to 268,426l. and in 1773 to half a million.

The exports to all the Colonies in 1744 were 640,114l.——In 1758, they were increafed to 1,832,948l. and in 1773, to three millions. (*a*) And the probability is, that, had it not been for the difcontents among the Colonies fince the year 1764, our trade with them would have been this year double to what it was in 1773; and that in a few years more, it would not have been poffible for the whole kingdom, though confifting only of manufacturers, to fupply the American demand.

This trade, it fhould be confidered, was not only thus an increafing trade; but it was a trade in which we had no rivals; a trade certain, conftant, and uninterrupted; and which, by the fhipping employed in it, and the naval ftores fupplied by it, contributed greatly to the fupport of that navy which is our chief national ftrength.——Viewed in thefe lights it was an objeft unfpeakably important. But it will appear ftill more fo if we view it in its connexions and dependencies. It is well known, that our trade with *Africa* and the *Weft-Indies* cannot eafily fubfift without it. And, upon the whole, it is undeniable, that it has been one of the

(*a*) Mr. Burke (in his excellent and admirable Speech on moving his refolutions for conciliation with the Colonies, P. 9. &c.) has fhewn, that our trade to the Colonies, including that to *Africa* and the *Weft-Indies*, was in 1772 nearly equal to the trade which we carried on with the whole world at the beginning of this Century.

main fprings of our opulence and fplendour; and that we have, in a great meafure, been indebted to it for our ability to bear a debt fo much heavier, than that which, fifty years ago, the wifeft men thought would neceffarily fink us.

This ineftimable prize, and all the advantages connected with *America*, we are now throwing away. Experience alone can fhew what calamities muft follow. It will indeed be aftonifhing if this kingdom can bear fuch a lofs without dreadful confequences.——Thefe confequences have been amply reprefented by others; and it is need-lefs to enter into any account of them——At the time we fhall be feeling them——The Empire difmembered; the blood of thoufands fhed in an unrighteous quarrel; our ftrength exhaufted; our merchants breaking; our manufacturers ftarving; our debts increafing; the revenue finking; the funds tottering; and all the miferies of a public bankruptcy impending——At fuch a *crifis* fhould our natural enemies, eager for our ruin, feize the op-portunity——The apprehenfion is too diftreffing. ——Let us view this fubject in another light.

On this occafion, particular attention fhould be given to the prefent SINGULAR fituation of this kingdom. This is a circumftance of the utmoft importance; and as I am afraid it is not much confidered, I will beg leave to give a diftinct ac-count of it.

7

At the REVOLUTION, the *specie* of the kingdom amounted, according to (*a*) *Davenant*'s account, to eighteen millions and a half.——From the ACCESSION to the year 1772, there were coined at the mint, near 29 millions of gold ; and in ten years only of this time, or from January 1759 to January 1769, there were coined eight millions and a half. (*b*)   But it has appeared lately, that the gold specie now left in the kingdom is no more than about twelve millions and a half.(*c*)—Not so much as half a million of *Silver specie* has been coined these sixty years ; and it cannot be supposed, that the quantity of it now in circulation exceeds two or three millions.   The whole specie of the kingdom, therefore, is probably at this time about fifteen millions.   Of this some millions must be hoarded at the *Bank.*——Our circulating *specie*, therefore, appears to be decreased. But our wealth, or the quantity of money in

(*a*) See Dr. Davenant's works, collected and revised by Sir Charles Whitworth, Vol. I. Page 363, &c. 443, &c.

(*b*) See Considerations on Money, Bullion, &c. Page 2 and 11.

(*c*) The coin deficient between one grain and three grains was not called in at the time this was written.   This call was made in the Summer of 1776 ; and it brought in above three millions more than was expected.   The quantity of gold coin should therefore have been stated at about SIXTEEN MILLIONS, and the whole coin of the kingdom at 18 or 19 millions.——The evidence from which I have drawn this estimate may be found in the first Section of the Second Part of the next Tract.

the

the kingdom, is greatly increafed. This is paper
to a vaft amount, iffued in almoft every corner of
the kingdom; and, particularly, by the BANK OF
ENGLAND. While this paper maintains its credit
it anfwers all the purpofes of fpecie, and is in all
refpects the fame with money.

Specie reprefents fome real value in goods or
commodities. On the contrary; paper reprefents
immediately nothing but fpecie. It is a promife
or obligation which the emitter brings himfelf under to pay a given fum in coin; and it owes its
currency to the credit of the emitter; or to an
opinion that he is able to make good his engage-
ment; and that the fum fpecified may be received
upon being demanded.——Paper, therefore, reprefents coin; and coin reprefents real value. That
is, the one is a *fign* of wealth. The other is the
fign of that *fign*.——But farther. Coin is an *univerfal* fign of wealth, and will procure it every
where. It will bear any alarm, and ftand any
fhock. ——On the contrary. Paper, owing its
currency to opinion, has only a local and ima-
ginary value. It can ftand no fhock. It is deftroyed by the approach of danger; or even the *fuf-
picion* of danger.

In fhort. Coin is the bafis of our paper-credit;
and were it either all deftroyed, or were only the
quantity of it reduced beyond a certain limit, the
paper circulation of the kingdom would fink at
once. But, were our paper deftroyed, the coin
would

would not only remain, but rife in value, in proportion to the quantity of paper deftroyed.

From this account it follows, that as far as, in any circumftances, fpecie is not to be procured in exchange for paper, it reprefents *nothing*, and is, worth *nothing*.——The fpecie of this kingdom is inconfiderable, compared with the amount of the paper circulating in it. This is generally believed; and, therefore, it is natural to enquire how its currency is fupported.——The anfwer is eafy. It is fupported in the fame manner with all other bubbles. Were all to demand fpecie in exchange for their notes, payment could not be made; but, at the fame time that this is known, every one trufts, that no alarm producing fuch a demand will happen, while he holds the paper he is poffeffed of; and that if it fhould happen, he will ftand a chance for being firft paid; and this makes him eafy. And it alfo makes all with whom he traffics eafy. —But let any events happen which threaten danger; and every one will become diffident. A run will take place; and a bankruptcy follow.

This is an account of what has often happened in *private* credit. And it is alfo an account of what *will* (if no change of meafures takes place) happen fome time or other in *public* credit. The defcription I have given of our paper-circulation implies, that nothing can be more delicate or hazardous. It is an immenfe fabrick, with its head in the clouds, that is continually trembling with

every

every adverfe blaft and every fluctuation of trade;
and which, like the bafelefs fabrick of a vifion,
may in a moment vanifh, and leave no wreck behind.——The deftruction of a few books at the
Bank; an improvement in the art of forgery; the
landing of a body of *French* troops on our coafts;
infurrections threatening a revolution in government; or any events that fhould produce a general panic, however groundlefs, would at once annihilate it, and leave us without any other medium of traffic, than a quantity of *fpecie* not
much more than the money now drawn from
the public by the taxes. It would, therefore,
become impoffible to pay the taxes. The revenue
would fail. Near a hundred and forty millions of
property would be deftroyed. The whole frame of
government would fall to pieces; and a ftate of nature would take place.——What a dreadful fituation? It has never had a parallel among mankind;
except at one time in *France* after the eftablifhment
there of the Royal *Miffiffipi* Bank. In 1720 this
bank broke; (*a*) and, after involving for fome
time the whole kingdom in a golden dream, fpread
through it in one day, defolation and ruin.——
The diftrefs attending fuch an event, in this free
country, would be greater than it was in *France*.
Happily for that kingdom, they have fhot this
gulph. Paper-credit has never fince recovered it

(*a*) See Sir James Steuart's Enquiry into the Principles of
political Œconomy, Vol. II. Book 4, Chap. 32.

felf

felf there ; and their circulating cafh confifts now all of folid coin, amounting, according to the loweft account, to no lefs a fum than 1500 millions of *Livres*; (*a*) or near 67 millions of pounds fterling. This gives them unfpeakable advantages ; and, joined to that quick reduction of their debts which is infeparable (*b*) from their nature, places them on a ground of fafety which we have reafon to admire and envy.

Thefe are fubjects on which I fhould have chofen to be filent, did I not think it neceffary, that this country fhould be apprized and warned of the danger which threatens it. This danger is created chiefly by the national debt. High taxes are neceffary to fupport a great public debt ; and a large fupply of cafh is neceffary to fupport high taxes. This cafh we owe to our paper ; and, in proportion to our paper, muft be the productivenefs of our taxes.——King William's wars drained the

(*a*) See the Second Tract, P. 65.

(*b*) Their debts confift chiefly of money raifed by annuities on lives, fhort annuities, anticipations of taxes for fhort terms, &c. During the whole laft war they added to their *perpetual* annuities only 12 millions fterling, according to Sir James Steuart's account ; whereas we added to thefe annuities near 60 millions. In confequence therefore of the nature of their debts, as well as of the management they are now ufing for haftening the reduction of them, they muft in a few years, if peace continues, be freed from moft of their incumbrances ; while we probably (if no event comes foon that will unburthen us at once) fhall continue with them all upon us.

kingdom

kingdom of its fpecie. This funk the revenue, and diftreffed government. In 1694 the BANK was eftablifhed; and the kingdom was provided with a fubftitute for fpecie. The taxes became again productive. The revenue rofe; and government was relieved.——Ever fince that period our paper and taxes have been increafing together, and fupporting one another; and one reafon, undoubtedly, of the late increafe in the productivenefs of our taxes has been the increafe of our paper.

Was there no public debt, there would be no occafion for half the prefent taxes. Our paper-circulation might be reduced. The balance of trade would turn in our favour. Specie would flow in upon us. The quantity of property deftroyed by a failure of paper-credit (fhould it in fuch circumftances happen) would be 140 millions lefs; and, therefore, the fhock attending it would be *tolerable*. But, in the prefent ftate of things, whenever any calamity or panic fhall produce fuch a failure, the fhock attending it will be *intolerable*.——May heaven foon raife up for us fome great ftatefman who fhall fee thefe things; and enter into effectual meafures, if not now too late, for extricating and preferving us.

Public banks are, undoubtedly, attended with great conveniencies. But they alfo do great harm; and, if their emiffions are not reftrained, and con-

7

ducted

ducted with great wisdom, they may prove the most pernicious of all institutions; not only, by substituting *fictitious* for *real* wealth; by increasing luxury; by raising the prices of provisions; by concealing an unfavourable balance of trade; and by rendering a kingdom incapable of bearing any *internal* tumults or *external* attacks, without the danger of a dreadful convulsion : But, particularly, by becoming instruments in the hands of ministers of state to increase their influence, to lessen their dependence on the people, and to keep up a delusive shew of public prosperity, when perhaps ruin may be near. There is, in truth, nothing that a government may not do with such a mine at its command as a public Bank, while it can maintain its credit; nor, therefore, is there any thing more likely to be IMPROPERLY and DANGEROUSLY used.——But to return to what may be more applicable to our own state at present.

Among the causes that may produce a failure of paper-credit, there are two which the present quarrel with *America* calls upon us particularly to consider.——The first is, " An unfavourable bal-" lance of trade." This, in proportion to the degree in which it takes place, must turn the course of foreign exchange against us; raise the price of bullion; and carry off our specie. The danger to which this would expose us is obvious; and it has
been

been much increased by the new coinage of the
gold specie which begun in 1773. Before this
coinage, the greatest part of our gold coin being
light, but the same in currency as if it had been
heavy, always remained in the kingdom. But,
being now nearly of full weight, whenever a wrong
balance of foreign trade alters the course of exchange, and gold in *coin* becomes of less value than
in *bullion*, there is reason to fear, that it will be
melted down in such great quantities, and exported
so fast, as in a little time to leave none behind ; (*a*)
the consequence of which must prove, that the whole
                                              super-

(*a*) Mr. *Lowndes* in the dispute between him and Mr. *Locke*,
contended for a reduction of the standard of silver. One of his
reasons was, that it would render the silver-coin more commen-
surate to the wants of the nation ; and CHECK HAZARDOUS
PAPER-CREDIT.—Mr. CONDUIT, Sir ISAAC NEWTON's suc-
cessor in the mint, has proposed, in direct contradiction to the
laws now in being, that all the bullion imported into the
kingdom should be carried into the mint to be coined ; and
only coin allowed to be exported. " The height, he says, of
" paper-credit is the strongest argument for trying this and *every*
" *other* method that is likely to increase the coinage. For
" whilst paper-credit does in a great measure the business of mo-
" ney at home, Merchants and Bankers are not under a necessi-
" ty, as they were formerly, of coining a quantity of specie for
" their home trade ; and as Paper-credit brings money to the
" Merchants to be exported, the money may go away insensi-
" bly, and NOT BE MISSED TILL IT BE TOO LATE: And
" where Paper-credit is large and increasing, if the money
" be exported and the coinage decrease, THAT CREDIT
" MAY SINK AT ONCE, for want of a proportionable quan-

" tity

superſtructure of paper-credit, now ſupported by
it, will break down.——The only remedy, in ſuch
circumſtances, is an increaſe of coinage at the
mint. But this will operate too ſlowly ; and, by
raiſing the price of bullion, will only increaſe the
evil.—It is the *Bank* that at ſuch a time muſt be
the immediate ſufferer : For it is from thence that
thoſe who want coin for any purpoſe will always
draw it.

For many years before 1773, the price of gold
in *bullion* had been, from 2 to 3 or 4 *per cent.*
higher than in *coin*. This was a temptation to melt
down and export the coin, which could not be reſiſted. Hence aroſe a demand for it on the BANK ;
and, conſequently, the neceſſity of purchaſing bullion at a loſs for a new coinage. But the more
coin the Bank procured in this way, the lower its
price became in compariſon with that of bullion,
and the faſter it vaniſhed ; and, conſequently, the
more neceſſary it became to coin again, and the
greater loſs fell upon the Bank.——Had things
continued much longer in this train, the conſequences might have proved very ſerious. I am by
no means ſufficiently informed to be able to aſſign
the cauſes which have produced the change that
happened in 1772. But, without doubt, the ſtate
of things which took place before that year muſt be

"tity of *Specie*, which alone can ſupport it in a time of dif-
"treſs."——See Mr. *Conduit*'s Obſervations on the ſtate of
our Gold and Silver Coins in 1730, Page 36, to 46.

expected

expected to return. The fluctuations of trade, in its beſt ſtate, render this unavoidable. But the con-teſt with our Colonies has a tendency to bring it on ſoon; and to increaſe unſpeakably the diſtreſs attending it. All know that the balance of trade with them is greatly in our favour; (a) and that this balance is paid partly by direct remittances of bul-lion; and partly by circuitous remittances through *Spain*, *Portugal*, *Italy*, &c. which diminiſh the ba-lance againſt us with theſe countries.—During the laſt year they have been employed in paying their debts, without adding to them; and their expor-tations and remittances for that purpoſe have con-tributed to render the general balance of trade more favourable to us, and, alſo, (in conjunction with the late operations of the Bank) to keep up our funds. Theſe remittances are now ceaſed; and a few years will determine, if this conteſt goes on, how far we can ſuſtain ſuch a loſs without ſuffering the conſequences I have de-ſcribed.

The ſecond event, ruinous to our paper circu-lation, which may ariſe from our rupture with *America*, is a deficiency in the revenue. As a fai-lure of our paper would deſtroy the revenue, ſo a

(a) According to the accounts of the exports to, and im-ports from the North-American Colonies, laid before Parlia-ment, the balance in our favour appears to have been, for 11 years before 1774, near a *million and a half* annually.

failure

failure of the revenue, or any confiderable diminution of it, would deftroy our paper. The BANK is the fupport of our paper; and the fupport of the BANK is the credit of government. Its principal fecurities, are a capital of eleven millions lent to government; and money continually advanced to a vaft amount on the Land-tax and Malt-tax, Sinking Fund, Exchequer Bills, Navy Bills, &c. Should, therefore, deficiencies in the revenue bring government under any difficulties, all thefe fecurities would lofe their value, and the *Bank* and Government, and all private and public credit, would fall together.—— Let any one here imagine, what would probably follow, were it but fufpected by the public in general, that the taxes were fo fallen, as not to produce enough to pay the intereft of the public debts, befides bearing the *ordinary* expences of the nation; and that, in order to fupply the deficiency and to hide the calamity, it had been neceffary in any one year to anticipate the taxes, and to borrow of the Bank.——In fuch circumftances I can fcarcely doubt, but an alarm would fpread of the moft dangerous tendency.——The next foreign war, fhould it prove *half* as expenfive as the laft, will probably occafion fuch a deficiency; and bring our affairs to that crifis towards which they have been long tending.——But the war with *America* has a greater tendency to do this; and the reafon is, that it affects our refources more; and is

7   attended

attended more with the danger of internal difturb-
ances.

Some have made the proportion of our trade de-
pending on *North America* to be near ONE HALF. A
moderate computation makes it a THIRD. (*a*) Let
it, however, be fuppofed to be only a FOURTH. I
will venture to fay, this is a proportion of our foreign trade, the lofs of which, when it comes to be
felt, will be found infupportable.——In the article
of *Tobacco* alone it will caufe a deduction from the
Cuftoms of at leaft 300,000*l. per ann.* (*b*) including
the duties paid on foreign commodities purchafed
by the exportation of tobacco. Let the whole deduction from the revenue be fuppofed to be only
half a million. This alone is more than the kingdom can at prefent bear, without having recourfe

(*a*) See the fubftance of the evidence on the petition prefented by the *Weft-India* Planters and Merchants to the Houfe
of Commons as it was introduced at the BAR, and fummed
up by Mr. GLOVER.

(*b*) The annual average of the payments into the Exchequer,
on account of the duties on tobacco, was for five years, from
1770 to 1774, 219,117*l.* exclufive of the payments from *Scotland.*——Near one half of the *tobacco* trade is carried on from
Scotland; and above *four fifths* of the tobacco imported is afterwards exported to *France, Germany* and other countries. From
France alone it brings annually into the Kingdom, I am informed, about 150,000*l.* in money.

In 1775, being, alas! the *parting* year, the duties on tobacco
in ENGLAND brought into the *Exchequer* no lefs a fum than
298,292*l.*

to

to lotteries, and the land-tax at 4 s, in order to defray the common and neceffary expences of peace. But to this muft be added a deduction from the produce of the *Excifes*, in confequence of the increafe of the poor, of the difficulties of our merchants and manufacturers, of lefs national wealth, and a retrenchment of luxury. There is no poffibility of knowing to what thefe deductions may amount. When the evils producing them begin, they will proceed rapidly; and they may end in a general wreck before we are aware of any danger.

In order to give a clearer view of this fubject, I will in an Appendix*, ftate particularly the national expenditure and income for eleven years, from 1764 to 1774. From that account it will appear, that the money drawn every year from the public by the taxes, does not fall greatly fhort of a fum equal to the whole *fpecie* of the kingdom; and that, notwithftanding the late increafe in the productivenefs of the taxes, the whole furplus of the national income has not exceeded 338,759l. *per ann.* See the Second Tract, p. 160. This is a furplus fo inconfiderable as to be fcarcely fufficient to guard againft the deficiencies arifing from the common fluctuations of foreign trade, and of home confumption. It is NOTHING when confidered as the

* All the accounts and calculations in the *Appendix* here referred to, have been transferred to the 2d and 4th Sections of the 3d Part of the Second Tract.

only

only fund we have for paying off a debt of near
140 millions.—Had we continued in a ftate of
profound peace, it could not have admitted of
any diminution. What then muft follow, when
one of the moft profitable branches of our trade is
deftroyed ; when a THIRD of the Empire is loft ;
when an addition of many millions is made to the
public debt ; and when, at the fame time, perhaps
fome millions are taken away from the revenue ?
——I fhudder at this profpect.——A KINGDOM
ON AN EDGE SO PERILOUS, SHOULD THINK OF NO-
THING BUT A RETREAT.

S E C T. IV.

Of the Honour of the Nation as affected by
the War with America.

ONE of the pleas for continuing the conteft
with *America* is, " That our honour is en-
" gaged ; and that we cannot now recede without
" the moft humiliating conceffions."

With refpect to this, it is proper to obferve, that
a diftinction fhould be made between the nation,
and its rulers. It is melancholy that there fhould be
ever any reafon for making fuch a diftinction. A government is, or ought to be, nothing but an inftitution for collecting and for carrying into execution the
will of the people. But fo far is this from being in

G 4   general

general the fact, that the meafures of government, and the fenfe of the people, are fometimes in direct oppofition to one another; nor does it *often* happen that any certain conclufion can be drawn from the one to the other.———I will not pretend to determine, whether, in the prefent inftance, the difhonour attending a retreat would belong to the nation at large, or only to the perfons in power who guide its affairs. Be this as it will, no good argument can be drawn from it againft receding. The difgrace which may be implied in making conceffions, is nothing to that of being the aggreffors in an unrighteous quarrel; and dignity, in fuch circumftances, confifts in retracting freely and fpeedily.———For, (to adopt on this occafion, words which I have heard applied to this very purpofe, in a great affembly, by a peer to whom this kingdom has often looked as its deliverer, and whofe ill ftate of health at this awful moment of public danger every friend to *Britain* muft deplore) to adopt, I fay, the words of this great man——" RECTITUDE IS DIGNITY. OPPRESSION ONLY IS MEANNESS ; AND JUSTICE, HONOUR."

I will add, that PRUDENCE, no lefs than true HONOUR, requires us to retract. For the time may come when, if it is not done voluntarily, we may be *obliged* to do it; and find ourfelves under a neceffity of granting that to our diftreffes, which

we

we now deny to equity and humanity, and the
prayers of *America*. The poffibility of this appears plainly from the preceding pages; and
fhould it happen, it will bring upon us difgrace
indeed, difgrace greater than the worft rancour
can wifh to fee accumulated on a kingdom already
too much difhonoured.———Let the reader think
here what we are doing.———A nation, once the
protector of Liberty in diftant countries, and the
fcourge of tyranny, changed into an enemy to
Liberty, and engaged in endeavouring to reduce
to fervitude its own brethren.———A great and enlightened nation, not content with a controuling
power over millions of people which gave it every
reafonable advantage, infifting upon fuch a fupremacy over them as would leave them nothing
they could call their own, and carrying defolation and death among them for difputing it.
———What can be more ignominious?———How
have we felt for the brave *Corficans*, in their
ftruggle with the *Genoefe*, and afterwards with the
French government? Did GENOA or FRANCE
want more than an abfolute command over their
property and legiflations ; or the power of binding
them in all cafes whatfoever?———The *Genoefe*,
finding it difficult to keep them in fubjection,
CEDED them to the *French*.———All fuch ceffions
of one people by another are difgraceful to human

man nature. But if our claims are just, may not we also, if we please, CEDE the Colonies to *France?* ——There is, in truth, no other difference between these two cases than that the *Corsicans* were not descended from the people who governed them, but that the *Americans* are.

There are some who seem to be sensible, that the authority of one country over another, cannot be distinguished from the servitude of one country to another; and that unless different communities, as well as different parts of the same community, are united by an equal representation, all such authority is inconsistent with the principles of Civil Liberty.——But they except the case of the Colonies and *Great Britain*; because the Colonies are communities which have branched forth from, and which, therefore, as they think, belong to *Britain.* Had the colonies been communities of *foreigners*, over whom we wanted to acquire dominion, or even to extend a dominion before acquired, they are ready to admit that their resistance would have been just.——In my opinion, this is the same with saying, that the Colonies ought to be worse off than the rest of mankind, because they are our own *Brethren.*

Again. The United Provinces of *Holland* were once subject to the *Spanish* monarchy; but, provoked by the violation of their charters; by levies of money, without their consent; by the introduc-

tion

tion of Spanish troops among them; by innovations in their antient modes of government; and the rejection of their petitions; they were driven to that resistance which we and all the world have ever since admired; and which has given birth to one of the greatest and happiest Republics that ever existed. ———— Let any one read also, the history of the war which the *Athenians*, from a thirst of Empire, made on the *Syracusans* in *Sicily*, a people derived from the same origin with them; and let him, if he can, avoid rejoicing in the defeat of the *Athenians*.

Let him, likewise, read the account of the social war among the Romans. The allied states of *Italy* had fought the battles of *Rome*, and contributed by their valour and treasure to its conquests and grandeur. They claimed, therefore, the rights of Roman citizens, and a share with them in legislation. The Romans, disdaining to make those their *fellow-citizens*, whom they had always looked upon as their *subjects*, would not comply; and a war followed, the most horrible in the annals of mankind, which ended in the ruin of the Roman Republic. The feelings of every *Briton* in this case must force him to approve the conduct of the Allies, and to condemn the proud and ungrateful Romans.

But not only is the present contest with *America* thus disgraceful to us, because inconsistent

with

with our own feelings in similar cases; but also because condemned by our own practice in former times. The Colonies are persuaded that they are fighting for Liberty. We see them sacrificing to this persuasion every private advantage. If mistaken, and though guilty of irregularities, they should be pardoned by a people whose ancestors have given them so many examples of similar conduct. ENGLAND should venerate the attachment to Liberty amidst all its excesses; and, instead of indignation or scorn, it would be most becoming them, in the present instance, to declare their applause, and to say to the Colonies——" We ex-
" cuse your mistakes. We admire your spirit.
" It is the spirit that has more than once saved
" *ourselves*. We aspire to no dominion over you.
" We understand the rights of men too well to
" think of taking from you the inestimable privi-
" lege of governing yourselves; and, instead of
" employing our power for any such purpose,
" we offer it to you as a friendly and guardian
" power, to be a mediator in your quarrels; a
" protection against your enemies; and an aid
" to you in establishing a plan of Liberty that shall
" make you great and happy. In return, we
" ask nothing but your gratitude and your com-
" merce."

This would be a language worthy of a brave and enlightened nation. But alas! it often hap-

pens

pens in the *Political World* as it does in *Religion*, that the people who cry out moſt vehemently for Liberty to themſelves are the moſt unwilling to grant it to others.

But farther. This war is diſgraceful on account of the perſuaſion which led to it, and under which it has been undertaken. The general cry was laſt winter, that the people of NEW-ENGLAND were a body of cowards, who would at once be reduced to ſubmiſſion by a hoſtile look from our troops. In this light were they held up to public deriſion in both Houſes of Parliament; and it was this perſuaſion that, probably, induced a Noble-man of the firſt weight in the ſtate to recommend, at the paſſing of the *Boſton Port Bill*, coercive meaſures; hinting at the ſame time, that the *appearance* of hoſtilities would be ſufficient, and that all would be ſoon over, SINE CLADE.——Indeed no one can doubt, but that had it been believed ſome time ago, that the people of *America* were brave, more care would have been taken not to provoke them.

Again. The manner in which this war has been hitherto conducted, renders it ſtill more diſgraceful.——Engliſh valour being thought inſuf-ficient to ſubdue the Colonies, the laws and religion of *France* were eſtabliſhed in *Canada*, on purpoſe to obtain the power of bringing upon them from thence an army of *French Papiſts*. The wild *Indi-ans*

ans and their own Slaves have been inftigated to attack them ; and attempts have been made to gain the affiftance of a large body of *Ruffians.*——— With like views, *German* troops have been hired ; and the defence of our Forts and Garrifons trufted in their hands.

Thefe are meafures which need no comment. The laft of them, in particular, having been carried into execution without the confent of parliament, threatens us with imminent danger ; and fhews that we are in the way to lofe even the *Forms* of the conftitution.———If, indeed, our minifters can at any time, without leave, not only fend away the national troops, but introduce *foreign* troops in their room, we lie entirely at mercy ; and we have every thing to dread.

S E C T. V.

Of the Probability of Succeeding in the War with America.

LET us next confider how far there is a poffibility of fucceeding in the prefent war.

Our own people, being unwilling to enlift, and the attempts to procure armies of *Ruffians, Indians,* and *Canadians* having mifcarried ; the utmoft force we can employ, including foreigners, does not exceed, if I am rightly informed, 40,000 effective men. This is the force that is to conquer half a million *at*

7

leaſt (*a*) of determined men fighting on their own ground, within fight of their houſes and families, and for that ſacred bleſſing of Liberty, without which man is a beaſt, and government a curſe. All hiſtory proves, that in ſuch a ſituation, a handful is a match for millions.

In the *Netherlands*, a few ſtates thus circum-ſtanced, withſtood, for a long courſe of years, the whole force of the Spaniſh monarchy, when at its zenith; and at laſt humbled its pride, and emanci-pated themſelves from its tyranny.—The citizens of SYRACUSE alſo, thus circumſtanced, withſtood the whole power of the *Athenians*, and almoſt ruined them.—The ſame happened in the conteſt be-tween the houſe of *Auſtria*, and the cantons (*b*) of *Switzerland*.——There is in this caſe an infinite difference between attacking and being attacked; between fighting to *deſtroy*, and fighting to *preſerve* or *acquire* Liberty.——Were we, therefore, ca-pable of employing a *land* force againſt *America* equal to its own, there would be little probability of ſucceſs. But to think of conquering that whole continent with 30,000 or 40,000 men to be tranſ-

(*a*) A quarter of the inhabitants of every country are fight-ing men.——If, therefore, the Colonies conſiſt only of two millions of inhabitants, the number of fighting men in them will be half a million.

(*b*) See the Appendix to Dr. Zubly's Sermon, preached at the opening of the Provincial Congreſs of *Georgia*.

ported acrofs the *Atlantic*, and fed from hence, and incapable of being recruited after any defeat ———This is indeed a folly fo great, that language does not afford a name for it.

With refpect to our naval force, could it fail at land as it does at fea, much might be done with it ; but as that is impoffible, *little* or *nothing* can be done with it, which will not hurt *ourfelves* more than the *Colonifts.*———Such of their maritime towns as they cannot guard againft our fleets, and have not been already deftroyed, they are determined either to give up to our refentment, or (*a*) deftroy themfelves : The confequence of which will be, that thefe towns will be rebuilt in fafer fituations ; and that we fhall lofe fome of the principal pledges by which we have hitherto held them in fubjection.——As to their trade ; having all the neceffaries and the chief conveniencies of life within themfelves, they have no dependence upon it ; and the lofs of it will do them unfpeakable good, by preferving them from the evils of luxury and the temptations of wealth ; and keeping them in that ftate of virtuous fimplicity which is the greateft happinefs. I know that I am now fpeaking the fenfe of fome of the wifeft men in America. It has been long their wifh that *Britain* would fhut up all their ports. They will rejoice, particularly, in the laft reftraining act. It might have happened, that the people would have grown weary of

their

their agreements not to export or import. But this act will oblige them to keep thefe agreements; and confirm their unanimity and zeal: It will alfo furnifh them with a reafon for confifcating the eftates of all the friends of our government among them, and for employing their failors, who would have been otherwife idle, in making reprifals on Britifh property. Their fhips, before ufelefs, and confifting of many hundreds, will be turned into fhips of war; and that attention, which they have hitherto confined to trade, will be employed in fitting out a naval force for their own defence; and thus the way will be prepared for their becoming, much fooner than they would otherwife have been, a great maritime power. This act of parliament, therefore, crowns the folly of all our late meafures.(*a*)—None who know me, can believe me to be difpofed to fuperftition. Perhaps, however, I am not in the prefent inftance, free from this weaknefs.——I fancy I fee in thefe meafures fomething that cannot be accounted for merely by human ignorance. I am inclined to think, that the hand of Providence is in them working to bring about fome great ends.—But this leads me to one confideration more, which I

(*a*) The apprehenfions here expreffed have been verified by the events which have happened fince this was written. American privateers have fpread themfelves over the Atlantick. They have frightened us even on our own coafts, and feized millions of Britifh property.

H   cannot

cannot help offering to the public, and which appears to me in the higheſt degree important.

In this hour of tremendous danger, it would become us to turn our thoughts to Heaven. This is what our brethren in the Colonies are doing. From one end of *North America* to the other, they are FASTING and PRAYING. But what are we doing?—We are ridiculing them as *Fanatics*, and ſcoffing at religion.——We are running wild after pleaſure, and forgetting every thing ſerious and decent at *Maſquerades*.——We are trafficking for Boroughs; perjuring ourſelves at Elections; and ſelling ourſelves for places.—Which ſide then is Providence likely to favour?

In *America* we ſee a number of riſing ſtates in the vigour of youth, inſpired by the nobleſt of all paſſions, the paſſion for being free; and animated by piety.——*Here* we ſee an old ſtate, great indeed, but inflated and irreligious; enervated by luxury; encumbred with debts; and hanging by a thread.——Can any one look without pain to the iſſue? May we not expect calamities that ſhall recover to *reflection* (perhaps to *devotion*) our *Libertines* and *Atheiſts*?

Is our cauſe ſuch as gives us reaſon to aſk God to bleſs it?——Can we in the face of Heaven declare, " that we are not the aggreſſors in this war; " and that we mean by it, not to acquire or even " preſerve dominion for its own ſake; not con-
" queſt

" queft, or Empire, or the gratification of refent-
" ment; but folely to deliver ourfelves from op-
" preffion; to gain reparation for injury; and
" to defend ourfelves againft men who would plun-
" der or kill us?"—Remember, reader, whoever
thou art, that there are no other juft caufes of war;
and that blood fpilled, with any other views, muft
fome time or other be accounted for.——But not
to expofe myfelf by faying more in this way, I will
now beg leave to recapitulate fome of the arguments I have ufed; and to deliver the feelings
of my heart in a brief, but earneft addrefs to my
countrymen.

I am hearing it continually urged——" Are
" they not our fubjects?"——The plain anfwer is,
they are not your fubjects. The people of *America* are no more the fubjects of the people of *Britain*, than the people of *Yorkfhire* are the fubjects
of the people of *Middlefex*. They are your *fellow-fubjects*.

" But *we* are taxed; and why fhould not *they*
be taxed?"——*You* are taxed by yourfelves. *They*
infift on the fame privilege.——They are taxed
to fupport their own governments; and they help
alfo to pay your taxes by purchafing your manufactures, and giving you a monopoly of their
trade. Muft they maintain *two* governments?
Muft they fubmit to be *triple* taxed?—Has your
moderation in taxing yourfelves been fuch as en-

courages

courages them to truft you with the power of taxing them?

" But they will not obey the *Parliament* and
the *Laws*."——Say rather, they will not obey *your*
parliament and *your* laws.   Their reafon is : They
have no voice in your parliament.   They have no
fhare in making (*a*) your laws.——" Neither have
moft of us."——Then you fo far want Liberty ;
and your language is, " *We* are not free, Why
will *they* be free ?"——But *many* of you have a
voice in parliament : *None* of them have.   *All*
your freehold land is reprefented : But not a foot
of *their* land is reprefented.   At worft, therefore,
you are only enflaved *partially*.——Were they
to fubmit, they would be enflaved *totally*.——
They are governed by parliaments chofen by themfelves, and by legiflatures fimilar to yours.   Why
will you difturb them in the enjoyment of a bleffing fo valuable ? Is it reafonable to infift, that
your difcretion alone fhall be their law ; that they

(*a*) " I have no other notion of flavery, but being bound
" by a law to which I do not confent." See the cafe of
Ireland's being bound by acts of Parliament in *England*, ftated
by William Molyneux, Efq; Dublin.——In arguing againft
the authority of Communities, and all people not incorporated, over one another; I have confined my views to taxation
and internal legiflation.   Mr. Molyneux carried his views
much farther ; and denied the right of *England* to make any
laws even to regulate the trade of *Ireland*.   He was the inti-
mate friend of Mr. Locke ; and writ his book in 1698, foon
after the publication of Mr. Locke's Treatife on Government.

fhall

fhall have no conftitutions of government, except
fuch as you fhall be pleafed to give them; and no
property except fuch as your parliament fhall be
pleafed to leave them?—What is your parliament?
—Is there not a growing intercourfe between
it and the court? Does it awe minifters of ftate
as it once did?—Inftead of contending for a controuling power over the governments of *America*,
fhould you not think more of watching and reform-
ing your own?—Suppofe the worft. Suppofe, in
oppofition to all their own declarations, that the Colonifts are now aiming at independence.(*a*)—" If
they can fubfift without you;" is it to be wondered
at? Did there ever exift a *community*, or even an *individual*, that would not do the fame?—" If they
cannot fubfift without you;" let them alone. They
will foon come back.————" If you cannot
fubfift without them," reclaim them by (*b*) kindnefs; engage them by moderation and equity. It
is madnefs to refolve to butcher them. This will

make

(*a*) See on this fubject the fecond Section of the fecond
Part of the next Tract, Page 77.

(*b*) Some perfons, convinced of the *folly* as well as *barbarity*
of attempting to keep the Colonies by flaughtering them,
have very humanely propofed giving them up. But the higheft authority has informed us, with great reafon, " That
" they are too important to be given up."—Dr. TUCKER has
infifted on the depopulation, produced by migrations from the
country to the Colonies, as a reafon for this meafure. In

H 3

make them deteſt and avoid you for ever. Freemen are not to be governed by force ; or dragooned into compliance. If capable of bearing to be
ſo treated, it is a diſgrace to be connected with
them.

" If *they* can ſubſiſt without *you* ; and alſo *you*
without *them*," the attempt to ſubjugate them,
by confiſcating their effects, burning their towns,
and ravaging their territories, is a wanton exertion
of cruel ambition, which, however common it has
been among mankind, deſerves to be called by
harder names than I chuſe to apply to it.—Sup-
poſe ſuch an attempt was to be ſucceeded :
Would it not be a fatal preparation for ſubduing
yourſelves ? Would not the diſpoſal of *American*
places, and the diſtribution of an *American* revenue,
render that influence of the crown irreſiſtible, which
has already ſtabbed your liberties ?

Turn your eyes to *India :* There more has been
done than is now attempted in *America.* There
ENGLISHMEN, actuated by the love of plunder and

unleſs the kingdom is made a priſon to its inhabitants, theſe
migrations cannot be prevented ; nor do I think that they have
any great tendency to produce depopulation. When a number of people quit a country, there is more employment and
greater plenty of the means of ſubſiſtence left for thoſe who remain ; and the vacancy is ſoon filled up. The grand cauſes
of depopulation are, not migrations, or even famines and
plagues, or any other *temporary* evils ; but the permanent and
ſlowly working evils of debauchery, luxury, high taxes, and
oppreſſion.

the

the spirit of conquest, have depopulated whole kingdoms, and ruined millions of innocent people by the most infamous oppression and rapacity.— The justice of the nation has slept over these enormities. Will the justice of heaven sleep?——Are we not now execrated on both sides of the globe?

With respect to the Colonists; it would be folly to pretend they are faultless. They were running fast into our vices. But this quarrel gives them a salutary check: And it may be permitted on purpose to favour them, and in *them* the rest of mankind; by making way for establishing, in an extensive country possessed of every advantage, a plan of government, and a growing power that will astonish the world, and under which every subject of human enquiry shall be open to free discussion, and the friends of Liberty, in every quarter of the globe, find a safe retreat from civil and spiritual tyranny.——I hope, therefore, our brethren in *America* will forgive their oppressors. It is certain *they know not what they are doing.*

CONCLUSION.

HAVING said so much of the war with America, and particularly of the danger with which it threatens us, it may be expected that I should propose some method of escaping from this danger, and of restoring this once happy Empire to a state of peace and security.—Various plans of pacification have been proposed; and some of them, by persons so distinguished by their rank and merit, as to be above my applause. But till there is more of a disposition to attend to such plans; they cannot, I am afraid, be of any great service. And there is too much reason to apprehend, that nothing but calamity will bring us to repentance and wisdom.——In order, however, to complete my design in these observations, I will take the liberty to lay before the public the following sketch of one of the plans just referred to, as it was opened before the holidays to the house of Lords by the *Earl of Shelburne*; who, while he held the seals of the Southern Department, with the business of the Colonies annexed, possessed their confidence, without ever compromising the authority of this country; a confidence which discovered itself by peace among themselves, and duty and submission to the Mother-country. I hope I shall not take an unwarrantable liberty, if, on this occasion, I use his Lordship's own words, as nearly as I have been able to collect them.

" Meet the Colonies on their own ground, in
" the last petition from the Congress to the king.
" The surest, as well as the most dignified
" mode of proceeding for this country.—Suspend
" all hostilities——Repeal the acts which imme-
" diately distress America, namely, the last re-
" straining act,—the charter act,—the act for the
" more impartial administration of justice;—and
" the Quebec act.—All the other acts (the custom
" house act, the post office act, &c.) leave to a tem-
" perate revisal.——There will be found much
" matter which both countries may wish repealed.
" *Some* which can never be given up, the prin-
" ciple being that regulation of trade for the
" common good of the Empire, which forms our
" *Palladium. Other* matter which is fair subject of
" mutual accommodation.——Prescribe the most
" explicit acknowledgment of your right of regu-
" lating commerce in its most extensive sense; if
" the petition and other public acts of the Colonies
" have not already, by their declarations and ac-
" knowledgments, left it upon a sufficiently secure
" foundation.—Besides the power of regulating the
" general commerce of the Empire, something
" further might be expected; provided a due and
" tender

" tender regard were had to the means and abili-
" ties of the feveral provinces, as well as to thofe
" fundamental, unalienable rights of *Englifhmen*,
" which no father can furrender on the part of his
" fon, no reprefentative on the part of his elector,
" no generation on the part of the fucceeding one ;
" the right of judging not only of the *mode* of
" raifing, but the *quantum*, and the appropriation
" of fuch aids as they fhall grant.——To be more
" explicit ; the debt of *England*, without entering
" into invidious diftinctions how it came to be
" contracted, might be acknowledged the debt of
" every individual part of the whole Empire,
" *Afia*, as well as America, included.——Pro-
" vided, that full fecurity were held forth to them,
" that fuch free aids, together with the Sinking
" Fund (Great Britain contributing her fuperior
" fhare) fhould not be left as the privy purfe of
" the minifter, but be unalienably appropriated to
" the original intention of that fund, the difcharge
" of the debt ;—and that by an honeft application
" of the *whole* fund, the taxes might in time be lef-
" fened, and the price of our manufactures confe-
" quently reduced, fo that every contributory part
" might feel the returning benefit—always fuppo-
" fing the laws of trade duly obferved and enforced.
" The time *was*, I am confident—and per-
" haps *is*, when thefe points might be obtain-
" ed upon the eafy, the conftitutional, and,
" therefore, the indifpenfible terms of an exemp-
" tion

" tion from parliamentary taxation, and an ad-
" miffion of the facrednefs of their charters; inftead
" of facrificing their good humour, their affec-
" tion, their effectual aids, and the act of NAVI-
" GATION itfelf, (which you are now in the direct
" road to do) for a commercial quit-rent, (*a*) or a
" barren metaphyfical chimæra.——How long
" thefe ends may continue attainable, no man can
" tell.——But if no words are to be relied on ex-
" cept fuch as make againft the Colonies—If
" nothing is acceptable, except what is attainable
" by force; it only remains to apply, what has
" been fo often remarked of unhappy periods,
" ——*Quos deus vult, &c.*"

Thefe are fentiments and propofals of the laft importance; and I am very happy in being able to give them to the public from fo refpectable an authority as that of the diftinguifhed Peer I have mentioned; to whom, I know, this kingdom, as

(*a*) See the Refolutions on the *Nova-Scotia* petition reported to the Houfe of Commons, November 29, 1775, by Lord North, Lord George Germaine, &c. and a bill ordered to be brought in upon the faid Refolutions.——There is indeed, as Lord Shelburne has hinted, fomething very aftonifhing in thefe Refolutions. They offer a relaxation of the authority of this country, in points to which the Colonies have always con-fented, and by which we are great gainers; at the fame time, that, with a rigour which hazards the Empire, we are main-taining its authority in points to which they will never con-fent; and by which nothing can be gained.

well

4

well as America, is much indebted for his zeal to promote those grand public points on which the preservation of Liberty among us depends; and for the firm opposition which, jointly with many others (Noblemen and Commoners of the first character and abilities,) he has made to the present measures.

Had such a plan as that now proposed been adopted a few months ago, I have little doubt but that a pacification would have taken place, on terms highly advantageous to this kingdom.—— In particular. It is probable, that the Colonies would have consented to grant an annual supply, which, increased by a saving of the money now spent in maintaining troops among them, and by contributions which might have been gained from other parts of the Empire, would have formed a fund considerable enough, if unalienably applied, to redeem the public debt; in consequence of which, agreeably to Lord Shelburne's ideas, some of our worst taxes might be taken off, and the Colonies would receive our manufactures cheaper; our paper-currency might be restrained; our whole force would be free to meet at any time foreign danger; the influence of the Crown would be reduced; our Parliament would become less dependent; and the kingdom might, perhaps, be restored to a situation of permanent safety and prosperity.

To

To conclude.——An important revolution in the affairs of this kingdom feems to be approaching. If ruin is not to be our lot, all that has been lately done muft be undone, and new meafures adopted. At that period, an opportunity (never perhaps to be recovered, if loft) will offer itfelf for ferving effentially *this country*, as well as *America*; by putting the national debt into *a fixed* courfe of payment; by fubjecting to new regulations, the adminiftration of the finances; and by eftablifhing meafures for exterminating corruption and reftoring the conftitution.——For my own part; if this is not to be the confequence of any future changes in the minif'ry, and the fyftem of corruption, lately fo much improved, is to go on; I think it totally indifferent to the kingdom who are *in*, or who are *out* of power.

THE

THE following fact is of so much importance, that I cannot satisfy myself without
laying it before the public.——In a Committee
of the American CONGRESS in *June* 1775, a declaration was drawn up containing an offer to
GREAT BRITAIN, " that the Colonies would not
" only continue to grant extraordinary aids in
" time of war, but also, if allowed a free com-
" merce, pay into the SINKING-FUND such a sum
" annually for ONE HUNDRED YEARS, as should
" be *more* than sufficient in that time, if faithfully
" applied, to extinguish all the present debts of
" BRITAIN. Or, provided this was not accepted,
" that, to remove the groundless jealousy of *Bri-*
" *tain* that the Colonies aimed at Independence
" and an abolition of the Navigation Act, which
" in truth, they had never intended ; and also, to
" avoid all future disputes about the right of mak-
" ing that and other Acts for regulating their
" commerce for the general benefit, they would
" enter into a covenant with *Britain*, that she
" should fully possess and exercise that right for
" *one hundred years* to come."

At the end of the preceding Tract I have had
the honor of laying before the public the
Earl of *Shelburne*'s plan of Pacification with the
Colonies. In that plan, it is particularly proposed, that the Colonies should grant an annual

supply

supply to be carried to the Sinking Fund, and unalienably appropriated to the difcharge of the public
debt.——It muſt give this excellent Peer great pleaſure to learn, from this reſolution, that even this
part of his plan, as well as all the other parts,
would, moſt probably, have been accepted by
the Colonies. For though the reſolution only
offers the alternative of either a *free* trade, with
extraordinary aids and an annual ſupply, or an
exclvſive trade confirmed and extended; yet there
can be little reaſon to doubt, but that to avoid
the calamities of the preſent conteſt, BOTH would
have been conſented to; particularly, if, on our
part, ſuch a reviſal of the laws of trade had been
offered as was propoſed in Lord Shelburne's plan.

The preceding reſolution was, I have ſaid,
drawn up in a Committee of the Congreſs. But
it was not entered in their minutes; a ſevere Act
of Parliament happening to arrive at that time,
which determined them not to give the ſum pro-
poſed in it.

F I N I S.

ADDITIONAL OBSERVATIONS

On the NATURE and VALUE of

CIVIL LIBERTY,

AND THE

WAR WITH AMERICA:

ALSO

OBSERVATIONS on Schemes for raifing Money
by PUBLIC LOANS;

An Hiftorical Deduction and Analyfis of the
NATIONAL DEBT;

And a brief Account of the DEBTS and RESOURCES
of FRANCE.

Should the morals of the Englifh be perverted by luxury;—
fhould they lofe their Colonies by reftraining them, &c.—
they will be enflaved; they will become infignificant and
contemptible; and *Europe* will not be able to fhew the
world one nation in which fhe can pride herfelf.

ABBE' RAYNAL.

TO

THE RIGHT HONOURABLE

THE LORD MAYOR,

THE ALDERMEN, AND THE COMMONS

OF THE

CITY OF LONDON,

THIS TRACT,

Containing ADDITIONS to thofe OBSERVATIONS
on CIVIL LIBERTY,

which they have honoured with their Approbation,

Is, with the greateft Refpect and Gratitude,

INSCRIBED,

BY

Their moft obedient

and humble Servant,

RICHARD PRICE.

CONTENTS.

A 3

Published by the same Author,

And printed for T. CADELL, in the Strand.

I. OBSERVATIONS on REVERSIONARY PAYMENTS; on Schemes for providing Annuities for Widows, and Persons in Old Age; on the Method of calculating the Values of Assurances on Lives; and on the National Debt. To which are added, Four Essays on different Subjects in the Doctrine of Life-Annuities and Political Arithmetic. Also, an Appendix, containing a complete Set of Tables; particularly four New Tables, shewing the Probabilities of Life in LONDON, NORWICH, and NORTHAMPTON, and the Values of two joint Lives. The 3d Edition, with a Supplement, containing (besides several New Tables) additional Observations on the Probabilities of Human Life in different Situations; on the LONDON Societies for the Benefit of Widows and of Old Age; and on the present State of Population in this Kingdom. Price 6s.

II. A Review of the principal Questions and Difficulties in MORALS. Particularly, those relating to the Original of our Ideas of Virtue, its Nature, Foundation, Reference to the Deity, Obligation, Subject-matter, and Sanctions. The Second Edition corrected. Price 6s.

III. FOUR DISSERTATIONS.——I. On Providence.—— II. On Prayer.—III. On the Reasons for expecting that virtuous Men shall meet after Death in a State of Happiness. —IV. On the Importance of Christianity, the Nature of Historical Evidence, and Miracles. The 4th Edition. Price 6s.

IV. An APPEAL to the PUBLIC, on the Subject of the NATIONAL DEBT. The 2d Edition; with an Appendix, containing Explanatory Observations and Tables; and an Account of the present State of Population in Norfolk. Price 2s.

V. OBSERVATIONS on the Nature of CIVIL LIBERTY, the Principles of GOVERNMENT, and the Justice and Policy of the WAR with AMERICA. To which is added an Appendix, containing a State of the National Debt, an Estimate of the Money drawn from the Public by the Taxes, and an Account of the National Income and Expenditure since the last War. The 7th Edition. Price 2s.

INTRODUCTION.

BEFORE the reader enters on the following tract, I shall beg leave to detain him while I give a general account of the contents of it, and make a few introductory observations.

In the first part of the *Observations on Civil Liberty*, published last winter, I gave a brief account of the nature of Liberty in general, and of *Civil Liberty* in particular. That account appears to me, after carefully reconsidering it, to be just; nor do I think it in my power to improve it. In order, however, to be as explicit as possible on this subject, and to remove those misapprehensions of my sentiments into which some have fallen, I have thought proper to add the *supplemental* and *explanatory* observations, which will be found in the FIRST part of this pamphlet.——In writing with this view, I have been led to refer often to my former pamphlet, and to repeat some of the observations in it. But as this could not have been avoided, it will, I hope, be excused.

The remarks in the SECOND part, I offer to the public with all the deference due to the high station and abilities of the noble Lord, whose speech at opening the Budget in *April* last, has occasioned them.——These remarks, having been

A 4   promised

promifed long ago, fhould have been publifhed
fooner. The reafons which have produced this
delay are of little confequence to the public; and,
therefore, need not be mentioned.

In the firft fection of this *fecond* part, it will,
I think, appear, that I went upon as good grounds
as the nature of the cafe admitted, when I ftated
the gold coin (*a*) of the kingdom at ABOUT
TWELVE MILLIONS AND A HALF. It appears now,
indeed, to be fome millions more. But this is a
difcovery made by the call of laft fummer; which,
I find, has brought in near double the fum that
the beft judges expected. Nothing, however,
very encouraging can be inferred from hence.
It only fhews that a great deal of gold has been
hoarded; and will, probably, be again hoarded.
This is the natural confequence of public diffi-
dence; and it is a circumftance which may, hereafter, greatly increafe diftrefs. Before the REVO-
LUTION, according to Dr. *Davenant*, near half the
coin was hoarded; and the fame, undoubtedly,
will be done again, whenever the nation comes to
be thoroughly alarmed.

In the next fection of this part, I have made
fome further obfervations on the conteft with
America.——I cannot expect any other than a
tragical and deplorable iffue to this conteft. But
let events turn out as they will, I fhall always

(*a*) See Obfervations on Civil Liberty, page 74.

reflect

reflect with satisfaction, that I have, though a private perfon of little confequence, bore my teftimony, from deep-felt conviction, againft a war which muft fhock the feelings and the reafon of every confiderate perfon ; a war in which rivers of blood muft be fhed, not to repel the attacks of enemies, or to maintain the authority of government *within* the realm, but to maintain fovereignty and dominion in another world (*a*).—I wifh the advocates for the meafures againft *America* would attend to the diftinction now intimated.—The fupport of juft government *within* the realm is always neceffary, and therefore right. But to maintain, by fire and fword, dominion over the perfons and the property of a people *out* of the realm, who have no fhare in its legiflature, contradicts every principle of liberty and humanity.—Legitimate government, let it be remembered, as oppofed to oppreffion and tyranny, confifts " only in the dominion of " EQUAL LAWS made with COMMON CONSENT, or of " men over THEMSELVES ; and not in the dominion " of communities over communities, or of ANY " MEN OVER OTHER MEN."—This is the great truth I have endeavoured to explain and defend ; and

(*a*) Of all the writers againft this war, the learned Dr. TUCKER is the fevereft. For if, as he maintains, contrary to repeated declarations from the throne, a feparation from the Colonies would be an advantage to us, the attempt to keep them, by invafion and bloodfhed, deferves a harfher cenfure than words can convey.

happy

happy would the world be, were a due conviction of it impreſſed on every human heart.

The repreſentation I have given in this ſection and elſewhere, of the ſtate of this kingdom, is, without doubt, gloomy. But it is not the effect, as ſome have intimated, of either a natural diſpoſition to gloo](mineſs, or of ſiniſter views. Few, who know me, will entertain ſuch a ſuſpicion. Valuing *moſt* what politicians and ſtateſmen generally value *leaſt*, I feel myſelf perfectly eaſy with reſpect to my intereſt as a citizen of this world ; nor is there any change of ſituation that can make me happier, except a return to privacy and obſcurity. The opinion I have entertained of the preſent danger of the kingdom is, therefore, the effect of evidence which appears to me irreſiſtible. This evidence I have ſtated to the public ; and every one may judge of it as he pleaſes. I am ſenſible of my own liableneſs to error. The meaſures which I condemn as the worſt that ever diſgraced and hazarded a great kingdom, others, whoſe integrity I cannot queſtion, approve ; and that very ſituation of our affairs which I think alarming, others think proſperous. Time will determine which of theſe opinions is right. But ſuppoſing the latter to be ſo, no harm can ariſe from any repreſentations which have a tendency to put us on our guard.

I have beſtowed particular attention on the obſervations in the third ſection of this ſecond part ;

and I think the fubject of this fection fo important, that it is probable, I fhould not have refolved on the prefent publication, had it not been for the opportunity it gives me to lay the obfervations it contains before the public.——An intimation of them was given in the Introduction to the third edition of the Treatife on *Reverfionary Payments.* The nation being now once more got into a courfe of borrowing; and our firft ftep having been a return to a mode of borrowing, which had appeared to me abfurd and detrimental, I was induced to refume the fubject, and to examine it with more care. And the refult of an examination of only a *part* of the public loans, will be found to be, " that a capital of more than " TWENTY MILLIONS has been a needlefs addition " to the public debt, for which no money, or any " fort of equivalent has been received; and which " might have been avoided, together with a great " expence of intereft, by only forming differently " the fchemes of the public loans."

The intention of the firft fection of the THIRD PART is to give, in as fhort a compafs as poffible, a view of the progrefs of our *foreign trade,* and its effect on the nation, from the beginning of this century; and, particularly, to point out an unfavourable change which feems to have taken place fince 1764.

In the fecond fection of this part, an explanation and analyfis are given of all the different
articles

articles of the national debt, which will probably inform every perſon of moſt that he can wiſh to know concerning them.—I have added a general account of the debts and reſources of FRANCE. This is a ſubject at preſent particularly intereſting to this country ; and, having been informed of ſome important facts relating to it, I have thought proper to lay them before the public, with ſuch reflexions as have offered themſelves in mentioning them.

The laſt ſection contains ſuch of the calculations in the APPENDIX to the *Obſervations on Civil Liberty* as were neceſſary to be reprinted, in order to introduce the remarks I have added on ſome particulars in the ſtate of the *public income and expenditure,* publiſhed not long ago by the *Earl of Stair.* I have alſo meant to accommodate the purchaſers of the different editions of the *Obſervations on Civil Liberty,* who will be enabled, by this ſection, to poſſeſs themſelves of all the material alterations and improvements which were made in that pamphlet after its firſt publication.— The accounts, in the latter part of this tract, are ſo various and extenſive, that it is ſcarcely poſſible there ſhould not be ſome incorrectneſſes in them. But the pains I have taken, and the means of information which I have poſſeſſed have been ſuch, that I cannot ſuſpect that I have fallen into any miſtakes of conſequence. Should, however, any ſuch have eſcaped me, it will be kind in any

perſon

perſon to point them out with candour; and to
aſſiſt in making thoſe accounts ſo correct and
perfect, as that they may ſerve for a baſis to all
future accounts of the ſame kind.

The following note in Mr. *Hume*'s Hiſtory of
England was written by him a little before
his death, and left with other additions to be
inſerted in the new edition of that hiſtory
juſt publiſhed. It contains, therefore, a kind
of dying warning from Mr. *Hume* to this kingdom; and I have thought proper to tranſcribe
it, and to inſert it in this place, as a confir-
mation of ſimilar ſentiments frequently ex-
preſſed in theſe tracts.

" The ſupplies granted Queen *Elizabeth*, du-
" ring a reign of FORTY-FIVE YEARS, amounted
" to three millions. The miniſter, in the war
" which begun in 1754, was, in ſome periods,
" allowed to laviſh a ſum equal to this in TWO
" MONTHS. The extreme frivolous object of
" the late war, and the great importance of hers,
" ſet this matter in ſtill a ſtronger light. Money
" too was in moſt particulars of the ſame value
" in both periods: ſhe paid eight-pence a day
" to every foot ſoldier;—but our LATE DELU-
" SIONS have much exceeded any thing known
" in hiſtory, not even excepting thoſe of the
" Cruſades.

" Crufades. For, I fuppofe, there is no mathe-
" matical, ftill lefs an arithmetical demonftration,
" that the road to the holy land was not the road
" to Paradife ; as there is, that the endlefs in-
" creafe of national debt is the direct road to
" national ruin. But having now completely
" reached that goal, it is needlefs at prefent to
" reflect on the paft. It will be found in the
" prefent year (1776) that all the revenues of
" this ifland, north of the *Trent*, and weft of
" *Reading*, are mortgaged or anticipated for
" ever. Could the fmall remainder be in a
" worfe condition, were thefe provinces feized
" by *Auftria* and *Pruffia?* There is only this
" difference, that fome event might happen in
" *Europe*, which would oblige thofe great mo-
" narchs to difgorge their acquifitions. But no
" imagination can figure a fituation which will
" induce our creditors to relinquifh their claims,
" or the public to feize their revenues.———So
" egregious, indeed, has been our folly, that
" we have even loft all title to compaffion, un-
" der the numberlefs calamities that are waiting
" us."———Mr. *Hume*'s Hiftory, vol. 5th, page
475.

I   PART

PART I.

SUPPLEMENTAL OBSERVATIONS

ON THE

NATURE and VALUE of CIVIL LIBERTY
and FREE GOVERNMENT.

SECT. I.

Of the Nature of Civil Liberty, and the Essentials of a Free Government.

WITH refpect to Liberty in general there are two queftions to be confidered: Firft, What it is?—And Secondly, How far it is of value?

There is no difficulty in anfwering the firft of thefe queftions.—To be FREE, is " to be able to " act or to forbear acting, as we think beft ;" or " to be mafters of our own refolutions and con- " duct."——It may be pretended, that it is not defirable to be thus free; but, without doubt, this it is to be *free*; and this is what all mean

B   when

when they fay of themfelves or others that they
are *free*.

I have obferved, that all the different kinds of
Liberty run up into the general idea of felf-government (a).——The Liberty of men as *agents*
is that power of felf-determination which all
agents, as fuch, poffefs.—Their Liberty as *moral*
agents is their power of felf-government in their
moral conduct.—Their Liberty as *religious* agents
is their power of felf-government in *religion*.——
And their Liberty, as members of communities af-
fociated for the purpofes of civil government, is
their power of felf-government in all their civil
concerns. It is Liberty, in the laft of thefe views
of it, that is the fubject of my prefent enquiry;
and it may, in other words, be defined to be
" the power of a ftate to govern itfelf by its own
" will."——In order, therefore, to determine
whether a ftate is free, no more is neceffary than
to determine whether there is any will, different
from its own, to which it is fubject.

When we fpeak of a ftate, we mean the *whole*
ftate, and not any *part* of it; and the will of the
ftate, therefore, is the will of the whole.——
There are two ways in which this will may be
expreffed. Firft, by the fuffrages of all the members given in perfon. Or fecondly, by the fuf-

(a) See Obfervations on Civil Liberty, Part I. fect. 1.

frages

frages of a body of Reprefentatives, in appointing
whom all the members have voices.——A ftate
governed by its own will in the firft of thefe ways
enjoys the moft complete and perfect Liberty;
but fuch a government being impracticable, except in very fmall ftates, it is neceffary that civil
communities in general fhould fatisfy themfelves
with that degree of Liberty which can be obtained
in the laft of thefe ways; and Liberty fo obtained
may be fufficiently ample, and at the fame time
is capable of being extended to the largeft
ftates (*a*).

But here, before I proceed, I muft defire, that
an obfervation may be attended to, which appears
to me of confiderable confequence.——A diftinction fhould be made between the *Liberty* of a
ftate, and its not fuffering oppreffion; or between
a free government, and a government under which
freedom is enjoyed.   Under the moft defpotic government liberty may happen to be enjoyed.   But
being derived from a will over which the ftate
has no controul, and not from its own will; or
from an accidental mildnefs in the *adminiftration*,
and not from a *conftitution* of government; it is
nothing but an indulgence of a precarious nature,
and of little importance.——Individuals in pri-

(*a*) See Obfervations, Part I. fect. 2.

vate

vate life, while held under the power of masters, cannot be denominated free, however equitably and kindly they may be treated. This is strictly true of *communities* as well as of *individuals*.—— Civil Liberty (it should be remembered) must be enjoyed as a right derived from the Author of nature only, or it cannot be the blessing which merits this name. If there is any human power which is considered as *giving* it, on which it depends, and which can invade or recall it at pleasure, it changes its nature, and becomes a species of slavery.

But to return——The force superseding self-government in a state, or the power destroying its Liberty, is of two kinds. It may be either a power *without* itself, or a power *within* itself. The former constitutes what may be properly called *external*, and the latter *internal* slavery.—— Were there any distant state which had acquired a sovereignty over this country, and exercised the power of making its laws and disposing its property, we should be in the first kind of slavery; and, if not totally depraved by a habit of subjection to such a power, we should think ourselves in a miserable condition; and an advocate for such a power would be considered as insulting us, who should attempt to reconcile us to it by telling us, that we were *one* community with that distant

state,

ftate, though deftitute of a fingle voice in its legiflature; and, on this ground, fhould maintain,
that all refiftance to it was no lefs criminal than
any refiftance *within* a ftate to the authority of
that ftate.—In fhort, every ftate, not incorporated
with another by an equal reprefentation, and yet
fubjeƈt to its dominion, is enflaved in this fenfe.—
Such was the flavery of the provinces fubjeƈt to
antient *Rome*; and fuch is the flavery of every
community, as far as any other community is
mafter of it; or as far as, in refpeƈt of taxation
and internal legiflation, it is not independent of
every other community. Nor does it make any
difference to fuch a community, that it enjoys
within itfelf a free conftitution of government, if
that conftitution is itfelf liable to be altered, fuf-
pended or over-ruled at the difcretion of the ftate
which poffeffes the fovereignty over it.

But the flavery moft prevalent in the world has
been internal flavery.——In order better to explain
this, it is proper to obferve, that all civil government being either the government of a *whole*
by *itfelf*, or of a *whole* by a *power extraneous* to
it, or of a *whole* by a *part*; the firft *alone* is Liberty, and the two laft are Tyranny, producing the two forts of flavery which I have mentioned. Internal flavery, therefore, takes place
wherever a whole community is governed by a
part; and this, perhaps, is the moft concife and

compre-

comprehenfive account that can be given of it.—
The part that governs may be either a *single* man,
as in *abfolute Monarchies* ; or, a body of grandees,
as in *Ariftocracies*. In both thefe cafes the
powers of government are commonly held for
life withcut delegation, and defcend from father
to fon ; and the people governed are in the fame
fituation with cattle upon an eftate, which defcends
by inheritance from one owner to another.——
But farther. A community may be governed by
a body of delegates, and yet be enflaved.——
Though government by reprefentation alone is
free, unlefs when carried on by the perfonal fuffrages of all the members of a ftate, yet *all* fuch
government is by no means free. In order to
render it fo, the following requifites are neceffary.

First, The reprefentation muft be *complete*. No
ftate, a *part* of which only is reprefented in the
Legiflature that governs it, is *self*-governed.
Had *Scotland* no reprefentatives in the Parliament
of *Britain*, it would not be free ; nor would it be
proper to call *Britain* free, though *England*, its
other part, were adequately reprefented. The
like is true, in general, of every country fubject to
a Legiflature in which *fome* of its parts, or fome
claffes of men in it, are reprefented, and others
not.

Secondly, The reprefentatives of a free ftate
muft be *freely* chofen. If this is not the cafe, they
are

are not at all reprefentatives; and government by them degenerates into government by a junto of men in the community, who happen to have power or wealth enough to command or pur-chafe their offices.

Thirdly, After being *freely* chofen, they muft be themfelves *free*. If there is any higher will which directs their refolutions, and on which they are dependent, they become the inftruments of that will; and it is that will alone that in reality governs the ftate.

Fourthly, They muft be chofen for fhort terms; and, in all their acts, be accountable to their conftituents. Without this a people will have no controul over their reprefentatives; and, in chufing them, they will give up entirely their Liberty; and only enjoy the poor privilege of naming, at certain intervals, a fet of men whom they are to *ferve*, and who are to difpofe, at their difcretion, of their property and lives.

The caufes of internal flavery now mentioned prevail, fome of them more and others lefs, in dif-ferent communities. With refpect, in particular, to a government by reprefentation; it is evident, that it deviates more or lefs from Liberty, in pro-portion as the reprefentation is more or lefs im-perfect. And, if imperfect in every one of the inftances I have recited; that is, if inadequate and partial; fubject to no controul from the

people;

people ; corruptly chofen for long terms ; and, after being chofen, venal and dependent ;—in thefe circumftances, a reprefentation becomes an impofition and a nufance ; and government by it is as inconfiftent with true Liberty as the moft arbitrary and defpotic government.

I have been fo much mifunderftood (a) on this fubject, that it is neceffary I fhould particularly obferve here, that my intention in this account has been merely to fhew what is requifite to con-ftitute a ftate or a government free, and not at all to define the beft form of government. Thefe are two very different points. The firft is at-tended with few difficulties. A free ftate is a ftate felf-governed in the manner I have de-fcribed. But it may be free, and yet not enjoy the beft conftitution of government. Li-berty, though the moft effential requifite in go-vernment, is not the only one. Wifdom, union, difpatch, fecrefy, and vigour are likewife requi-fite ; and that is the beft form of government which beft unites all thefe qualities ; or which, to an equal and perfect Liberty, adds the greateft

(a) The greateft part of Mr. *Goodricke's* remarks are founded on this mifunderftanding. He is fo candid that I know he did not mean to mifreprefent me ; and yet I can-not help thinking it hard, after repeated declarations of my preference of fuch a conftitution as our own, to be confidered as an advocate for a pure Democracy. See *Obfervations on Dr. Price's Theory and Principles of Civil Liberty and Govern-ment,* by Mr. GOODRICKE.

wifdom

wifdom in deliberating and refolving, and the greateft union, force and expedition in executing (a).

In fhort, my whole meaning is, that the will of
the Community alone ought to govern ; but that
there are different methods of obtaining and executing this will ; of which thofe are the beft which
collect into it moft of the knowledge and experience of the community, and at the fame time
carry it into execution with moft difpatch and
vigour.

It has been the employment of the wifeft men in
all ages to contrive plans for this purpofe ; and the
happinefs of fociety depends fo much on civil
government, that it is not poffible the human un-
derftanding fhould be better employed.

I have faid in the Obfervations on Civil Liberty,
that " in a free ftate every man is his own le-
" giflator."—I have been happy in fince finding
the (b) fame affertion in *Montefquieu*, and alfo in

(a) One of the beft plans of this kind has been with much
ability, defcribed by Mr. De Lolme, in his account of the
Conftitution of England.

(b) " As in a free ftate, every man who is fuppofed a free
" agent, ought to be his own governor ; fo the legiflative
" power fhould refide in the whole body of the people."
Spirit of Laws, Book XI. chap. vi. See likewife Juftice
Blackftone's Commentaries on the Laws of England, page 158.
1ft Vol. oct. edition.———*Demofthenes* fpeaking in his firft
Philippic, fect. 3d. of certain free ftates, calls them *their own
legiflators, αυτονομευμύα καὶ ελευθερα.*

Mr.

Mr. Juſtice *Blackſtone*'s Commentaries. It expreſſes the fundamental principle of our conſtitu-
tution; and the meaning of it is plainly, that
every independent agent in a free ſtate ought to
have a ſhare in the government of it, either by
himſelf *perſonally*, or by a body of repreſentatives,
in chuſing whom he has a free vote, and therefore all the concern and weight which are
poſſible, and conſiſtent with the equal rights
of every other member of the ſtate. —— But
though the meaning of this aſſertion is ſo obvious, and the truth of it undeniable, it has
been much exclaimed againſt, and occaſioned no
ſmall part of the oppoſition which has been
made to the principles advanced in the *Obſer-*
vations on Civil Liberty. —— One even of the moſt
candid, as well as the ableſt of my opponents,
(whoſe difference of opinion from me I ſincerely
lament) has intimated, that it implies, that, in
a free ſtate, *(a) thieves and pick-pockets have a*
right to make laws for themſelves. —— The public
will not, I hope, wonder that I chuſe to take
little notice of ſuch objections.

It has been ſaid, that the liberty for which I
have pleaded, is " a right or power in every one

(a) See *Remarks*, printed for Mr. Cadell, *on a pamphlet*
publiſhed by Dr. Price. In a letter from a gentleman in the
country to a member of parliament, page 10.

" to

" to act as he likes without any reftraint."——
However unfairly this reprefentation has been
given of my account of liberty, I am ready to
adopt it, provided it is underftood with a few
limitations.——MORAL LIBERTY, in particular,
cannot be better defined than by calling it " a
" power in every one to do as he likes." My
opponents in general feem to be greatly puzzled
with this; and I am afraid it will fignify little to
attempt explaining it to them by faying, that
every man's will, if perfectly free from reftraint,
would carry him invariably to rectitude and
virtue; and that no one who acts wickedly acts
as he *likes*, but is confcious of a tyranny within
him overpowering his judgment, and carrying
him into a conduct, for which he condemns and
hates himfelf. *The things that he would he does
not*; (a) *and the things that he would not, thofe he
does.* He is, therefore, a flave in the propereft
fenfe.

RELIGIOUS LIBERTY, likewife, is a power of
acting as we *like* in religion; or of profeffing and
practifing that mode of religious worfhip which we
think moft acceptable to the Deity.——But here
the limitation to which I have referred muft be
attended to. ALL have the fame unalienable right
to this Liberty; and confequently, no one has a
right to fuch a ufe of it as fhall take it from others.

(a) Rom. vii.

Within

Within this limit, or as far as he does not encroach on the equal liberty of others, every one
has a right to do as he pleafes in religion.———
That the right to religious Liberty goes as far as
this every one muft allow, who is not a friend to
perfecution; and that it cannot go farther, is
felf-evident; for if it did, there would be a contradiction in the natures of things; and it would
be true, that every one had a right to enjoy
what every one had a right to deftroy.———If,
therefore, the religious faith of any perfon leads
him to hurt another becaufe he profeffes a different
faith; or if it carries him, in any inftances, to in-
tolerance, Liberty itfelf requires he fhould be reftrained, and that, in fuch inftances, he fhould lofe
his liberty.

All this is equally applicable to the Liberty of
man in his *civil* capacity; and it is a maxim true
univerfally, " that as far as any one does not
" moleft *others*, others ought not to moleft *him*."
———All have a right to the free and undifturbed
poffeffion of their good names, properties and
lives; and it is the right all have to this that
gives the right to eftablifh civil government,
which is or ought to be nothing but an inftitution
(by laws and provifions made with *common* confent)
for guarding this right againft invafion; for giving to every one, in *temporals* and *fpirituals*, the
power of commanding his own conduct; or, of
acting

acting as he pleafes, and going where he will, provided he does not run foul of others.——Juft government, therefore, does not *infringe* liberty, but *eftablifh* it.——It does not *take away* the rights of mankind, but *proteƈ* and *confirm* them.—— I will add, that it does not even create any new fubordinations of particular men to one another, but only gives fecurity in thofe feveral ftations, whether of authority and pre-eminence, or of fub-ordination and dependence, which nature has efta-blifhed, and which muft have arifen among man-kind whether civil government had been infti-tuted or not. But this goes beyond my purpofe in this place, and more will be faid of it prefently.

To fum up the whole—Our ideas of Civil Li-berty will be rendered more diftinƈ by confidering it under the three following views:—The Liberty of the *citizen*—The liberty of the *government*— And the liberty of the *community*.——A *citizen* is free when the power of commanding his own conduƈ and the quiet poffeffion of his life, per-fon, property and good name are *fecured* to him by being his own legiflator in the fenfe explained in page 10 (*a*).——A *government* is free when
                                                  conftituted

(*a*) Dr. PRIESTLY, in his Effay on the *firft principles of Government*, makes a diftinƈion between *civil* Liberty and *political* Liberty ; the former of which he defines to be " the
                                                  " power

conftituted in fuch a manner as to give this *fe-curity*.——And the freedom of a community or nation is the fame among nations, that the freedom of a citizen is among his fellow-citizens.——It is not, therefore, as obferved in page 3, the mere poffeffion of Liberty that denominates a citizen or a community free; but that *fecurity* for the poffeffion of it which arifes from fuch a free go-vernment as I have defcribed; and which takes place, when there exifts no power that can take it away.——It is in the fame fenfe that the mere performance of virtuous actions is not what deno-minates an agent virtuous; but the temper and habits from whence they fpring; or that *inward conftitution*, and right balance of the affections, which *fecure* the practice of virtue, produce ftabi-lity of conduct, and conftitute a *character*.

I cannot imagine how it can be difputed whe-ther this is a juft account of the nature of Li-berty. It has been already given more briefly in the Obfervations on Civil Liberty; and it is with reluctance I have repeated fo much of what

" power which the members of a ftate ought to enjoy over " their actions;" and the latter, " their power of arriving at " public offices, or, at leaft, of having votes in the nomina-" tion of thofe who fill them."—This diftinction forms a very proper fubdivifion of *the liberty of the citizen* here menti-oned; and it may be accommodated to all I have faid on this fubject, by only giving fome lefs general name to that which Dr. Prieftly calls *civil* Liberty.

has

has been there faid. But the wrong apprehenfions which have been entertained of my fentiments have rendered this neceffary. And, for the fame reafon, I am obliged to go on to the fubject of the next fection.

S E C T. II.

Of the VALUE *of Liberty, and the* EXCELLENCE *of a Free Government.*

HAVING fhewn in the preceding fection " what Liberty is ;" the next queftion to be confidered is, " how far it is valuable."

Nothing need be faid to fhew the value of the three kinds of liberty which I have diftinguifhed under the names of *Phyfical*, *Moral*, and *Religious* Liberty. They are, without doubt, the foundation of all the happinefs and dignity of men, as reafonable and moral agents, and the fubjects of the Deity.—It is, in like manner, true of *Civil* Liberty, that it is the foundation of the whole happinefs and dignity of men as members of civil fociety, and the fubjects of civil government.

Firft. It is Civil Liberty, or fuch free government as I have defcribed, that alone can give juft fecurity againft oppreffion. One government is better than another in proportion as it gives more of this fecurity. It is, on this account, that the fupreme government of the Deity is perfect.

There

There is not a poffibility of being oppreffed or aggrieved by it. Subjection to it is the fame with complete freedom.

Were there any men on whofe fuperior wifdom and goodnefs we might abfolutely depend, they could not poffefs too much power; and the love of liberty itfelf would engage us to fly to them, and to put ourfelves under their direction. But fuch are the principles that govern human nature; fuch the weaknefs and folly of men; fuch their love of domination, felfifhnefs, and depravity; that none of them can be raifed to an elevation above others without the utmoft danger. The conftant experience of the world has verified this; and proved, that nothing intoxicates the human mind fo much as power, and that men, when they have got poffeffion of it, have feldom failed to employ it in grinding their fellow-men, and gratifying the vileft paffions.—In the eftablifh-ment, therefore, of civil government, it would be prepofterous to rely on the difcretion of any men. If a people would obtain fecurity againft oppreffion, they muft feek it in *themfelves*, and never part with the powers of government out *of their own* hands. It is there only they can be fafe.— A people will never opprefs themfelves, or invade their own rights. But if they truft the arbitrary will of any body or fucceffion of men, they truft

ENEMIES,

ENEMIES, and it may be depended on that the worſt evils will follow.

It follows from hence, that a free government is the only government which is conſiſtent with the ends of government.——Men combine into communities and inſtitute government to obtain the peaceable enjoyment of their rights, and to defend themſelves againſt injuſtice and violence: And when they endeavour to ſecure theſe ends by ſuch a free government as I have deſcribed, improved by ſuch arrangements as may have a tendency to preſerve it from confuſion, and to concentrate in it as much as poſſible of the wiſdom and force of the community; In this caſe, it is a moſt rational and important inſtitution.——But when the contrary is done; and the benefits of government are ſought by eſtabliſhing a government of *men*, and not of *laws* made with common conſent; it becomes a moſt abſurd inſtitution.—— It is ſeeking a remedy for oppreſſion in *one* quarter, by eſtabliſhing it in *another*; and avoiding the outrages of *little* plunderers, by conſtituting a ſet of *great* plunderers.——It is, in ſhort, the folly of *giving up* liberty in order to *maintain* Liberty; and, in the very act of endeavouring to ſecure the moſt valuable rights, to arm a body of enemies with power to deſtroy them.

C

I can

I can eafily believe, that mankind, in the firft and rude ftate of fociety, might act thus irrationally. Abfolute governments, being the fimpleft forms of government, might be the firft that were eftablifhed. A people having experienced the happy effects of the wifdom or the valour of particular men, might be led to truft them with unlimited power as their rulers and legiflators. But they would foon find reafon to repent : And the time, I hope, may come, when mankind in general, taught by long and dear experience, and *weary* of the abufes of power under *flavifh* governments, will learn to deteft them, and never to give up that SELF-GOVERNMENT, which, whether we confider men in their private or collective capacities, is the firft of all the bleffings they can poffefs.

Again. Free governments are the only governments which give fcope to the exertion of the powers of men, and are favourable to their improvement.——The members of free ftates, knowing their rights to be fecure, and that they fhall enjoy without moleftation the fruits of every acquifition they can make, are encouraged and incited to induftry. Being at liberty to pufh their refearches as far as they can into all fubjects, and to guide themfelves by their own judgments in all their religious and civil concerns, while they

allow

allow others to do the fame ; error and fuperftition muft lofe ground. Confcious of being their own governors, bound to obey no laws except fuch as they have given their confent to, and fubject to no controul from the arbitrary will of any of their fellow-citizens ; they poffefs an elevation and force of mind which muft make them great and happy.——How different is the fituation of the vaffals of defpotic power ?——Like cattle inured to the yoke, they are driven on in one track, afraid of fpeaking or even thinking on the moft inte-refting points ; looking up continually to a poor creature who is their mafter ; their powers fettered ; and fome of the nobleft fprings of action in human nature rendered ufelefs within them. There is nothing indeed more humiliating than that de-bafement of mankind which takes place in fuch fituations.

It has been obferved of free governments, that they are often torn by violent contefts, which render them dreadful fcenes of diftrefs and anarchy. But it ought to be confidered, that this has not been owing to the *nature* of fuch governments ; but to their having been ill-modelled, and wanted thofe arrangements and fupplemental checks which are neceffary to conftitute a wife form of government.——There is no reafon to doubt, but that free governments may be fo contrived, as to exclude the greateft part of the ftruggles and

tumults

tumults which have arisen in free states ; and, as far as they cannot be excluded, they will do more good than harm. They will occasion the display of powers, and produce exertions which can never be seen in the *still* scenes of life. They are the active efforts of health and vigour; and always tend to preserve and purify. Whereas, on the contrary, the *quiet* which prevails under slavish governments, and which may seem to be a recommendation of them, proceeds from an ignominious tameness, and stagnation of the human faculties. It is the same with the *stillness* of midnight, or the *silence* and torpor of death.

Further. Free governments are the only governments which are consistent with the natural equality of mankind. This is a principle which, in my opinion, has been assumed, with the greatest reason, by some of the best writers on government. But the meaning of it is not, that all the subordinations in human life owe their existence to the institution of civil government. The superiorities and distinctions arising from the relation of parents to their children ; from the differences in the personal qualities and abilities of men ; and from servitudes founded on voluntary compacts, must have existed in a state of nature, and would now take place were all men so virtuous as to leave no occasion for civil government.——The maxim,

therefore,

therefore, " that all men are naturally equal," refers to their ſtate when grown up to maturity, and
become independent agents, capable of acquiring
property, and of directing their own conduct.
And the ſenſe of it is, that no one of them is conſtituted by the author of nature the vaſſal or
ſubject of another, or has any right to give law to
him, or, without his conſent, to take away any
part of his property, or to abridge him of his
liberty.——In a ſtate of nature, one man may
have received benefits from another ; and this
would lay the perſon obliged under an obligation
of gratitude, but it would not make his *benefactor*
his *maſter* ; or give him a right to judge for him
what grateful returns he ought to make, and to
extort theſe from him.——In a ſtate of nature,
alſo, one man may poſſeſs more ſtrength, or more
knowledge, or more property than another ; and
this would give him weight and influence ; but it
would not give him any degree of authority.
There would not be one human being who would
be bound to *obey* him.——A perſon likewiſe, in a
ſtate of nature, might let out his labour, or give
up to another, on certain ſtipulated terms, the
direction of his conduct ; and this would ſo far
bring him into the ſtation of a *ſervant* ; but being
done by himſelf, and on ſuch terms only as he
chuſes to conſent to, it is an *inſtance* of his liberty ;

and

and he will always have it in his power to quit
the service he has chosen, or to enter into another.

This equality or independence of men is one of
their essential rights. (*a*) It is the same with that
equality or independence which now actually takes
place among the different states or kingdoms of
the world with respect to one another. Mankind
came with this right from the hands of their
Maker.——But all governments, which are not
free, are totally inconsistent with it. They imply,
that there are some of mankind who are born
with an inherent right of dominion ; and that the
rest are born under an obligation to subjection ;
and that civil government, instead of being founded
on any compact, is nothing but the exercise of this
right. Some such sentiments seem to be now re-
viving in this country, and even to be growing
fashionable. Most of the writers against the *Observations on Civil Liberty* argue on the supposition
of a right in the *few* to govern the *many* (*b*), independently

(*a*) See on this Subject an excellent Sermon entitled, *The
Principles of the* REVOLUTION *vindicated*. By Dr. Watson,
Regius Professor of Divinity, at Cambridge.

(*b*) Some who maintain this doctrine concerning government, overthrow their own system by acknowledging the
right of resistance in certain cases. For, if there is such a
right, the people must be judges *when* it ought to be exercised ;
a right to resist only when civil governors *think* there is reason,
being a gross absurdity and nullity.——The right of resistance,

pendently of their own choice. Some of thefe
writers have gone fo far as to affert, in plain language, that civil governors derive their power
immediately from the Deity; and are *his* agents
or reprefentatives, accountable to him only. And
one courtly writer, in particular, has honoured
them with the appellation of OUR POLITICAL GODS.
——Probably, this is the idea of civil governors
entertained by the author of the *Remarks on the
Acts of the Thirteenth Parliament of Great Britain*:
for it is not eafy to imagine on what other ground
he can affert, that *property* and *civil rights* are derived from civil governors, and their *gifts* to mankind (*a*).

fiftance, therefore, cannot mean lefs than a right in the people,
whenever they think it neceffary, to change their governors,
and to limit their power. And from the moment this is done,
government becomes the work of the people, and governors
become their truftees or agents.

(*a*) It has been commonly reckoned, that it is the end of
civil government and civil laws to protect the *property* and
rights of men; but, according to this writer, civil government and civil laws create *property* and *rights*. It follows
therefore, that, antecedently to civil laws, men could have no
property or *rights*; and that civil governors, being the makers
of civil laws, it is a contradiction to fuppofe, that mankind can
have any property or rights which are valid againft the claims
of their governors. See Three Letters to Dr. *Price*, p. 21, &c.
And Remarks on the principal Acts of the 13th Parliament
of Great-Britain, p. 58, &c. and p. 191.

If

If thefe fentiments are juft, civil governors are indeed an awful order of beings ; and it becomes us to enquire with anxiety who they are, and how we may diftinguifh them from the reft of mankind.——Shall we take for fuch all, whether *men* or *women*, whom we find in actual poffeffion of civil power, whatever may be their characters ; or however they may have acquired their power ?—— This is too extravagant to be afferted. It would legalize the *American* Congrefs.——There muft then be fome *pretenders* among civil governors ; and it is neceffary we fhould know how to difcover them. It is incredible, that the Deity fhould not have made this eafy to us, by fome particular marks and diftinctions, which point out to our notice his *real* vicegerents ; juft as he has pointed out man, by his figure and fuperior powers, to be the governor of the lower creatures.——In particular ; thefe perfons muft be poffeffed of wifdom and goodnefs fuperior to thofe of the reft of mankind (*a*) ; for, without this, a grant of the powers they are fuppofed to poffefs would be nothing but a grant of power to injure and opprefs, without remedy and without bounds. But this is a teft by which they cannot be tryed. It would leave but few of them in poffeffion of the places they

(*a*) This has been done in a lower inftance. Parents have been furnifhed with a particular affection for their children, in order to prevent any abufe of their power over them.

hold

hold and the rights they claim. It is not in the high ranks of life, or among the great and mighty, that we are to feek wifdom and goodnefs. Thefe love the fhade, and fly from obfervation. They are to be found chiefly in the middle ranks of life, and among the contemplative and philo-fophical, who decline public employments, and look down with pity on the fcramble for power among mankind, and the reftleffnefs and mifery of ambition.——It is proper to add, that it has never been hitherto underftood that any fuperi-ority in intellectual and moral qualifications lays the foundation of a claim to *dominion*.

It is not then, by their fuperior endowments, that the Deity intended to point out to us the *few* whom he has deftined to command the *many*. —But in what other manner could they be diftin-guifhed?——Muft we embrace Sir *Robert Filmer*'s *Patriarchal* fcheme? One would have thought, that Mr. *Locke* has faid more than enough to expofe this ftupid fcheme. One of my opponents, however, has adopted it; and the neceffary infe-rence from it is that, as there is but now one lineal defcendent from Adam's eldeft fon, there can be but one rightful monarch of the world.— But I will not abufe my reader's patience by faying more on this fubject. I am forry that in this country there fhould be any occafion for taking notice of principles fo abfurd, and at the

fame

same time ſo pernicious (a).   I ſay, PERNICIOUS ;
for they imply, that King *James* the Second was
depoſed at the Revolution unlawfully and im-
piouſly ; that the preſent King is an uſurper ; and
that the preſent government, being derived from
rebellion and treaſon, has no right to our allegiance.

Without all doubt, it is the choice of the
people that makes civil governors.—The people
are the ſpring of all civil power, and they have
a right to modify it as they pleaſe.

(a) " In ages of darkneſs, and too often alſo in thoſe of
" greater knowledge, by the perfidious arts of deſigning
" princes, and by the baſe ſervility of too many eccleſiaſtics,
" who managed the ſuperſtition of the populace, by the vio-
" lent reſtraints put upon divulging any juſter ſentiments
" about the rights of mankind, the natural notions of polity
" were eraſed out of the minds of men ; and they were filled
" with ſome confuſed imaginations of ſomething adorable in
" monarchs, ſome repreſentation of the Divinity ; and that
" even in the worſt of them ; and of ſome certain Divine
" claims in certain families.——No wonder this ! that mil-
" lions thus look upon themſelves as a piece of property to
" one of their fellows as ſilly and worthleſs as the meaneſt
" of them ; when the like arts of ſuperſtition have made mil-
" lions, nay the very artificers themſelves, fall down before
" the block or ſtone they had ſet up ; or adore monkies, cats,
" and crocodiles, as the ſovereign diſpoſers of their fortunes."
See Dr. HUTCHESON's Syſtem of Moral Philoſophy. Vol. ii.
p. 289.

Mankind

Mankind being naturally equal according to the foregoing explanation, civil government, *in its genuine intention*, is an inftitution for maintaining that equality, by defending it againft the encroachments of violence and tyranny. All the fubordinations and diftinctions in fociety previous to its eftablifhment, it leaves as it found them, only confirming and protecting them. It makes no man *mafter* of another. It elevates no perfon above his fellow citizens. On the contrary, it levels all by fixing all in a ftate of fubjection to one common authority.——The authority of the laws.—The will of the community.——TAXES are *given*; not *impofed*. LAWS are regulations of common choice; not injunctions of fuperior power.——The authority of magiftrates is the authority of the State; and their falaries are wages paid by the State for executing its will and doing its bufinefs. *They* do not govern the *State*. It is the *State* governs *them*; and had they juft ideas of their own ftations, they would confider themfelves as no lefs properly *fervants* of the Public, than the labourers who work upon its roads, or the foldiers who fight its battles.—— A KING, in particular, is only the firft executive officer; the creature of the law; and as much accountable and fubject to the law as the meaneft peafant (*a*). And were Kings properly attentive

(*a*) " Let not, therefore, thefe *pretended mafters* of the " people be allowed even to do good againft the general " confent.

to their duty, and as anxious as they fhould be
about performing it, they could not eafily avoid
finking under the weight of their charge.

The account now given is, I am fully perfuaded, in every particular, a true account of
what civil government *ought* to be; and it
teaches us plainly the great importance and excellence of FREE Government.——It is this only
that anfwers the defcription I have given of government; that fecures againft oppreffion; that gives
room for that elevation of fpirit and that exertion
of the human powers which is neceffary to human
improvement; or that is confiftent with the ends of
government, with the rights of mankind, and their
natural equality and independence. *Free* Government, therefore, only, is *juft* and *legitimate*
government.

It follows farther from the preceding account,
that no people can lawfully furrender or cede
their Liberty. This muft appear to any one

" confent.——Let it be confidered, that the condition of
" rulers is exactly the fame as that of the Cacique, who being
" afked whether he had any flaves, anfwered; *Slaves? I*
" *know but one flave in all my diftrict, and that is myfelf.*"
See the Philofophical and Political Hiftory of the Settlements
and Trade of the *Europeans* in the EAST AND WEST INDIES.
Tranflated from the French of the Abbe *Raynal*, by Mr.
Juftamond. Vol. v. page 414.

who

who will confider, that when a people make fuch
a ceffion, and the extenfive powers of government
are trufted to the difcretion of any man or body
of men, they part with the powers of life and
death, and give themfelves up a prey to oppreffion; that they make themfelves the inftruments
of any injuftice in which their rulers may chufe
to employ them, by arming them againft neighbouring ftates; and alfo, that they do this not
only for *themfelves*, but for their *pofterity*.——I will
add, that if fuch a ceffion has been made; or if
through any caufes, a people have loft their Liberty, they muft have a right to emancipate
themfelves as foon as they can (*a*). In attempting
this, indeed, they ought to confider the fufferings
which may attend the ftruggle, and the evils
which may arife from a defeat. But at the fame
time, it will be proper to confider, that the
fufferings attending fuch a ftruggle muft be temporary, whereas the evils to be avoided are permanent; and that Liberty is a bleffing fo ineftimable, " that whenever there appears any pro-
" bability of recovering it, a people fhould be
" willing to run many hazards, and even not to

(*a*) See Obf. p. 25. " The rights of mankind are fo facred
" that no prefcription of tyranny or arbitrary power can have
" authority enough to abolifh them." Mr. *Hume*'s Effays,
vol. iii. Effay on the Coalition of Parties.

" repine

" repine at the greateſt expence of blood or trea-
" ſure." (a)

I am very ſenſible, that civil government, as it
actually exiſts in the world, by no means anſwers
to the account I have given of it.——Inſtead of
being an inſtitution for guarding the weak againſt
the ſtrong, we find it an inſtitution which makes
the ſtrong yet ſtronger, and gives them a ſyſte-
matical power of oppreſſing. Inſtead of promoting virtue and reſtraining vice, encouraging free
enquiry, eſtabliſhing Liberty, and protecting alike
all peaceable perſons in the enjoyment of their
civil and religious rights; we ſee a ſavage deſpotiſm, under its name, laying waſte the earth, unreaſonably elevating ſome and depreſſing others,
diſcouraging improvement, and trampling upon
every human right. That force of ſtates, which
ought to be applied only to their own defence,
we ſee continually applied to the purpoſe of attack, and uſed to extend dominion by conquering
neighbouring communities.——Civil governors
conſider not themſelves as *ſervants* but as *maſters.*
Their ſtations they think they hold in their own
right. The people they reckon their property;

(a) " Mankind have been generally a great deal too tract-
" able; and hence ſo many wretched forms of power have
" always enſlaved nine tenths of the nations of the world,
" where they have the fulleſt right to make all efforts for a -
" change." Dr. *Hutcheſon's* Moral Philoſophy. Vol. ii. p. 280.

and

and their poffeffions, a common *ftock* from which
they have a right to take what (*a*) they will, and
of which no more belongs to any individual than
they are pleafed to *leave* him.

What a miferable perverfion is this of a moft
important inftitution ? What a grievance is government fo degenerated ?——But this perverfion
furnifhes no juft argument againft the truth of the
account I have given. Similar degeneracies have
prevailed in other inftances of no lefs importance.

Reafon in man, like the will of the community
in the political world, was intended to give law
to his whole conduct, and to be the fupreme controuling power within him. The paffions are
fubordinate powers, or an *executive force* under
the direction of reafon, kindly given to be, as it
were, wind and tide to the veffel of life in its
courfe through this world to future honour and
felicity.——How different from this is the *actual*
ftate of man ?——Thofe powers which were deftined to *govern* are made to *ferve* ; and thofe
powers which were deftined to *ferve*, are allowed
to *govern*. Paffion guides human life ; and moft

(*a*) See Remarks on the Acts of the Thirteenth Parliament
of *Great Britain*. P. 34, &c.——" Is not the fame reafoning
" applicable to taxes paid for the fupport of civil government?
" Are not thefe too the property of the civil magiftrate ?"
Ibid. p. 56.——If I underftand this writer, his meaning is, not
only that the taxes which the civil magiftrate *has* impofed are
his property ; but alfo, *any* which he fhall pleafe to impofe.

men

men make no other use of their reason than to justify whatever their interest or their inclinations determine them to do.

RELIGION likewise (the perfection of REASON) is, in its true nature, the inspirer of humanity and joy, and the spring of all that can be great and worthy in a character; and were we to see its genuine effects among mankind, we should see nothing but peace and hope and justice and kindness, founded on that regard to God and to his will, which is the noblest principle of action.— But how different an aspect does religion actually wear? What is it, too generally, in the practice of mankind, but a gloomy and cruel superstition, rendering them severe and sour; teaching them to compound for wickedness by punctuality in religious forms; and prompting them to harrass, persecute and exterminate one another?

The same perversion has taken place still more remarkably in CHRISTIANITY; the perfection of RELIGION.—JESUS CHRIST has established among Christians an absolute equality. He has declared, that they have but *one* master, even himself; and that they are all *brethren*; and, therefore, has commanded them not to be called *masters*; and, instead of assuming authority over one another, to be ready to *wash one another's feet* (*a*). The

(*a*) Matth. xxiii. 8—12.——John xiii. 14.

princes

princes of the Gentiles, he fays, exercife lordfhip over them, and are flattered with (a) high
titles; but he has ordained, that it fhall not be
fo amongft his followers; and that if any one of
them would be *chief*, he muft be the *fervant* of
all.———The clergy in his church are, by his appointment, no more than a body of men, chofen
by the different focieties of Chriftians, to conduct
their worfhip, and to promote their fpiritual improvement, without any other powers than thofe
of perfuafion and inftruction. It is exprefsly directed, that they fhall not make themfelves
Lordsof *God's heritage*, or exercife dominion
over the faith of Chriftians, but be *helpers
of their joy* (b).———Who can, without aftonifh-
ment, compare thefe appointments of Chriftianity, with the events which have happened in
the Chriftian church?———That religion which
thus inculcates humility and forbids all domination, and the end of which was to produce *peace
on earth, and good-will among men*, has been turned
into an occafion of animofities the moft dreadful,
and of ambition the moft deftructive. Notwithftanding its mildnefs and benignity, and the tendency it has to extinguifh in the human breaft
pride and malevolence; it has been the means of
arming the fpirits of men with unrelenting fury

(a) Luke xxii. 25; &c.   (b) 1 Pet. v. 3.———2 Cor. i. 24;

D   againft

againſt one another. Inſtead of *peace*, it has brought a *ſword*; and its profeſſors, inſtead of waſhing one another's feet, have endeavoured to tread on one another's necks.——The miniſters, in particular, of Chriſtianity, became, ſoon after its eſtabliſhment, an independent body of ſpiritual rulers, nominating one another in perpetual ſuc-ceſſion; claiming, by divine right, the higheſt powers; and forming a HIERARCHY, which by degrees produced a deſpotiſm more extravagant than any that ever before exiſted on this earth.

A conſiderate perſon muſt find difficulties in enquiring into the cauſes and reaſons of that depravity of human nature which has produced theſe evils, and rendered the beſt inſtitutions liable to be ſo corrupted. This enquiry is much the ſame with the enquiry into the origin of moral evil, which has in all ages puzzled human wiſdom. I have at preſent nothing to do with it. It is enough for my purpoſe in theſe obſervations, that the facts I have mentioned prove undeniably, that the ſtate of civil govern-ment in the world affords no reaſon for concluding, that I have not given a juſt account of its true nature and origin.

I have ſhewn at the beginning of this ſection, that it is free government alone that can preſerve from oppreſſion, give ſecurity to the rights of a

people,

people, and anfwer the ends of government. It
is neceffary I fhould here obferve, that I would
not be underftood to mean, that there can be
no *kind* or *degree* of fecurity for the rights of
a people, under any government which cannot be
denominated free. Even under an abfolute Monarchy or an Ariftrocracy, there may be laws and
cuftoms which, having gained facrednefs by time,
may reftrain oppreffion, and afford fome important fecurities.——Under governments by reprefentation, there muft be ftill greater checks on
oppreffion, provided the reprefentation, though
partial, is uncorrupt, and alfo frequently changed.
In thefe circumftances, there may be fo much of
a common intereft between the body of reprefentatives and the people, and they may ftand fo
much on one ground, that there will be no temptations to oppreffion.——The taxes which the reprefentative body impofe, they will be obliged
themfelves to pay ; and the laws they make, they
will make with the profpect of foon returning to
the fituation of thofe for whom they make them,
and of being themfelves governed by them.

It feems particularly worth notice here, that
as far as there are any fuch checks under any
government, they are the confequence of its par-
taking fo far of Liberty, and that the fecurity attending them is more or lefs in proportion as a
government partakes more or lefs of Liberty.

If,

If, under an abfolute government, fundamental laws and long eftablifhed inftitutions give fecurity in any inftances, it is becaufe they are held fo facred that a defpot is afraid to violate them ; or, in other words, becaufe a people, not being completely fubdued, have ftill fome controul over the government.——The like is more evidently true under mixed governments of which a houfe of reprefentatives, fairly chofen and freely deliberating and refolving, forms a part ; and it is one of the higheft recommendations of fuch governments that, even when the reprefentation is moft imperfect, they have a tendency to give more fecurity than any other governments.—— Under other governments, it is the fear of exciting infurrections by contradicting eftablifhed maxims, that reftrains oppreffion. But, as, in general, a people will bear much, and are feldom driven to refiftance till grievances become intolerable, their rulers can venture far without danger ; and therefore, under fuch governments, are very imperfectly reftrained. On the contrary ; If there is an honeft reprefentation, vefted with powers like to thofe of our *Houfe of Commons*, the redrefs of grievances, as foon as they appear, will be always eafily attainable, and the rulers of a ftate will be under a neceffity of regarding the firft beginnings of difcontent.——Such, and greater than can be eafily defcribed, are the advantages

of

of even an *imperfect reprefentation* in a government. How great then muft be the bleffing of a
COMPLETE REPRESENTATION ?———(*a*) It is this
only gives full fecurity; and that can properly
denominate a people free.

It deferves to be added here, that as there can
be no private character fo abandoned as to want
all virtue; fo there can be no government fo flavifh, as to exclude *every* reftraint upon oppreffion.———The moft flavifh and, therefore, the
worft governments are thofe under which there is
nothing to fet bounds to oppreffion, befides the
difcretion and *humanity* of thofe who govern.———
Of this kind are the following governments.

First, All governments *purely* defpotic. Thefe
may be either monarchical, or ariftocratical. The
latter are the worft, agreeably to a common obfervation, that it is better to have *one* mafter than
many. The appetites of a fingle defpot may be
eafily fatiated; but this may be impoffible where
there is a multitude.

Secondly, All provincial governments.—The
hiftory of mankind proves thefe to be the worft of
all governments; and that no oppreffion is equal

to that which one people are capable of practising towards another. I have mentioned some of the reasons of this in the *Observations on Civil Liberty*, Part I. sect. 3. Bodies of men do not feel for one another as individuals do. The *odium* of a cruel action, when shared among many, is not regarded. The master of slaves working on a plantation, though he may keep them down to prevent their becoming strong enough to emancipate themselves, yet is led by *interest*, as well as *humanity*, to govern them with such moderation, as to preserve their use : But these causes will produce more of this good effect, when the slaves are under the eye of their proprietor, and form a part of his family, than when they are settled on a distant plantation, where he can know little of them, and is obliged to trust them to the management of rapacious servants.

It is particularly observable here, that *free* governments, though happier in themselves, are more oppressive to their provinces than despotic governments. Or, in other words, that the *subjects* of free (*a*) states are worse slaves than the subjects of states not free. This is one of the observations which Mr. HUME represents as an universal axiom in politicks (*b*).——" Though,

(*a*) " A *free* subject of a free state" is a contradiction in terms. See the Proclamation for a Fast.

(*b*) Mr. Hume's Essays. Vol. i. Essay iv. p. 31.

" says

" fays he, free governments have been commonly
" the moft happy for thofe who partake of their
" freedom, yet are they the moft oppreffive and
" ruinous to their provinces ; and this obfervation
" may be fixed as an univerfal axiom in politics.
" What cruel tyrants were the Romans over the
" world during the time of their commonwealth ?
" ——After the diffolution of the commonwealth
" the Roman yoke became eafier upon the pro-
" vinces, as *Tacitus* informs us ; and it may be
" obferved, that many of the worft Emperors
" (*Domitian*, for inftance) were very careful to
" prevent all oppreffion of the provinces.——
" The oppreffion and tyranny of the *Carthaginians*
" over their fubject ftates in *Africa* went fo far,
as we learn from *Polybius* (Lib. 1. cap. 72.)
" that not content with exacting the *half* of all
" the produce of the ground, which of itfelf was a
" very high rent, they alfo loaded them with many
" other taxes.——If we pafs from antient to modern
" times we fhall always find the obfervation to
" hold. The provinces of abfolute monarchies
" are always better treated than thofe of free
" ftates."

Thirdly, Among the worft forts of governments I reckon all governments by a corrupt reprefentation.——There is no inftance in which
the trite obfervation is more true than in this,
" that the beft things when corrupted become the

D 4   " worft."

" worſt." A corrupt repreſentation is ſo far from being any *defence* againſt oppreſſion, that it is a *ſupport* to it. Long eſtabliſhed cuſtoms, in this caſe, afford no ſecurity, becauſe, under the ſanction of ſuch a repreſentation, they may be eaſily undermined or counteracted ; nor is there any injury to a people which, with the help of ſuch an inſtrument, may not be committed with ſafety. It is not, however, every degree of corruption, that will deſtroy the uſe of a repreſentation, and turn it into an evil ſo dreadful. In order to this, corruption muſt paſs a certain limit. But *every degree* of it *tends* to this, ſaps the foundation of Liberty, and poiſons the fountain of Legiſlation. And when it gets to its laſt ſtage, and has proceeded its utmoſt length ; When, in particular, the means by which candidates get themſelves choſen are ſuch as admit the *worſt*, but exclude the *beſt* men ; a Houſe of Repreſentatives becomes little better than a ſink into which is collected all that is moſt worthleſs and vile in a kingdom.——— There cannot be a greater calamity than ſuch a government.——It is impoſſible there ſhould be a condition more wretched than that of a nation, once free, ſo degenerated.

CONCLUSION.

IT is time to difmifs this fubject. But I cannot take a final leave of it, (and probably of all fubjects of this kind) without adding the following reflections on our own ftate in this kingdom.

It is well known, that MONTESQUIEU has paid the higheft compliment to this country, by defcribing its conftitution of government, in giving an account of a perfect government; and by drawing the character of its inhabitants, in giving an account of the manners and characters of a free people.——— " All (he fays) having, in free ftates, a fhare in " government, and the laws not being made for " fome more than others, they confider themfelves " as *monarchs,* and are more properly *confederates* " *than fellow-fubjects.*———No one citizen being " fubject to another, each fets a greater value on " his Liberty than on the glory of any of his fel- " low-citizens.———Being independent, they are " proud ; for the pride of kings is founded on " their independence.———They are in a conftant " ferment, and believe themfelves in danger, " even in thofe moments when they are moft " fafe.———They reafon ; but it is indifferent whe- " ther they reafon well or ill. It is fufficient

" that

" that they *do* reafon. Hence fprings that Li-
" berty which is their fecurity.——This ftate,
" however, will lofe its Liberty. It will perifh,
" when the *Legiflative* power fhall become more
" corrupt than the *executive*." (a)

Such is the account which this great writer
gave, many years ago, of the *Britifh* conftitution
and people. We may learn from it, that we have
nothing to fear from that difpofition to examine
every public meafure, to cenfure minifters of ftate,
and to be reftlefs and clamorous, which has hitherto characterized us.——On the contrary ;
we fhall have every thing to fear, when this
difpofition is loft. As foon as a people grow
fecure, and ceafe to be quick in taking alarms,
they are undone. A free conftitution of government cannot be preferved without an earneft and unremitting jealoufy. Our Conftitution,
in particular, is fo excellent, that it is the propereft object of fuch a jealoufy. For my own
part, I admire fo much the general frame and
principles of it, that I could be almoft fatisfied
with that reprefentation of the kingdom, which
forms the moft important part of it, had I no
other objection to this reprefentation than its *inadequatenefs.* Did it confift of a body of men, fairly
elected for a fhort term, by a number of independent perfons, of all orders in every part of the king-

(a) Spirit of Laws. Book xix. ch. 27.

dom,

dom, equal to the number of the prefent voters ;
and were it, after being elected, under no undue
influence ; it would be a fecurity of fuch importance, that I fhould be lefs difpofed to complain
of the injuftice done, by its inadequatenefs, to the
greateft part of the kingdom by depriving them
of one their natural and unalienable rights. To
fuch a body of reprefentatives we might commit,
with confidence, the guardianfhip of our rights,
knowing, that having one intereft with the reft
of the ftate, they could not violate them ; or
that if they ever did, a little time would bring
the power of gaining redrefs without tumult or
violence,——Happy the people fo bleffed.——
If wife, they will endeavour, by every poffible
method, to preferve the purity of their reprefentation ; and, fhould it have degenerated, they will
lofe no time in effecting a reformation of it.——
But if, unhappily, infection fhould have pervaded
the whole mafs of the ftate, and there fhould be
no room to hope for any reformation, it will be
ftill fome confolation to reflect, that flavery, in all
its rigour, will not immediately follow. Between
the time in which the fecurities of Liberty are
undermined, and its final fubverfion, there is commonly a flattering interval during which the *enjoyment* of Liberty may be continued, in confequence of fundamental laws and rooted habits
which cannot be at once exterminated. And this

interval

interval is longer or shorter, according as the progress of corruption is more or less rapid; and men in power more or less attentive to improve favourable opportunities. ———— The government of this country, in particular, is so well balanced, and the institutions of our common law are so admirable, and have taken such deep root, that we can bear much decay before our liberties fall. ———Fall, however, they must, if our public affairs do not soon take a new turn. That very evil, which, according to the great writer I have quoted, is to produce our ruin, we see working every where and increasing every day.———The following facts, among many others, shew too plainly whither we are tending and how far we are advanced.

First. It seems to me, that a general indifference is gaining ground fast among us.———This is the necessary effect of increasing luxury and dissipation; but there is another cause of it, which I think of with particular regret.—In consequence of having been often duped by false patriots; and found, that the leaders of opposition, when they get into places, forget all their former declarations; the nation has been led to a conviction, that all patriotism is imposture, and all opposition to the measures of government nothing but a struggle for power and its emoluments. The honest and independent part of the nation entertain at present

most

moſt of this conviction ; and, therefore, having
few public men to whom they can look with
confidence, they give up all zeal, and ſink into
inactivity and deſpondence.

Secondly. At the Revolution, the Houſe of
Commons acquired its juſt weight in the conſtitution; and, for ſome years afterwards, it was often
giving much trouble to men in power. Of late,
it is well known, that means have been tryed and
a ſyſtem adopted for quieting it.——I will not ſay
with what ſucceſs——But I muſt ſay, that the
men whoſe policy this has been, have ſtruck at
the very *heart* of public liberty, and are the worſt
traitors this kingdom ever ſaw.——". If ever,
" (ſays Judge *Blackſtone*) it ſhould happen, that
" the independency of any one of the three
" branches of our legiſlature ſhould be loſt ; or
" that it ſhould become ſubſervient to the views
" of either of the other two, there would ſoon be
" an end of our conſtitution. The legiſlature
" would be changed from that which was origi-
" nally ſet up by the general conſent and funda-
" mental act of the ſociety ; and ſuch a change,
" however effected, is according to Mr. *Locke*
" (who perhaps carries his theory too far) at
" once an entire diſſolution of the bands of
" government, and the people are thereby
" reduced to a ſtate of anarchy, with liberty
" to

7

" to conſtitute to themſelves a new legiſlative
" power." (a)

Thirdly. Soon after the REVOLUTION, bills for
triennial parliaments paſſed both Houſes, in oppoſition to the court (b). At the ACCESSION, ſepten-
nial parliaments were eſtabliſhed. Since this laſt
period, many attempts have been made, by the
friends of the conſtitution, to reſtore triennial parliaments ; and, formerly, it was not without difficulty that the miniſtry were able to defeat theſe
attempts. The diviſion in the Houſe of Commons
in 1735, on a bill for this purpoſe, was 247 to
184.——I need not ſay, that *now* all ſuch attempts
drop of themſelves. So much are the ſentiments
of our repreſentatives changed in this inſtance, that
the motion for ſuch a bill, annually made by a
worthy member of the Houſe of Commons, can
ſcarcely produce a ſerious debate, or gain the leaſt
attention.——For ſeveral years, at the beginning
of the laſt reign, the HOUSE OF COMMONS conſtantly
paſſed *penſion* and *place* bills, which were as conſtantly rejected by the HOUSE OF LORDS. At preſent, no one is ſo romantic as ever to think of introducing any ſuch bills into the Houſe of Commons.

(a) Introduction to the Commentaries on the Laws of
England, p. 48. See alſo Book i. ch. 8.

(b) In 1692 King William rejected a bill for triennial
Parliaments, after it had paſſed both Houſes. But in a following year he thought proper to give his aſſent to it. .

Fourthly,

Fourthly. Standing armies have in all ages been deſtructive to the Liberties of the ſtates into which they have been admitted.—MONTESQUIEU (a) obſerves, that the preſervation of Liberty in ENGLAND requires, that it ſhould have no land forces.——Dr. FERGUSON calls the eſtabliſhment of ſtanding armies " A FATAL REFINEMENT in " the preſent ſtate of civil government." (b)—— Mr. *Hume* pronounces " our ſtanding army a " mortal diſtemper in the Britiſh conſtitution, of " which it muſt *inevitably* periſh." (c)—Formerly, the nation was apprehenſive of this danger ; and the *ſtanding army* was a conſtant ſubject of warm debate in both Houſes of Parliament. The prin- cipal reaſon then aſſigned for continuing it was, the ſecurity of the Houſe of HANOVER againſt the friends of the *Pretender*. This is a reaſon which now exiſts no more ; the Houſe of *Hanover* being ſo well eſtabliſhed as not to want any ſuch ſecurity.——The ſtanding army alſo is now more numerous and formidable than ever ; and yet all oppoſition to it is loſt, and it is become in a man- ner a part of the conſtitution.

Fifthly. For many years after the acceſſion the national debt was thought an evil ſo alarming, that the reduction of it was recommended every

(a) Spirit of Laws. Book xix. ch. 27.
(b) Hiſtory of Civil Society. Part vi. ſect. 5.
(c) *Political* Diſcourſes. Eſſay xii. p. 301.

year from the throne to the attention of Parliament as an object of the laft importance. The
FUND appropriated to this purpofe was called the
ONLY HOPE of the kingdom; and when the practice of alienating it begun, it was reckoned a
kind of facrilege, and zealoufly oppofed in the
Houfe of *Commons*, and protefted againft in the
Houfe of *Lords*. But now, though the debt is
almoft *tripled*, we fit under it with perfect indifference; and the facred fund, which repeated laws
had ordered to be applied *to no other purpofe* than
the redemption of it, is always alienated of courfe,
and become a conftant part of the current fupplies, and much more an encouragement to diffipation than a prefervative from bankruptcy.

Sixthly. Nothing is more the duty of the reprefentatives of a nation than to keep a ftrict eye
over the expenditure of the money granted for
public fervices.—In the reign of King William,
the Houfe of Commons paffed almoft every year
bills for appointing commiffioners for taking,
ftating and examining the public accounts; and,
particularly, the army and navy debts and contracts. In the reign of Queen Ann fuch bills
became lefs frequent. But fince the acceffion,
only two motions have been made for fuch bills;
one in 1715, and the other in 1741; and both
were rejected.

Seventhly.

Seventhly. I hope I may add, that there was a time when the kingdom could not have been brought to acquiesce in what was done in the case of the *Middlesex* election. This is a precedent which, by giving the House of Commons the power of excluding its members at discretion, and of introducing others in their room on a minority of votes, has a tendency to make it a self-created House, and to destroy entirely the right of representation: And a few more such precedents would completely overthrow the constitution.

Lastly. I cannot help mentioning here the addition which has been lately made to the power of the Crown, by throwing into its hands the *East-India Company*. Nothing more unfavourable to the security of public Liberty has been done since the REVOLUTION: And should our statesmen, thus strengthened by the patronage of the EAST, be farther strengthened by the conquest and patronage of the WEST, they will indeed have no small reason for triumph; and there will be little left to protect us against the encroachments and usurpations of power. ROME sunk into slavery, in consequence of enlarging its territories, and becoming the center of the wealth of conquered provinces, and the seat of universal empire. It seems the appointment of Providence, that free states, when, not contented with *self*-government,

E   and

and prompted by the love of domination, they make themfelves mafters of other ftates, fhall lofe Liberty at the fame time that they take it away; and, by fubduing, be themfelves fubdued. Diftant and dependent provinces can be governed only by a military force. And a military force which governs abroad, will foon govern at home. The *Romans* were fo fenfible of this, that they made it treafon for any of their generals to march their armies over the *Rubicon* into *Italy*. CÆSAR, therefore, when he came to this river, hefitated; but he paffed it, and enflaved his country.

" Among the circumftances (fays Dr. FERGU-
" SON) which in the event of national profperity
" and in the refult of commercial arts, lead to
" the eftablifhment of defpotifm, there is none
" perhaps that arrives at this termination with fo
" fure an aim as the perpetual enlargement of ter-
" ritory. In every ftate the freedom of its mem-
" bers depends on the balance and adjuftment of
" its interior parts; and the exiftence of any fuch
" freedom among mankind depends on the ba-
" lance of nations. In the progrefs of conqueft
" thofe who are fubdued are faid to have loft their
" liberties. But, from the hiftory of mankind,
" to conquer or to be conquered has appeared in
" effeƈt the fame." (*a*)

(*a*) Hiftory of Civil Society. Part iv. feƈt. 5.

Many

Many more facts of this kind might eafily be enumerated; but thefe are fufficient.——They fhew, with fad evidence, how faft we have, for fome time, been advancing towards the greateft of all public calamities.

We may, alfo, infer from the preceding ob-fervations, that there is only one way in which our deliverance is poffible; and that is, by RESTOR-ING OUR GRAND NATIONAL SECURITY. This is the object which our great men in oppofition ought to hold forth to the kingdom, and to bind themfelves by fome decifive tefts to do all they can to obtain. That patriotifm muft be fpurious which does not carry its views princi-pally to this. Without it, nothing is of great importance to the kingdom; and even an ac-commodation with *America* would only preferve a limb, and fave from prefent danger, while a gangrene was left to confume the vitals.

But, probably, we are gone too far; and cor-ruption has ftruck its roots too deep to leave us much room for hope.——Mr. HUME has ob-ferved, (*a*) that as the affairs of this country are not likely to take a turn favourable to the eftab-lifhment of a perfect plan of Liberty, " an ab-" folute monarchy is the eafieft death, the true " EUTHANASIA of the Britifh conftitution."——

(*a*) See Mr. Hume's Effays. Vol. i. p. 91.

If

If this obfervation is juft, our conftitution (fhould no great calamity intervene) is likely, in fome future period, to receive a very quiet diffolution. ——At prefent, however, it muft be acknow-ledged, that we enjoy a degree of Liberty, civil and religious, which has feldom been paralleled among mankind. We ought to rejoice in this happinefs; and to be grateful to that benevolent difpofer of all events who bleffes us with it. But, at the fame time, our hearts muft bleed when we reflect, that, the fupports of it having given way, it is little more than a *fufferance* which we owe to the temper of the times; the lenity of our go-vernors; and fome awe, in which the friends of defpotifm are ftill held, by the voice and fpirit of the uncorrupted part of the kingdom.——May thefe caufes, if no better fecurities can be hoped for, long delay our fate.

It muft not be forgotten, that all I have now faid is meant on the fuppofition, that our affairs will proceed fmoothly till, by a common and na-tural progrefs, we have gone the round of other nations once free, and are brought to their end. ——But it is poffible this may not happen.—— Our circumftances are fingular; and give us reafon to fear, that we have before us a death which will not be eafy or common.

PART

PART II.

CONTAINING

REMARKS on some Particulars in a
SPEECH at opening the BUDGET in
April 1776.

SECT. I.

*Supplemental Observations on the Surplus of the
Revenue; the Quantity of Coin in the
Kingdom; and Paper-Credit.*

IT is well known, that the great minister who
presides over our finances, took occasion, at
opening the Budget in April last, to enter into a
particular account of the state of the nation. In
this account, he represented us as in a condition the
most sound and happy; our trade and revenue
flourishing; our common people well provided
for; our debts and taxes light; our current
specie sufficiently ample; our paper-circulation
safe; and the BANK, in particular, as little less
firm and durable than the world.

E 3

This

This account, fo encouraging and flattering,
was generally underftood to be given in defigned
oppofition to another account very different, which
had been given in the *Obfervations on Civil Li-*
berty.——It cannot, therefore, I hope, be thought
too prefuming in me to offer the following remarks in my own defence.

I have grounded my opinion of the hazardous
ftate of the kingdom, partly on the fmallnefs of
the furplus in the revenue, and the nature and
circumftances of our paper-circulation, compared
with the quantity of *fpecie* in the kingdom, and
the weight of our debts and taxes.

The furplus of the revenue I have made out in
two different methods ; and by a deduction fo
minute, that it is, I think, fcarcely poffible it
fhould be materially wrong. One of thefe methods
brings it out 338,759*l. per ann.* (*a*) : and the
other, 300,000*l. per ann.* fuppofing the expence
of calling in the gold coin, and the profits of
lotteries excluded ; the land-tax at three fhillings
in the pound ; and the peace eftablifhment the
fame that it has been at a medium for eleven years,
from 1764 to 1775.

Nothing more was faid in oppofition to this,
than a general intimation, that had it not been for
the war with *America*, the peace-eftablifhment for

(*a*) See the conclufion of the Third Part.

the

the navy would have been reduced, and a fufficient furplus gained (including lotteries) to enable parliament to pay off a million every year of the public debt.

I am very fenfible that reductions of the public expences and improvements in the revenue are practicable, which would give fuch a furplus. But I am afraid, they will never take place. Nor can I think it proper, in determining what permanent furplus we poffefs, to include thofe pernicious profits of lotteries, by which infinitely more is upon the whole loft than gained; or, to form our judgment of the expence of *future* years, by any other rule than the medium expence of *paft* years. ———It would, however, give little confolation, were there a certainty that, had peace continued, a MILLION annually of the public debt would have been difcharged. This would have made a very flow progrefs in difcharging our debts. A million every year difcharged in peace, and eight or ten millions every year added in war, would leave us under the neceffity of breaking at laft. But hitherto we have not proceeded in a courfe fo favourable. The great perfon to whom I refer, muft know, that in 1772, he announced in the *Houfe of Commons*, his intention to pay off a *million and a half* every year, and SEVENTEEN MILLIONS in ten years; that yet only 2.800,000*l.* was paid off in the three fubfequent years; and

that,

that, on account of the increase of the *navy* and *civil-list* debts, there has not been in fact the ability (without the help of lotteries) to pay half that sum.

In page 74th of the *Observations on Civil Liberty*, I have said, " that it has appeared lately, " that the gold specie of the kingdom, is no " more than about TWELVE MILLIONS AND A " HALF."——This assertion has been much controverted ; and it is therefore necessary I should give a distinct account of the reasons on which it was grounded.

I had learnt from unquestionable authority, that the quantity of gold coin brought into the mint, by the Acts of Parliament and Proclamations in 1773 and 1774, was about NINE MILLIONS (*a*); or as much as, when recoined, amounted nearly to that sum.——I find also, that it was expected by the best judges, that the proclamation lately issued would bring in about *three* millions. These two sums make up *twelve* millions ; and they include the gold coin of *Ireland*. Let this be estimated at a (*b*) million ; and the whole gold coin

(*a*) This was confirmed by the account of the noble Lord at opening the last Budget.

(*b*) I have mentioned this sum at random. It is not of great consequence whether it is half a million too little or half a million too much.

of

of *Britain*, to be brought in by all the calls, will be ELEVEN millions; and none will remain, except that part which was deficient lefs than a grain in a guinea, and remained in the kingdom, at the time the coin Act took effect in June 1773. We are here left entirely to conjecture. But it fhould be remembered, that for many years before 1773, the heavy coin was catched up as foon as iffued, and either clipped, or melted down and exported; and that from hence arofe fuch a fcarcity of heavy coin, that, in fome counties, heavy guineas might be difpofed of at a premium.———In fuch circumftances, an allowance of about a million and a half, for the coin deficient lefs than a grain in a guinea before the coin Act in 1773, feems to be fufficient; and therefore, it might, I think, with reafon be faid, that it appeared that the gold coin of the kingdom was about TWELVE MIL-LIONS AND A HALF.

But there is another reafon, by which I have been convinced, that this is a moderate eftimate.

The quantity of gold coin, deficient between three and fix grains in a guinea, was 4.800,000*l*. and this, when recoined, made 4.600,000*l*.———The coin deficient lefs than three grains could not have been fo much, for the following reafons. Firft, new coin being rougher, wears fafter than old coin; and therefore, does not remain fo long

in

in any given degree of deficiency.—Secondly, coin, deficient lefs than three grains, is fubjeét to feveral peculiar caufes of diminution and deftruction.— Clipping and fweating remove part of it to greater degrees of deficiency; and part is deftroyed by being melted down and exported ; whereas, lighter coin is diminifhed only by being worn (a).

(a) The quantity of coin within all equal degrees of defi- ciency would be equal, were equal quantities iffued every year, and were there alfo no caufe which diminifhed or de- ftroyed it, except the *uniform* operation of time in wearing it. Any caufe, therefore, which deftroys it more, or diminifhes it fafter at firft than at laft, muft render the quantity lefs in the firft degrees of deficiency. And the fame muft be the confe- quence of a greater proportion iffued formerly, in any given time, than of late.——The caufes of diminution never pro- bably operated fo much on the gold coin as they did for about twelve years before 1773 ; and this will balance the greater proportion coined during that time. The very reafon of the increafe of coinage in thofe years was, a neceffity created by the lofs of the new coin, and never before felt in an equal degree. The coinage, however, in thofe years, was not fo much more than ufual as fome may imagine. In ten years before 1770, eight millions and a half were coined ; and in twelve years after the *Acceffion*, the fame quantity was coined ; and in twenty-feven years after the *Acceffion*, more was coined than in twenty-feven years before 1770. See *Confiderations on Money, Bullion*, &c. p. 2.——The whole quantity of gold coined from the Acceffion to 1770, was near 29 millions·; more than one half of which muft have been melted and exported ; and, the greateft part of the remainder muft have been precipitated in its progrefs towards deficiency by being clipped and fweated.

Thefe

Thefe reafons feem to prove, that if the gold coin, deficient in June 1773 lefs than three grains, is eftimated at *five millions*, (that is, at a little more than the coin deficient between three and fix grains) it will be rated rather too high ; and the conclufion will be, that the whole of our gold coin (exclufive of the *Irifh)* might poffibly be *lefs*, but could not have been *much more*, than the fum at which I have reckoned it.

Such have been the facts and arguments by which my judgment has been determined in this inftance.——But it muft not be overlooked, that it helps only to afcertain the quantity of *circulating* fpecie in the kingdom, as diftinguifhed from that which is *hoarded*. When the *Obfervations on Civil Liberty* were publifhed, I did not apprehend, that this part of the coin could be confiderable enough to deferve regard. But the contrary has lately appeared. The Proclamation iffued laft fummer, and which it was expected would bring in about three millions, has, I am informed, brought in about *fix millions and a half*. This exceeds the fum at which I have been led to ftate the *whole* gold coin deficient lefs than three grains ; and proves, that feveral millions muft have been hoarded *(a)*. Nor, I think,

(a) When the filver *fpecie* was recoined in King William's time, it appeared, that a great treafure had been hoarded before

I think, will this appear incredible, when it is re-
collected, that only gold coin under three grains
of deficiency is likely to be hoarded; and alfo,
that diſtruſt of the *Funds* and of Paper-money has
a particular tendency to increaſe the practice of
hoarding.

Affifted, therefore, by this new light, I would
now ſtate the *circulating* gold coin of the kingdom
before 1773, nearly as I did before; and call it
TWELVE or THIRTEEN MILLIONS. But the whole
gold coin (including the hoarded part) I would
reckon at SIXTEEN or SEVENTEEN MILLIONS (*b*).

An account very different from this was given
at opening the Budget; the fubſtance of which
I will ſtate as faithfully as my memory will
enable me; and juſt as I underſtood it.

" From the beginning of the year 1772, to
" the 23d of April laſt, 13.200,000*l*. had been
" coined at the Tower; and on that day there
" was 600,000*l*. more ready to be coined.——

before the *Revolution*, in conſequence of the danger of public
liberty at that time. See Davenant's Works, Vol. I. p. 439, &c.

In *Ruſſia* it is reckoned, that as much money lies buried
under ground, as exiſts above ground.

(*b*) In theſe fums is included all the coin which the late
Proclamations have brought in from HOLLAND and other
foreign countries; and which, I think, ought not to be
deemed a part of the reſting ſtock of the kingdom.

All

" All this, (it was intimated) is now left in the
" kingdom. The laſt Proclamation, it was ex-
" pected, would bring in three millions more;
" which, added to the coin deficient leſs than a
" grain reſting in the kingdom at the time of the
" Coin Act in 1773, and iſſued before 1772,
" will make the whole, EIGHTEEN OR NINETEEN
" MILLIONS (a)."

On this account I would obſerve,

Firſt. That if juſt, it proves that, in 1773, a
third at leaſt of the *circulating* coin was in the beſt
ſtate poſſible. For the late calls having ſhewn,
that there was then, in *Britain* and *Ireland*, no
more than about twelve *millions* deficient *more*
than a grain; ſix millions (that is, a third of
eighteen millions) or ſeven millions (that is, more
than a third of nineteen millions) muſt have been
deficient *leſs* than a grain. (b)—It will alſo follow,

(a) Or deducting a million for the *Iriſh* coin, ſeventeen or
eighteen millions.

(b) This is ſaid on the ſuppoſition, that the laſt call would
bring in no more than was expected, or about three millions. Its having brought in above double this ſum makes
little difference. For it proves, that the whole quantity of
gold coin muſt have been (according to Lord NORTH's method of computing) 21 or 22 millions; and the quantity deficient more than a grain about 15 millions; and, conſequently,
ſix or ſeven millions (that is, near a *third*) will ſtill remain
to be the quantity deficient leſs than a grain.

(ſince

(fince the quantity brought in by the firft call is known to have been 4,900,000 l.) that but little more than a *fourth* could have been deficient fo much as fix grains, or a fhilling in a guinea.——— No perfon can think this credible who recollects the diftrefs of traffic, and the complaints of the kingdom before 1773.

Secondly. The truth of the account I have ftated depends, in a great meafure, on the fuppofition, that all the gold coined fince the beginning of 1772 is now in the kingdom. I cannot conceive on what grounds this was taken for granted. ———From the beginning of 1772 to June 1773, the practice of clipping was more prevalent than it had ever been. During the greateft part of 1772, the price of gold was fo much above mint price, that a profit, from 2 to 4 *per cent.* might be got by melting heavy guineas (*a*). And, in February in that year, the price of gold was at

(*a*) It has been thought very ftrange, that a piece of metal fhould bear a higher price, merely becaufe it wants the ftamp of the mint. But the reafon is, that bullion alone being exportable in any confiderable quantity, the price of it muft vary as the demand for it varies ; or, in other words, as the *balance of payment* between us and the reft of the world is favourable or unfavourable.———This will be explained at the beginning of the Third Part, where it will appear that, in confequence of the increafe of luxury and the national debt, this balance has been generally againft us ever fince the end of the laft war.

4l. 1s.

4l. 1s. 6d. per ounce; and $4\frac{1}{2}$ *per cent.* might be got by melting heavy guineas. Inftead, therefore, of believing, that all the gold coined fince the beginning of 1772 remains with us; I think it almoft certain, that the greateft part of all coined during the firft year and a half of this period, has been either clipped or melted into bullion. That part which was clipped has been recoined; and that part which was melted has been either recoined or expofted; and, therefore, neither has made any addition to the coin of the kingdom.

Thefe obfervations demonftrate, that the amount of the gold coin at the time of the Coin Act in 1773, muft have been near the fum at which I have reckoned it. There may, for ought I know, have been an increafe fince; but I fhall not believe there has, till I know, whether the coin brought in by the laft proclamation has been all recoined and iffued. But this cannot be expected; for fhould it be done, FOUR MILLIONS (*a*) more will have been coined and iffued, than has been brought in.——The truth, therefore, may be, that the coinage, fince June 1773, has been car-

(*a*) The coin brought in laft Summer, added to near 14 millions coined from the beginning of 1772 to the time of the laft call, amounts to about 20 millions and a half; but only 16 millions and a half have been brought in, including the coin from *Ireland* and foreign countries.

ried,

ried on only to provide a supply of new coin to be exchanged for old; in which case, the quantity of coin in the kingdom, even according to this method of computing it, will come out nearly the same with that which I have given.

After all, let the *specie* of the kingdom, including the silver, be allowed to be as considerable as some have asserted; or about four millions more than I have reckoned it; the difference arising from hence will not be of particular consequence; and it will be still true, that notwithstanding all our increase of trade and apparent opulence, the *specie* of the kingdom (*a*) is not much more than it was at the *Revolution.*——What then is all the rest of our circulating cash? What is it keeps up rents; feeds our luxury; pays our taxes; supplies the revenue, and supports government? ——Paper, chiefly, emitted, not only at the Bank, but by tradesmen, merchants, and bankers in every corner of the kingdom.——And is this a solid

(*a*) Or EIGHTEEN MILLIONS AND A HALF. See Dr. DAVENANT's Works, Vol. i. p. 363, &c. 443, &c. A great part of this specie was carried out of the nation in King WILLIAM's wars; and the consequence was, that the taxes became unproductive; and that Government fell under great difficulties, from which it was afterwards relieved by the establishment of the *Bank* and the increase of trade. See the beginning of the Third Part.

and

and permanent fupport ? (*b*) Is there, in the annals of the world, another inftance of a great
kingdom fo fupported ?——The caufes are numberlefs which may fuddenly deftroy it; and were
this

(*b*) The paper currency of the Colonies is one of the greateft
difadvantages under which they labour; but it is of a more
fafe and permanent nature than ours. Were it not fo, it
could not have been of the leaft ufe to them for the laft year
and a half. He who doubts this, need only confider what
our paper would be worth were we now invaded as they are.
This difference depends chiefly, on the following circumftances.——Their paper is not payable on demand.—It is a
legal tender.——It reprefents fixed property which is mortgaged for it.——It does not fupport fuch a monftrous debt
as ours.—And when public emergencies require any extraordinary emiffions, they are generally funk by taxes in
four or five years.—— It is the firft of thefe circumftances that
gives our paper its currency; and it is alfo this circumftance
that creates the danger attending it, by rendering it incapable
of fuftaining any great fhock or panic.——The poffeffion of
fecurities equal in nominal value to the amount of the paper
emitted, or the debts contracted, is of little confequence when
the value of thefe fecurities depends on the paper, and is created by it; that is, in other words, when the debts themfelves are the very cafh which muft pay the debts.——Nothing
can be more unnatural than fuch a ftate of things; and it may
hereafter be a curious object of enquiry, how it could be ever
poffible that it fhould fubfift any long time.
In page 78 of the *Obfervations on Civil Liberty*, I have faid,
" that the kingdom of FRANCE has no fuch dependence as
" we have on paper-credit; and that its fpecie amounts to
" 67 millions fterling." In mentioning this fum I took the

F   loweft

this to happen, we fhould fall at once, with a
debt of 140 millions upon us, to the ftate we were
in before the REVOLUTION.————Imagination cannot paint to itfelf the fhock this would give.————

lowest of different accounts which I had then received from
different authorities. I have fince received accounts which
make it 87 millions and a half; or 2000 millions of *livres*.
This, in particular, is the account of an author whom all
know to be likely to be well informed on this fubject; I mean
the author of the Treatife on the *Legiflation* and *Commerce of
Corn*, Part I. chap. v.——In the fame treatife it is faid,
(Part I. chap. viii,) that it appears, from the returns made by
the intendants of the different Provinces, that the number of
annual deaths in the whole kingdom of France, for three
yeats ended in 1772, was 780,040. I have been informed
by the ingenious author, that this account may be depended
on; and if fo, *France* muft contain 26 millions of inhabitants; for the beft obfervations prove, that no more than a
thirty-third part of a whole kingdom dies annually. See Obfervations on Reverfionary Payments, page 200.—In *Sweden*,
though a nineteenth part die in the capital every year, only
a thirty-fifth part die in the whole kingdom. See Philofophical Tranfactions, Vol. lxv. for 1775, p. 426. The
particulars now mentioned, added to the nature of the
debts of FRANCE as mentioned in page 78 of the *Obfervations on Civil Liberty*, form a ftriking contraft between
the ftate of that kingdom and ours. Nothing gives us our fu-
periority but the advantages we derive from our RELIGION
and our LIBERTY. Even in thefe refpects, however, they
feem to be improving, while we are declining. *Montefquieu*,
Abbe Raynal, and others of their moft admired writers, incul-
cate principles of government, and breathe a fpirit of Liberty,
which, to the fhame of this country, are become offenfive in it.

I muft

I muſt repeat here what I have ſaid in the *Ob-ſervations on Civil Liberty*, page 73, &c. that we ſhould think of nothing but guarding ourſelves againſt the danger of ſuch a ſituation, by reſtrict-ing our paper currency, and gradually diſcharging our public debts.——In giving this admonition, I look upon myſelf as doing my country one of the beſt offices in my power; and acting in the character of one who calls to another to awake who is ſleeping over a precipice.——But I know I call in vain.——The great miniſter who di-rects our finances has aſſured us all is well; and, under this perſuaſion, we are advancing, with unſuſpicious and careleſs ſpeed, to the cataſtrophe I have pointed out; and purſuing meaſures which muſt increaſe the difficulty of avoiding it, and the diſtreſs attending it.

Among theſe meaſures I have mentioned the preſent new coinage.——Before this coinage, I have obſerved, the light money always remained, becauſe nothing could be got by melting and ex-porting it. But now, as ſoon as gold riſes to the price it bore for many years before 1773, the melters and exporters of coin will be ſaved the trouble of ſelection; and every piece on which they can lay their hands will be proper for their purpoſe.——It ſeems, therefore, obvious, that, in conſequence of this meaſure, all our coin may be carried away, and the whole ſuperſtructure of

paper

paper fupported by it, break down, before we are aware of any danger.

I will take this opportunity to add, that this meafure will at the fame time increafe our paper. This has been the confequence of the two former calls; but it will probably be more the confequence of the laft call. For, as no coin is now to be current which is more than a grain deficient; and as alfo a great deal of it is already at or near that limit; the vexation attending it will be fo intolerable, that it will be generally cried down, and paper fubftituted in its room.——— Certain it is, that nothing can prevent this evil, but another evil; I mean, the deficient coin forcing itfelf again into circulation, and furnifhing clippers with more employment than ever; and, confequently, a return, with increafed violence, of the confufion and diftrefs which took place before the Coin Act in 1773.———This, indeed, will be much the leaft of the two evils; nor, in my opinion, are there any methods of preventing the diminution of the coin, which will not produce greater evils, except fuch alterations in its form (a) as fhall render clipping lefs practicable, joined to the execution of fevere laws againft clippers, and a ftrict vigilance in detecting them.

Upon the whole. It feems to me, that enough had been done by the firft coin act to reftore the

(a) See the propofals and obfervations in a pamphlet lately publifhed by Lord Vifcount Mahon on this fubject.

gold

gold coin; and that all which has been done fince, at the expence of about 650,000l. has been nothing but a preparation of the coin for melters and exporters, to the dreadful hazard of the kingdom.——Thefe are my prefent views of this fubject. But I muft fay, that I fufpect my own judgment in this inftance. The noble Lord, who is furnifhed with infinitely more of the means of information than I am, intimated, if I remember rightly, that there is no fuch danger: And though I did not underftand the reafon he affigned for this affertion, I muft believe, that, in a matter fo particularly interefting to the kingdom, he has gone upon the beft evidence.

S E C T. II.

Of the State of the Nation; and the War with America.

AT the beginning of the preceding fection, I have taken notice of the flattering account which was given, at opening the Budget in April laft, of the ftate of the kingdom with refpect to its commerce, revenue, and opulence. On that account I fhall beg leave to offer the following reflections.

Firft. The obfervations in the laft fection prove, I think, that it is not fo well fuppotted by facts, as

F 3   there

there is reaſon to wiſh. I am ſenſible, indeed,
that we never made a more gay and ſplendid appearance. But no conſiderate perſon will draw
much encouragement from hence. That pride
and ſecurity; that luxury, venality and diſſipation
which give us this appearance, are melancholy
ſymptoms; and have hitherto been the forerunners
of diſtreſs and calamity.

Secondly. When this account was given there
was a particular end to be anſwered by it. Additional taxes were to be impoſed; and it was neceſſary
to reconcile the public to the proſpect of a great
increaſe of its burthens, in order to carry on the
war with *America*.———On other occaſions, different accounts had been given. In order to
prove the juſtice of taxing the *Americans*, the
weight of our own taxes had been often inſiſted
upon; and the difficulty of raiſing a ſufficient
force among ourſelves to reduce them, had been
urged as a reaſon for ſeeking and employing, at
a great expence, the aſſiſtance of foreign powers.
On ſuch occaſions, I have heard our unhappy and
embarraſſed ſituation mentioned; and, at the end
of the laſt ſeſſion of Parliament, one of our
greateſt men, whoſe opinion in favour of coercion, had contributed to bring us into our
preſent ſituation, acknowledged the diſtreſs attending it, and repreſented the veſſel of the ſtate
as having never before rode in ſo dangerous
a ſtorm.

a ftorm.——This is, without doubt, the truth. But, if the account on which I am remarking was juft, we were then fafe and happy; nor was the veffel of the ftate ever wafted by more gentle and profperous gales.

But the reflection which, on this occafion, has given me moft pain is the following.

If, without *America*, we can be in a ftate fo flourifhing, a war to reduce *America* muft be totally inexcufeable. I wifh I could engage attention to this. War is a dreadful evil; and thofe who involve a people in it *needlefsly*, will find they have much to anfwer for. Nothing can ever juftify it, but the neceffity of it to fecure fome *effential* intereft againft unjuft attacks. But, it feems, there is no intereft to be fecured by the prefent war. The revenue has never flourifhed fo much, as fince *America* has been rendered hoftile to us; and it is now reckoned by many a decided point, that little depends on the *American* trade. It follows then, that if the end of the prefent war is to " obtain a reve-" nue," it is a revenue we do not want; if " to " maintain authority," it is an authority of no ufe to us.——Muft not humanity fhudder at fuch a war?——Why not let *America* alone, if we can fubfift without it?——Why carry fire and fword into a happy country to do ourfelves no good?

Some

Some of, the very perfons who depreciate the value of the colonies, as a fupport to our revenue and finances, yet fay, that we are now under a neceffity of reducing them, or perifhing. I wifh fuch perfons would give an account of the caufes which, according to their ideas, create this dreadful neceffity. Is it the fame that led *Haman* of old to reckon all his honours and treafures nothing to him, while *Mordecai* the Jew would not bow to him?——Or, are we become fo luxurious, that luxury even in the revenue is become neceffary to us; and fo depraved, that, like many individuals in private life, having loft *felf*-dominion, we cannot fubfift without dominion over *others* ?

It muft not be forgotten, that I fpeak here on the fuppofition, that it is poffible for this country to be as fafe and profperous without *America* as fome have afferted, and as was implied in what was faid at opening the laft Budget.——This is far from being my own opinion.—Some time or other we fhall, in all probability, feel feverely, in our commerce and finances, the lofs of the colonies. As a fource of revenue they are, I think, of great importance to us; but they are ftill more important as fupports to our navy, and an aid to us in our wars. It appears now, that there is a force among them fo formidable and fo growing, hat, with its affiftance, any of the great *Euro-pean* powers may foon make themfelves mafters

of

of all the *Weſt-Indies* and *North-America* ; and nothing ought to be more alarming to us than that
our natural enemies fee this, and are influenced
by it.——With the colonies united to us, we
might be the greateſt and happieſt nation that
ever exiſted.   But with the colonies ſeparated
from us, and in alliance with *France* and *Spain,*
we are no more a people.——They appear, therefore, to be indeed worth any price.——Our exiſtence depends on keeping them.——But how
are they to be kept ?——Moſt certainly, not by
forcing them to unconditional ſubmiſſion at the
expence of many millions of money and rivers of
blood.   The reſolution to attempt this, is a
melancholy inſtance of that infatuation, which
ſometimes influences the councils of kingdoms.
It is attempting to keep them by a method, which,
if it ſucceeds, will deſtroy their uſe, and make
them not worth the having ; and which, if it does
not ſucceed, will throw them into the ſcale of
rival powers, kindle a general war, and undo the
empire.

   The extenſion of our territories in *America,* during the laſt war, increaſed the expence of our
peace-eſtabliſhment, from 2.400,000 l. *per ann.* to
four millions *per ann.*—Almoſt all the provinces
in *America,* which uſed to be ours, are now to be
conquered.   Let the expence of this be ſtated at
25 or 30 millions; or, at a capital bearing a million

lion *per annum* intereft.——*America* recovered by
the fword muft be kept by the fword, and forts
and garrifons muft be maintained in every province to awe the wretched inhabitants, and to
hold them in fubjection. This will create another addition of expence; and both together cannot, I fuppofe, be ftated at lefs than two millions
per annum.——But how is fuch an increafe of revenue to be procured?——The colonies, defo-
lated and impoverifhed, will yield no revenue.——
The furpluffes of the finking fund have, for many
years, formed a neceffary part of the current and
ordinary fupplies.——It muft, therefore, be drawn
from *new* taxes.——But can the kingdom bear
fuch an increafe of taxes? Or, if it can, where
fhall we find a furplus for difcharging an enormous debt of above 160 millions? And what
will be our condition, when the next foreign war
fhall add two millions *per annum* more to our expences?——Indeed this is a frightful profpect.
But it will be rendered infinitely more frightful
by carrying our views to that increafe of the
power of the Crown which will arife from the
increafe of the army, from the difpofal of new
places without number, and the patronage of the
whole continent of *North-America.*

These confequences have been ftated moderately
on the fuppofition, that we fhall fucceed in fubduing *America*; and that, while we are doing it,
our

c r natural enemies will neglect the opportunity
of red them, and continue to satisfy themselves
w n that no *America indirectly*.——But should
the contrary happen.——I need not say what will
follo /

Some time ago this horrid danger might have
been avoided, and the colonies kept by the
easiest means.——By a prudent lenity and moderation.——By receiving their petitions.——By
giving up the right we claim to dispose of their
property, and to alter their governments.——By
guarantying to them, in these respects, a legislative independence ; (*a*) and establishing them in
the

(*a*) " There is something (says a great writer) so unnatural
" in supposing a large society, sufficient for all the good pur-
" poses of an independent political union, remaining subject
" to the direction and government of a distant body of men
" who know not sufficiently the circumstances and exigencies
" of this society ; or in supposing this society obliged to be
" governed solely for the benefit of a distant country ; that it
" is not easy to imagine there can be any foundation for it
" in justice or equity. The insisting on *old claims* and *tacit
" conventions*, to extend civil power over distant nations, and
" form grand unwieldy empires, without regard to the ob-
" vious maxims of humanity, has been one great source of
" human misery." *System of Moral Philosophy*, by Dr. HUT-
CHESON, vol. ii. p. 309. In the section from whence this
quotation is taken, Dr. HUTCHESON discusses the question,
" When colonies have a right to be released from the domi-
" nion of the parent state?" And his general sentiment seems

the poffeffion of equal liberty with ourfelves.——
This a great and magnanimous nation fhould
have done. This, fince the commencement
of hoftilities, would have brought them back
to their former habits of refpect and fubordination; and might have bound them to us for
ever.

Montesquieu has obferved, that England, in
planting colonies, fhould have *commerce*, not *dominion*, in view; the increafe of dominion being incompatible with the fecurity of public liberty.——
Every advantage that could arife from commerce
they have offered us without referve; and their
language to us has been——" Reftrict us, as much
" as you pleafe, in *acquiring* property by regu-
" lating our trade for your advantage; but claim
" not the difpofal of that property after it has
" been acquired.—Be fatisfied with the authority
" you exercifed over us before the prefent reign.——
" Place us where we were in 1763."——On
thefe terms they have repeatedly fued for a reconciliation. In return, we have denounced
them *Rebels*; and with our fleets in their ports,

to be, that they acquire fuch a right, " Whenever they are
" fo increafed in numbers and ftrength, as to be fufficient by
" themfelves for all the good ends of a political union."——
Such a decifion given by a wife man, long before we had any
difputes with the colonies, deferves, I think, particular
notice.

5 and

and our bayonets at their breaſts, have left
them no other alternative than to acknowledge
our ſupremacy, and give up rights they think
moſt ſacred; or ſtand on the defenſive, and appeal to heaven.—They have choſen the latter.

In this ſituation, if our feelings for *others* do not
make us tremble, our feelings for *ourſelves* ſoon
may.———Should we ſuffer the conſequences I
have intimated, our pride will be humbled.———
We ſhall admire the plans of moderation and
equity which, without bloodſhed or danger,
would have kept *America*.———We ſhall wiſh for
the happineſs of former times; and remember,
with anguiſh, the meaſures which many of us
lately offered their lives and fortunes to ſupport.

I muſt not conclude theſe obſervations, without taking particular notice of a charge againſt
the colonies, which has been much inſiſted on.—
" They have, it is ſaid, always had independency
" in view; and it is this, chiefly, that has pro-
" duced their preſent reſiſtance."———It is ſcarcely
poſſible there ſhould be a more unreaſonable
charge. Without all doubt, our connexion with
them might have been preſerved for ages to
come, (perhaps *for ever)* by wiſe and liberal
treatment. Let any one read a pamphlet publiſhed in 1761, by Dr. *Franklin*, and entitled,

The

The interest of Great Britain with respect to her Colonies ; and let him deny this if he can.—Before the prefent quarrel, there prevailed among them the purest affection for this country, and the warmest attachment to the House of HANOVER. And fince the prefent quarrel begun, and not longer ago than the beginning of laft winter, independency was generally dreaded among them. There is the fulleft evidence for this ; and all who are beft acquainted with *America*, muft know it to be true. As a fpecimen of this evidence, and of the temper of *America* till the period I have mentioned, I will juft recite the following facts.

In the refolutions of the *Affembly*, which met at *Philadelphia*, July 15, 1774, after making the ftrongeft profeffions of affection to *Britain*, and duty to their fovereign, they declare their ab- horrence of every idea of an unconftitutional in- dependence on the parent ftate.———An affembly of delegates from all the towns of the county of *Suffolk* (of which *Bofton* is the capital) delivered in September 1774, to General Gage, a remonftrance againft fortifying *Bofton-neck*. In this remon- ftrance, they totally difclaim every wifh of inde- pendence.———The fame is done in the inftructions given by the feveral colonies to the firft deputies chofen for a general Congrefs.———In the petition of the firft Congrefs to the King, they declare
they

they shall always, carefully and zealously, endeavour to support and maintain their connexion with *Great Britain.* In the memorial of the same Congress to the people of this country, they repeat this assurance. —— In the order of the *Congress*, which met in May 1775, for a general fast, they call upon all *America* to unite in beseeching the Almighty to avert the judgments with which they were threatened, and *to bless their rightful Sovereign*, that so *a reconciliation might be brought about with the parent state.*——And in their declaration setting forth the causes of their taking arms, they warn us, " that, should they " find it necessary, foreign assistance was undoubt- " edly attainable ;" but at the same time declare, " that they did not mean to dissolve the union " which had so long and so happily subsisted " between them and this country ; that necessity " had not yet driven them to that desperate " measure, or induced them to excite any other " nation to war against us ; and that they had " not raised armies with ambitious designs of " forming independent states, but solely for the " protection of their property against violence, " and the defence of that freedom which was their " birth-right."—— In the instructions, delivered Nov. 9, 1775, by a committee of the representatives of the province of *Pensylvania*, to their delegates in the third general congress ; they en-
join

join them, in behalf of the province, " utterly to
" reject any propofitions, fhould fuch be made,
" that might lead to a feparation from the mother
" country."

What reafon can there be for thinking the
colonies not fincere in all thefe declarations ?——
In truth ; it was not poffible they fhould be otherwife than fincere; for fo little did they think of
war, at the time when moft of thefe declarations
were made, that they were totally unprepared for
it : And, even when hoftilities were begun at
LEXINGTON in April 1775, they were fo deftitute
of every inftrument of defence, particularly ammu-
nition, that *half* the force which is now invading
them, would have been fufficient to conquer them
at once.

I will beg leave to add on this occafion, the
following extracts from letters, written by fome
leading perfons at NEW-YORK, the genuinenefs
of which may be depended on.

New-York, Auguft 3d. 1775. —— " I am
" fenfible of the many artifices and falfhoods
" which have been ufed to biafs the minds of
" your countrymen, who believe evil reports of
" us ; and, particularly, that we are aiming at
" independence. —— Of this be affured, that even
" HANCOCK and ADAMS are averfe to inde-
" pendence. There was a lye current laft week,
" that the congrefs had finally agreed upon inde-
                                        " pendence

" pendence to take place the 10th of March
" next, fhould not our grievances be redreffed
" before that time. I wrote to one of our
" delegates, to enquire whether this report
" was true. In his anfwer he declares, upon
" his honour, that he believed there was not
" one man in the Congrefs who would dare to
" make a motion tending to independence; or,
" that if any one did, two could not be found
" to fupport the motion.——None but thofe
" who are on the fpot can conceive what a fpirit
" is gone forth among all ranks and degrees of
" men.——We deferve to be free. It is a heavy
" facrifice we are making. Trade is at an end.
" We expect our city to be knocked about our
" ears. But I declare folemnly, I will fubmit to
" all, and die in a log-houfe in the wilds of
" America, and be free; rather than flourifh in
" fervitude."——In a fubfequent letter, dated
New-York, Jan. 3d. 1776, the fame perfon writes
as follows:—— " It is in the power of the
" miniftry to annihilate all our difputes, by re-
" ftoring us to the fituation we were in at the
" conclufion of the laft war. If this is done, we
" fhall immediately return to our allegiance.
" But if not, be affured, that an awful fcene will
" be opened in the fpring. Let me repeat a
" caution to you; believe not the infinuations

G   " of

" of our enemies, who would make you all believe
" that *independence* is what *America* aims at. It
" is an infidious falfhood. Madmen will be
" found in all large focieties. It would be
" fingular, were there none fuch to be found
" in a body of three millions of people and
" upwards. But they are like a grain of fand on
" the fea fhore."

Another perfon writes thus.——NEW-YORK,
Nov. 2d. 1775. " We love and honour our
" King. He has no fubjects in all his dominions
" more attached to his perfon, family and govern-
" ment, notwithftanding the epithet of rebels be-
" ftowed upon us. No charge is more unjuft
" than the charge that we defire an independence
" on *Great Britain*. Ninety-nine in a hundred
" of the inhabitants of this country deprecate
" this as the heavieft of evils. But if adminiftra-
" tion will perfift in their prefent meafures, this
" will and muft inevitably be the event; for
" fubmit to the prefent claims of the Britifh par-
" liament, while unreprefented in it, you may be
" affured they never will. And what deferves
" notice is, that all the violence of *Britain* only
" unites the *Americans* ftill more firmly together,
" and renders them more determined to be free
" or die. This fpirit is unconquerable by vio-
" lence; but they may be eafily won by kindnefs.
" Serious

" ——Serious people of all denominations among
" us, epifcopal and non-epifcopal, are much em-
" ployed in prayer to God for the fuccefs of the
" prefent ftruggles of *America*. They confider
" their caufe as the caufe of God ; and as fuch,
" they humbly commit it to him, confident of
" fuccefs in the end, whatever blood or treafure
" it may coft them.

Since thefe letters were written, the fentiments
of *America*, with refpect to *independence*, have been
much altered. But it fhould be remembered,
that this alteration has been owing entirely to OUR-
SELVES ; I mean, to the meafures of the laft winter
and fummer, and particularly the following.

Firft. The rejection of the petition from the
Congrefs brought over by Governor PENN. In
this petition they profeffed, in ftrong language,
that they ftill retained their loyalty to the King
and attachment to this country ; and only prayed,
" that they might be directed to fome mode by
" which the united applications of the Colonies
" might be improved into a happy reconciliation ;
" and that, in the mean time, fome meafures
" might be taken for preventing their farther de-
" ftruction, and for repealing fuch ftatutes as
" more immediately diftreffed them."——The
Colonies had often petitioned before without
being heard. They had, therefore, little hope

from

from this application; and meant that, if rejected, it fhould be their laft.

Secondly. The laft prohibitory bill, by which our protection of them was withdrawn; their fhips and effects confifcated; and open war declared againft them.

Thirdly. Employing *foreign* troops to fubdue them. This produced a greater effect in *America* than is commonly imagined. And it is remarkable, that even the writers in *America* who anfwered the pamphlet entitled COMMON SENSE, acknowledge, that fhould the *Britifh* miniftry have recourfe to foreign aid, it might become (*a*) proper to follow their example, and to embrace the neceffity of refolving upon *independence*.

I have, further, reafon to believe, that the anfwer to the laft petition of the City of London, prefented in March 1776, (*b*) had no fmall fhare in producing the fame effect.

By thefe meafures, and others of the fame kind, thofe Colonifts who had all along moft dreaded and abhorred independence, were at laft reconciled to it.——I can, however, fay from

(*a*) See COMMON SENSE, and PLAIN TRUTH, p. 44. Publifhed for Mr. *Almon*.

(*b*) The Colonies, I am affured, were not perfectly unanimous till they faw this anfwer.

particular

particular information, that even fo lately as the month of June laft, an accommodation might have been obtained with the Colonies, on a rea- fonable and moderate plan; without giving up any one of the rights claimed by this country, except that of altering their charters and difpofing of their property.——And, as it would have re- ftored peace and prevented the defolating cala- mities into which *America* and *Britain* are now plunged, no friend to humanity can avoid regret- ting that fuch a plan, when offered, was not adopted. But our rulers preferred coercion and conqueft: And the confequence has been, that the Colonies, aftei being goaded and irritated to the utmoft, refolved to difengage themfelves, and directed the Congress to declare them Inde- pendent States; which was accordingly done, as is well-known, on the 4th of July laft. Since that time, they have, probably, been making ap- plications to foreign powers; and it is to be feared, that *now* we may in vain offer them the very terms for which they once fued.——All this is the neceffary confequence of the principles by which human nature is governed.——There was a time when, perhaps, we fhould ourfelves have acted with more violence; and, inftead of remonftrat- ing and praying, as *America* has done, have re- fufed the moft advantageous terms when offered with defiance, and under an awe from a military

G 3   force.

force. Had King WILLIAM, inftead of coming over by invitation to deliver us, invaded us; and, at the head of an army, offered us the BILL OF RIGHTS; we fhould, perhaps, have fpurned at it; and confidered LIBERTY itfelf as no better than SLAVERY, when enjoyed as a boon from an infolent conqueror.——But we have all along acted as if we thought the people of *America* did not poffefs the feelings and paffions of *men*, much lefs of *Englifhmen*.——It is indeed ftrange our minifters did not long ago fee, that they had miftaken the proper method of treating the Colonies; and that though they might be gradually *influenced* to any thing, they could be dragooned to nothing.——Had King *James the Second* avoided violence; and been a little more patient and fecret in purfuing his views, he might have gained all he wifhed for. But an eager hafte and an open avowal of the odious claims of prerogative ruined him.——This has been fince confidered; and a plan both here and in *Ireland*, (*a*) lefs *expeditious* indeed, but more *fure*, has been purfued.

(*a*) I am forry to differ from thofe refpectable perfons who have propofed placing *America* on the fame ground with *Ireland*. If the fame ground of LAW is meant, it is already done; for our laws give us the fame power over *Ireland*, that we claim over *America*. If the fame ground of PRACTICE is meant; it has been moft unfortunate for *Ireland*, and would be equally fo for *America*.

And

And had the fame plan been purfued in *America*, the whole empire might in time have been brought, without a ftruggle, to reft itfelf quietly in the lap of corruption and flavery. It may, therefore, in the iffue prove happy to the Colonies, that they have not been thought worthy of any fuch cautious treatment. Our coercive meafures have done all for them that their warmeft patriots could have defired. They have united them among themfelves, and bound them together under one government. They have checked them in the career of vicious luxury; guarded them againft any farther infection from hence; taught them to feek all their refources within themfelves; inftructed them in the ufe of arms; and led them to form a naval and military power which may, perhaps, in time, become fuperior to any force that can attack them, and prove the means of preferving from invafion and violence, a government of juftice and virtue, to which the oppreffed in every quarter of the globe may fly, and find peace, protection, and liberty.———In fhort. Thefe meafures have, in all probability, haftened that difruption of the *new* from the *old* world, which will begin a new *æra* in the annals of mankind; (*a*) and produce a revolution more

(*a*) See the Abbe RAYNAL's Reflections on this fubject at the end of the 18th book of his Hiftory of the *European Settlements* in the Eaft and Weft-Indies.——" Is it not likely,

" fays

important, perhaps, than any that has happened in human affairs.——As a friend, therefore, to the general intereſt of mankind, I ought, pro- bably, to rejoice in theſe meaſures ; and to bleſs that all-governing Providence, which, often, out of the evil intended by wretched mortals, brings the greateſt good.——But when I conſider the *preſent* ſufferings which theſe meaſures muſt occa- ſion, and the *cataſtrophe* with which they threaten GREAT-BRITAIN ; I am ſhocked ; and feel my- ſelf incapable of looking forward, without diſtreſs, to the fate of an empire, once united and happy, but now torn to pieces, and falling a ſacrifice to deſpotic violence and blindneſs. Under the im- preſſion of theſe ſentiments, and dreading the

" ſays this writer, that the diſtruſt and hatred which have of " late taken place of that regard and attachment which the " *Engliſh* Colonies felt for the parent country, may haſten their " ſeparation from one another ? Every thing conſpires to pro- " duce this great diſruption ; the æra of which it is impoſ- " ſible to know.——Every thing tends to this point: The " progreſs of good in the new hemiſphere, and the progreſs " of evil in the old.——In proportion as our people are " weakened, and reſign themſelves to each other's dominion, " population and agriculture will flouriſh in *America* ; and " the arts make a rapid progreſs: And that country riſing out " nothing, will be fired with the ambition of appearing with " glory in its turn on the face of the globe—— O poſterity ! " ye, peradventure, will be more happy than your unfortunate " and contemptible anceſtors."——Mr. *Juſtamond*'s Tranſ- lation.

awful

awful *crisis* before us, I cannot help, however im-
potent my voice, crying out to this country——
" Make no longer war against *yourselves.* With-
" draw your armies from your Colonies. Offer
" your power to them as a *protecting*, not a *de-*
" *stroying* power. Grant the security they desire
" to their property and charters; and renounce
" those notions of dignity, which lead you to pre-
" fer the exactions of force to the offerings of
" gratitude, and to hazard *every thing* to gain
" *nothing.*——By such wisdom and equity *Ame-*
" *rica* may, perhaps, be still preserved; and that
" dreadful breach healed, which your enemies
" are viewing with triumph, and all *Europe* with
" astonishment."

But what am I doing?——At the moment
I am writing this, the possibility of a reconciliation may be lost.——*America* may have formed
an alliance with FRANCE——And the die may be
cast.

SECT. III.

Of Schemes for raising Money by Public Loans.

THE following observations were occasioned
by the scheme for the public loan of last
year, proposed to the *House of Commons* at opening
the *Budget*, and afterwards agreed to. I have
thought

thought proper, therefore, to introduce thefe
obfervations here; and, as they appear to me of
fome importance, I fhall endeavour to explain
them with as much care and perfpicuity as
poffible.

In order to raife *two millions*, the Legiflature
created laft year a new capital in the 3 *per
cent.* confolidated annuities, of 2.150,000l. Every
fhare of 77l. 10s. in this new capital was valued at 65l. 17s. 6d. or every 100l. *ftock* at
85l. For the whole new capital, therefore, Government has received in money, 1.827,500l.—
The remaining fum, neceffary to make up *two
millions*, was a compenfation advanced to Government for relinquifhing the profits of a Lottery,
confifting of 60,000 tickets, each of the fame value with 10l. *three per cent. ftock*; and might have
been obtained, without annexing the Lottery to
the annuities.——This new capital the public
may be obliged to redeem at *par*; in which
cafe, 322,500l. (being the difference between
1.827,500 and 2.150,000l.) that is 17 $\frac{1}{2}$ *per
cent.* will be paid by the public more than it has
received.——In this tranfaction, therefore, Government has acted as a private perfon would act,
who, in order to raife 850l. on a mortgage,
fhould promife for it 30l. *per ann.* (or 3 $\frac{1}{2}$ *per
cent.* intereft) and 150l. (that is 17 $\frac{1}{2}$ *per cent.*

3   nearly)

nearly) over and above the principal, when the
mortgage came to be difcharged.———Such a
premium (fhould the mortgage be difcharged foon)
would be very extravagant; but, if *never* to be
difcharged, would be infignificant: Nor would it
be poffible to account for fuch a bargain, except
by fuppofing, that the borrower, inftead of meaning to repay the fum he borrowed, chofe to continue *always* paying intereft for it, or returning
30 l. annually for 850 l. once advanced; and to
fubject his eftate, for that purpofe, to an eternal
incumbrance.

The public, I have faid, may be obliged to
difcharge the new capital, lately created, at *par*;
and, confequently, to fuffer a lofs by this year's
loan of 322,500 l. This will, undoubtedly, happen, fhould the nation profper, and the public
debts be put into a regular and fixed courfe of
redemption; for the 3 *per cents.* would then foon
rife to *par*.

The extravagance I have pointed out is the
more to be regretted, becaufe it was entifely
needlefs; for the fame fum might as well have
been borrowed by fchemes, which would not have
fubjected the public to the neceffity of paying,
when the loan came to be difcharged, more
money than had been received.———For inftance.
The fum advanced for the new capital of
2,150,000 l. *three per cent.* annuities, might have
beeb

been procured by offering 3 ½ *per cent.* on a capital equal to the sum advanced; or on 1.827,500 l. And the remainder, necessary to make up *two millions*, might have been obtained by the profits of a Lottery, consisting of 60,000 tickets each worth 10 l. in MONEY. This scheme would have differed but little in value from the other; and the interest, or the annuity payable by the public, would have been 63,962 l. at 3 ½ *per cent.* on a capital of 1.827,500; (*a*) instead of 64,500 l. at 3 *per cent.* on a capital of 2.150,000 l.

When a 100 l. *stock* in the 3 *per cent.* annuities is sold at 85 ¾, purchasers get 3 ½ *per cent.* interest for their money. When, therefore, the 3 *per cents* are at this price, 3 ½ *per cents* would be at *par*; and a capital of 1.827,500 l. might be redeemed by the public, (without losing any advantage arising from its debts being at a discount,) by paying this sum; or by returning the money borrowed (*b*). But in the same circumstances, a capital

(*a*) Had this interest been insufficient, it might have been increased a 16th or even an 8th *per cent.* without any material difference; or, (which would have been better) 3 ½ *per cent.* might have been offered for *four fifths* of the sum borrowed, and 4 *per cent.* for the remainder; in which case, the annuity payable by the public would have been 65,790 l.

(*b*) It should be remembered here, that tho' Government, when its debts are at a discount, may be able, with the consent

capital of 2.150,000l. in the 3 *per cent.* annuities, for which 85l. *per cent.* or, in the whole, 1.827,500l. had been received, could not be re-deemed without offering 86 or 87 *per cent.* for it; nor, therefore, without paying *more* than the ori-ginal sum borrowed.——When the 3 *per cents* are near *par*, there would be a loss of 322,500l. in redeeming the same capital; whereas, the for-mer annuities, for which the same sum had been advanced, might be always discharged by either paying the very sum (*a*) advanced, or a *less sum.*

In

fent of the creditors, to redeem a given capital by paying a less sum than that capital; yet it can never be obliged to pay *more.* ——In other words; a 100l. capital in the 3 *per cents*; 3 $\frac{1}{2}$ *per cents*; or 4, or 5 *per cents,* Government is always at liberty to redeem by paying 100l. whatever the market price of it may be, and whether the creditors will consent or not.

(*a*) There is another very great advantage which would at-tend these annuities.——One and the same *surplus* would dis-charge a given capital in less time. For example. A sur-plus of a million *per ann.* invariably applied, and the first payment to be made immediately, would discharge a capital of a *hundred millions* bearing 3 *per cent.* interest in 46 years. But if the same capital bore 3 $\frac{1}{2}$ *per cent.* interest, it would be discharged in 43 $\frac{1}{2}$ years; if 4 *per cent.* in 40 years; if 5 *per cent.* in 37 $\frac{1}{4}$ years.——A capital *less* than a 100 millions, in the same proportion that the interest is *more* than 3 *per cent.* and for which, therefore, the same annuity is paid, (as in the present case) the same surplus would discharge in 39 years, if the interest is 3 $\frac{1}{2}$; in 34 $\frac{1}{4}$ years, if the interest is 4 *per cent.*

———In all poſſible circumſtances, therefore, theſe annuities would have the advantage.———But we never, when contracting debts, carry our views to the diſcharge of the principal ; and the conſequences muſt prove fatal.

It

cent. in 27 ¼ years if the intereſt is 5 *per cent.*———Suppoſing, therefore, 75 millions borrowed in the manner of our Government, by creating a capital of a 100 millions bearing 3 *per cent.* (that is, by ſelling 3 *per cent.* ſtock for 75l. in money) which might have been borrowed by creating a capital of only 75 millions bearing 4 *per cent.* (that is by ſelling 4 *per cent.* ſtock at 100) there will not only be a loſs of 25 millions by a needleſs increaſe of the capital ; but alſo a loſs of 14 millions, by an increaſe of the time in which one and the ſame ſaving will diſcharge the two capitals.———This may be proved in the following manner.———A million *per ann.* will, in 34 years and a quarter, very nearly diſcharge a debt of 75 millions bearing intereſt at 4 *per cent*; but the ſame ſaving will, in the ſame time, diſcharge only a capital of 61 millions, if it bears intereſt at 3 *per cent.* When, therefore, ſuch a ſaving has compleated the redemption of the *one* capital, there will remain unpaid of the other, 39 millions. ———What has been now applied to a large ſum holds true in proportion of any ſmaller ſums.

It appears from hence to be a very wrong obſervation which ſome have made; " that provided the annual charge is the ſame, " it ſignifies little what the *principal* of the public debt is." ———As there is no way of removing the annual charge but by paying the *principal,* it is of juſt as much conſequence what it is, as whether it is practicable or impracticable, to remove a burden which weakens and cripples, and muſt in time ſink the public. An annuity of Six Millions, if the principal is
a Hun-

It is neceſſary I ſhould obſerve, in juſtice to our preſent miniſters, that in adopting the ſcheme on which I have made theſe remarks, they have only followed the example of former miniſters; and that, however needleſs a waſte it occaſions of public money, there is reaſon to fear it will be followed by future miniſters; for the increaſe of difficulty and expence in redeeming the public debts, which ſuch ſchemes create, being to be felt *hereafter*, it makes no impreſſion, and is little regarded.

In 1759, the fifth year of the laſt war, the lenders of 6.600,000 l. were granted a capital in the 3 *per cents* of 7,590,000 l. together with the profits of the Lottery. Subtract from the ſum advanced, 150,000 l. for the profits of the Lottery; and it will appear, that, in this inſtance, 1.140,000 l. was *needleſsly* added to the capital; there being no reaſon to doubt, but that lenders would then have

a HUNDRED MILLIONS borrowed at 6 *per cent.* might be redeemed in 33 years with a million *per ann.* ſurplus. But if the principal is Two HUNDRED MILLIONS bearing 3 *per cent.* the ſame ſurplus would, in the ſame time, pay off only 56 millions; and but little more than a *quarter* of the annuity would be redeemed. If, therefore, the ſame ſum might as well have been obtained by creating a principal of a hundred millions bearing 6 *per cent.* as by creating a capital of two hundred millions bearing 3 *per cent.* there will be a needleſs expence, in diſcharging the debt, of 144 millions.

readily

readily advanced 6.600,000l. for a capital of 6.450,000l. bearing 3 ¼ *per cent.* (*a*) intereſt, provided the profits of a Lottery were annexed ; inſtead of advancing the ſame ſum for a nominal capital near 18 *per cent.* greater, but bearing 3 *per cent* intereſt.

Again. In 1762, in order to raiſe 12 millions, every contributor of 80 l. was entitled to a capital of 100l. to bear 4 *per cent.* intereſt for 19 years ; and afterwards to become redeemable, and to bear intereſt at 3 *per cent.* And for the remaining 20 l. neceſſary to make up a 100l. contributors were entitled to an annuity of 1 l. for 98 years.——This was the ſame with promiſing, for every 60 l. advanced, a 100l. capital in the 3 *per cent.* annuities, not redeemable for 19 years; and, for the remaining 40 l. neceſſary to make up 100l. an annuity of 2 l. for 19 years ; and, after that, of 1 l. for 79 years.

By this ſcheme no leſs a ſum than 4.800,000l. was needleſsly added to the capital of the public debts.   For, had 5 *per cent.* been offered for for every 60 l. advanced ; (*b*) and, for the re-remaining

(*a*) The price of the 3 *per cents* at the time of this loan (in the beginning of Feb. 1759) was 88 ½ and 89.

(*b*) The 3 *per cents* juſt before this loan were at 69 l. and, conſequently, 5 *per cent.* intereſt, (or 3 l. *per ann.* for 60 l.) would

maining 40 l. an annuity of 2 l. during 19 years, and afterwards of 1 l. for 79 years; equal encouragement would have been given to contributors; the annuity payable by the public would have been the fame; and the new capital would have been 7.200,000 l. bearing 5 *per cent.* interest; which might, at any time, have been redeemed with a faving of a million *per ann.* (the firft payment to be made immediately) in *five* years and a *quarter* : Whereas now, this debt will not become redeemable till 1781 ; and then, it will form a capital of 12 millions, not capable of being redeemed with the fame faving, in lefs than *nine* years and a half. Five millions and a quarter, (*a*) therefore, will be wafted.

The capital of 12 millions four *per cent.* annuities created this year, were made irredeemable for 19 years, to guard againft the effects of an apprehenfion then unavoidable, that an intereft of 4 *per cent.* would, if the capitals were redeemable, be reduced, whenever peace came, to 3 *per cent.*

would have afforded fubfcribers a profit of 9 l. for every 60 l. advanced. The long annuity was worth, as the ftocks then ftood, 21 years purchafe, and the fhort annuity, 13 years purchafe. Upon the whole loan, therefore, the profit would have been 3 *per cent.*

(*a*) That is, the difference between 12 millions, and the fum bearing intereft at 3 *per cent.* which a million *per ann.* would pay off, in five years and a quarter.

as had been done in the preceding peace.—But this end would have been anfwered, with equal effect and more advantage to the public, by pledging the faith of Parliament, that whatever intereft was promifed on any capital, fhould not be *reduced* for 19 years; or (which comes to the fame) that the capital fhould not be *redeemed,* during that term, by borrowing money, and creating a new capital bearing *lower* intereft. This would have placed capitals bearing any intereft on the fame footing *nearly* with the 3 *per cent.* annuities; and an affurance, that no part of them fhould be dif-charged, without at the fame time difcharging an equal capital in the 3 *per cents,* would have placed them *entirely* on the fame footing.——Had it, however, been neceffary, on account of the fear of a reduction of intereft, to make the capital here propofed bearing 5 *per cent,* and the capitals to be mentioned prefently bearing 4 *per cent.* irredeemable, (and therefore the intereft irre-ducible) for any·term (fuppofe till 1781); had, I fay, even this been neceffary (and more could not have been neceffary) no advantage of great confequence would have been loft. Thefe capitals would, during that term, have been exactly the fame burden on the public with the capitals which were actually created; and after that term, they would have been a much lefs burden, as will be fhewn at the end of this fection.

Again.

Again. In January 1760, eight millions were borrowed by offering for this fum a capital of eight millions to carry 4 *per cent*. intereft for 21 years, and afterwards 3 *per cent*, together with a *premium* of 240,000l. ftock carrying the fame intereft, and divided into 80,000l. lottery tickets, each 3l. ftock.——This was the fame with offering, for 80l. of every 100l. advanced, a capital of 100l. in the 3 *per cent*. annuities, (*a*) not redeemable for 21 years; and for the remainder befides a lottery ticket an annuity of 1l. for 21 years.——The fame fum might have been raifed by offering 4 *per cent*, irreducible during 21 years, or 3l. *per ann*. for 75l. of every 100l. advanced, and for the remaining 25l. an annuity of 1l. for 21 years, together with a lottery ticket.——In this cafe, the new capital, inftead of 8.240,000l. bearing 3 *per cent*. not fubject to redemption, and having an annuity of 82,400l. annexed to it, for 21 years; would have been 6.000,000l. bearing 4 *per cent*. with

(*a*) The 3 *per cents* being at this time at 80l. an annuity of 3l. purchafed for 75 l. would have produced a profit of 5 l. Therefore thefe fchemes are of exactly the fame value. But they are too narrow; and the fubfcription this year fell immediately to one *per cent*. difcount. But in the fcheme I have propofed this might have been prevented by only offering 4 *per cent*. for 77 l. or 78 l. (inftead of 75 l.) of every 100 l.

the

the fame annuity annexed, but redeemable at *any* time; and 240,000*l.* (*a*) bearing 4 *per cent.* for 21 years, and afterwards 3 *per cent.*

By the fcheme likewife in 1761, for borrowing 11.400,000*l.* a capital of 100*l.* bearing 3 *per cent. interest*, was given for part of every 100*l.* advanced; and for the other part, an annuity of 1*l.* 2*s.* 6*d.* for 99 years. Had, in this cafe, 75*l.* FOUR *per cent.* STOCK, been offered for 75*l.* in *money*; and, for the remaining 25*l.* neceffary to make up 100*l.* the faid annuity of 1*l.* 2*s.* 6*d.* for 99 years; (*b*) the whole annual charge would have been the fame; fubfcribers could not have been fenfible of any difference in the encouragement offered them; and the public, in paying its debts, would have faved 2.850,000*l.*

There was alfo this year 600,000*l.* received by government for 600,000*l.* ftock, carrying 3 *per cent.* intereft, and divided into 60,000 lottery tickets, each worth 10*l.* in ftock.—As 150,000*l.* of this fum was paid for the profits of the lottery;

(*a*) It is plain, that this capital, as well as the former, might have been a quarter (or 60,000*l.*) lefs, which would have made the whole faving of capital 2.060,000*l.*

(*b*) At the time of this loan, the 3 *per cents.* were above 75; and, therefore, a perpetual annuity of 3l. could not be purchafed for 75*l.* and an annuity of 1*l.* 2*s.* 6*d.* for 99 years, was worth at leaft 27*l.* This, therefore, would have been a fcheme very profitable to fubfcribers.

and

and as 4 *per cent.* could not at this time be made of money laid out in the funds, it is out of doubt, that the fame fum (or 600,000 *l.*) would have been given for 450,000 *l.* ftock, carrying 4 *per cent.* and divided into 60,000 lottery tickets, each of the fame value with 7 *l.* 10 *s.* four *per cent.* ftock; and thus 150,000 *l.* more would have been faved.

In like manner; it will appear, that *three millions*, raifed in 1757, by creating a capital of *three millions* bearing 3 *per cent.* intereft, (*a*) with a life annuity annexed of 1 *l.* 2 *s.* 6 *d.* for every 100 *l.* advanced; and alfo, *four millions and a half* raifed in 1758, by creating a capital of *four millions and a half*, bearing 3 *per cent.* with an annuity of a *half per cent.* annexed for 24 years; might have been

(*a*) The life-annuity granted in this cafe could not have been worth fo little as 16 *l.* or 14 years purchafe; and, therefore, a capital of 100 *l.* in the 3 *per cents* was fold for 84 *l.*; or a capital of three millions, for 2.520,000 *l.*——A premium, therefore, was granted of 480,000 *l*; and this was done without the leaft reafon. For the 3 *per cents* being at that time at 87 and 88, 2.520,000 *l.* would undoubtedly have been lent at 3 ½ *per cent.* intereft; and the remaining 480,000 *l.* neceffary to make up three millions, would have been given for the life annuities; in which cafe, the annual charge occafioned by the new capital would have been fomewhat lefs; and 480,000 *l.* would have been faved, together with the additional expence occafioned by the longer time which a given furplus would require to difcharge a debt bearing 3 *per cent.* intereft, as explained in the note, p. 94.

raifed

raifed by creating, in the former cafe, a capital of
two millions and a half, and, in the latter, a
capital of four millions, bearing $3\frac{1}{2}$ *per cent.* intereft, with the fame annuities annexed.

In 1758, the additional fum of half a million
was borrowed at *3 per cent.* by a lottery, confifting
of 50,000 tickets, each of the fame real value
with 10*l. ftock*, but fold to the fubfcribers for 10*l.*
in *money* (a). As the *3 per cents.* were now at 94,

$3\frac{1}{4}$ *per*

(a) It is a general and certain maxim " that whenever
" money is borrowed by a lottery which gives a right
" to *ftock* equal to the fum advanced, there is a lofs
" equal to the fum which might have been received for
" the profits of the lottery."——When the *3 per cents.* are
at 76 or 77, half a million might be borrowed by a lottery,
confifting of 50,000 tickets, each of the fame value with
10*l.* three *per cent.* ftock: and hitherto fuch a method of
borrowing has been reckoned advantageous. But it only
gives a fallacious appearance of borrowing at *3 per cent.* It is
the fame with felling the profits of a lottery, and at the fame
time abfurdly converting the purchafe-money into a debt due
to the purchafer.——Since the laft war we have had feven
of thefe lotteries, including two in 1763 ; and above a million has been loft by them.

In Queen *Anne*'s time, there were feveral lotteries, confifting
of all *prizes* and no *blanks.* This is fo curious, and moft
perfons may be fo much at a lofs to conceive of the poffibility
of it, that I cannot help explaining it.

A capital, equal to the whole money advanced, was diftributed *equally* among all the tickets in the lottery ; and, in
order to make them prizes of different values, there was
farther diftributed among them different fhares of an additional

5   çapital,

$3\frac{1}{4}$ *per cent.* could not be made of money laid out in the funds. Therefore, 350,000 *l.* of this half

capital, to which a right was given, though no money had been paid for it.——For example——In 1711, two millions were raifed by a lottery of this kind, called a clafs lottery. The whole fum advanced was divided into 20,000 tickets, each 100*l.* ftock bearing 6 *per cent.* intereft. This capital was increafed by a gratuitous capital of 602,200*l.* bearing the fame intereft, and divided into fhares which were added to the tickets, in order to form prizes. ——This was the fame with giving near 8 *per cent.* for money, befides a *premium* of 30 *per cent.*——As the intereft of money was at this time 6 *per cent.* the fum borrowed would moft certainly have been advanced at 8 *per cent.* without any *premium*; but it was, I fuppofe, reckoned neceffary that government fhould not *feem* to give fuch high intereft.——In the fame year, 1.500,000*l.* was borrowed by another fuch lottery, and creating a capital of 1.928,570*l.* And in 1712, 3.600,000*l.* was borrowed by two more fuch lotteries, and creating a capital of 4.683,080*l.*——The greateft part of the debts contracted by thefe lotteries (amounting to 9.213,850*l.* though only 7.100,000*l.* was advanced) remains at this hour an incumbrance on the public; and the duties conftituting the *general fund* are charged with the intereft of it.

In 1714, the national intereft was reduced to 5 *per cent.* But in that very year 1.400,000*l.* was borrowed by a lottery, which gave a right to a capital of 1.876,000*l.* bearing 4 *per cent.* that is, by giving near $5\frac{1}{2}$ *per cent.* intereft, befides a *premium* of 34 *per cent.*——Thus have our debts been increafed. But even worfe has been done. The taxes charged with the intereft of the public debts proving often deficient, the fhorteft way of difcharging the arrears has been often taken, by adding them to the principal, and paying *compound* intereft for money.——Is it a wonder, that a nation which has been fo carelefs in contracting debts, fhould have done fo little towards difcharging them?

million

million might have been raifed at $3\frac{1}{2}$ *per cent.*
intereft, and the remaining 150,000 *l.* might have
been procured for the profits of the lottery. Or
(which is the fame) 10 *l.* each would have been
given for 50,000 tickets, of the fame value taken
all together, with 350,000 l. carrying $3\frac{1}{4}$ *per cent.*
intereft ; and a capital of 150,000 *l.* would have
been faved.

The fame is true of the lottery, by which half
a million was borrowed in 1756.——A million
and a half alfo borrowed in this year, by creating
a capital of a million and a half, bearing $3\frac{1}{2}$ *per
cent.* for 15 years, and afterwards 3 *per cent.*
might have been procured, by creating a capital
of only 1.400,000 *l.* bearing $3\frac{1}{4}$ *per cent.* intereft.
But I will not examine any more of thefe loans.
Let us next confider how detrimental they have
been to the public.

All the favings and furplus monies of the
kingdom from 1763 to 1775, have amounted
(deducting 400,000 *l.* gained by debts difcharged
at a difcount) to 10.739,793 *l.* and with this fum
11.139,793 *l.* of the national debt has been paid
off. (See the *Poftfcript* at the end of this work.)
——The needlefs addition which was made to
the capital of the national debt, by injudicious
fchemes for raifing money during the laft war,
exceeded this fum ; and it follows, therefore, that
the whole furplus of the revenue for twelve years,
has

has not been fufficient to difcharge the capital, to which in the laft war a right was given, without receiving any money for it, or obtaining the leaft advantage by it.

The attentive reader muft have obferved, as I have gone along, that the extravagance on which I have infifted, has been the confequence of not feparating, in the fchemes for raifing money, the premiums (confifting of fhort and long and life-annuities) from the perpetual annuities, and re-quiring them to be diftinctly paid for ; and alfo, of not attending to the difference between felling an *annuity*, and felling the *ftock* for which that annuity is paid. When a 100*l. ftock* in the 3 *per cents.* is at any given price, there is no one who would not be glad to purchafe from government a perpetual annuity of 3 *l.* at any *lower* price (*a*). But when government fells the *ftock*, inftead of the *annuity*, at that price, the public is injured in the manner I have reprefented.

Would any one, in felling any part of his pro-perty, offer to make the purchafe-money an out-ftanding principal which he fhall be bound to

---

(*a*) That is, in other words ; there is no one who would not be glad to lend to government on any higher intereft than that which he can make in the funds. There is no one, for inftance, who would not be glad to lend 75*l.* at 4 *per cent.* when the 3 *per cents.* are at 76, and when, therefore, he can-not make 4 *per cent.* by purchafing them.

return ?

return? (*a*) This is what government has uniformly done in its proposals for raising money.—Were I to desire any sum to be lent me *without* interest, offering as a *compensation* or *premium* an annuity for a given term, or an advantageous contract; the proposal would not be accepted, unless the annuity or the contract was worth the sum to be lent; and I should make myself a debtor to the purchaser for the very thing which I sold to him. ——The absurdity would be the same, if instead of borrowing *without* interest, I should in the same way borrow at a *low* inteteft. In every such bargain, I should bring upon myself a needlefs debt, equal to the value of the *premium*.

I am afraid I have tired my reader's attention on this subject. But as much depends upon a right understanding of it, I am anxious about shewing it in every possible light. In hopes, therefore, of being attended to a little longer, I shall endeavour to give a yet fuller view of this subject, and to prove its importance, by recapitulating some of the foregoing remarks, and comparing the *present* state of our public debts, with

(*a*) The expectation of receiving back some time or other the purchase-money would probably, in private loans, influence a purchaser. But in the cases to which I allude, this certainly was not considered, and did not at all influence. And if it had influenced, the observations I have made as I have gone along, demonstrate that the same loans would have been made without any such expectation.

that

that which would have been their ftate, had the errors I have pointed out, in the fchemes of the public loans during the laft war, been avoided.

The fum of 12 millions, borrowed in 1762, would have left, at the end of the war, a redeemable capital of 7.200,000l. carrying 5 *per cent.* intereft, with an annuity added of 120,000l. for 18 years from January 1763, inftead of an *ir*-redeemable capital of 12 millions carrying 4 *per cent.* for 18 years, and afterwards 3 *per cent.* See page 95, &c.

The fum of 12 millions, borrowed in 1761, would have left a redeemable capital of 9 millions bearing 4 *per cent.* intereft, with a long annuity annexed; inftead of 12 millions with the fame annuity annexed. Page 100.

The fum of 8 millions, borrowed in 1760, would have left a redeemable capital of 6.180,000l. carrying 4 *per cent.* with an annuity of 82,400l. for 18 years from January 1763; inftead of 8.240,000l. *ir*-redeemable, and carrying 4 *per cent.* for 18 years, and afterwards 3 *per cent.* Page 99.

The fum of 6.600,000l. borrowed in 1759, would have left a capital of 6.450,000l. carrying 3 $\frac{1}{2}$ *per cent*; inftead of a capital of 7.590,000l. carrying 3 *per cent.* Page 95.

The fum of five millions, borrowed in 1758, would have left a redeemable capital of 4.350,000l. bearing 3 $\frac{1}{2}$ *per cent.* intereft, with an annuity
added

added of 22,500 l. for 19 years from Midsummer
1763 ; instead of a capital of five millions irredeemable, and carrying 3 $\frac{1}{2}$ *per cent.* for 19 years,
and afterwards 3 *per cent.* Page 101, 102, &c.

The sum of three millions, borrowed in 1757,
would have left a capital of two millions and a
half bearing 3 $\frac{1}{2}$ *per cent.* interest, instead of three
millions bearing 3 *per cent.* interest.——And two
millions, borrowed in 1756, instead of leaving a
capital of two millions, would have left a capital
of only 1.750,000 l. Page 104.

The result, therefore, is, that the whole capital of the public debts would have been, at the
end of the last war, near TWELVE MILLIONS AND
A HALF less than it was ; and at the same time,
the annual charge not greater.——In 1775, the
difference would have been much more considerable. For,

Supposing all the same sums applied since the
last war to the discharge of the public debts that
we know have been so applied, not only the *capital* but the *annual charge* would have been con-
siderably less.——This will be demonstrated by the
following account.

It may be learnt from the *Postscript* at the
end of this Tract, that 11.139,793 l. of the public debts has been discharged with 10.739,793 l.
of the public money, derived from various savings
and surpluffes. All this money *might* have been
employed,

employed, and without doubt *would* have been
employed, in redeeming firſt the capital I have
mentioned in Page 107, of 7.200,000 l. bearing 5 *per cent.* intereſt; and afterwards, the
two other capitals there mentioned of 9 millions, and of 6,180,000l. bearing 4 *per cent.* intereſt. It would have been ſufficient to redeem
the whole of the former capital, and alſo
3.539,793 l. of the two laſt capitals; which would
have ſet free for the public an annual charge of
501,591 l.——To this ſum muſt be added an annual charge of 256,000l. ſaved in 1765, 1766,
1767 and 1768, by redeeming, with 6.400,000l.
borrowed in thoſe years, ſo much of a debt unfunded at the end of the war, but afterwards
funded, and carrying 4 *per cent.* intereſt. And
alſo 12,537 l. *per ann.* gained by changing
1.253,700l. from an intereſt of 4 to 3 *per cent.*
and 7,500l. *per ann.* gained in 1771, by the ceaſing
of an annuity of a $\frac{1}{2}$ *per cent.* annexed for 15 years
to 1.500,000l. borrowed in 1756.——The total
decreaſe, therefore, of the annual charge would
have been 777,628l.——But at the ſame time
there would have been the following additions to
it.——Firſt. There would have been the addition of 199,500l. *per ann.* being the intereſt of
6.650,000l. borrowed ſince 1763.——Secondly.
Of 69,187 l. *per ann.* being the intereſt of
2.306,240l. applied, in 1764 and 1765, to the diſcharge

charge of German and army debts derived from the war, and which might have been converted into a funded capital bearing 3 *per cent.* interest, by borrowing money to pay them off, in order to avoid diverting money employed in redeeming capitals bearing 5 *per cent.*

These two sums make 268,687 l. which deducted from 777,628 l. leaves 508,941 l. And this is the clear annual charge which would have been saved to the public, exclusive of the savings which have arisen from the falling in of life-annuities.

But the annual charge that has in fact been saved is only 382,129 (*a*).——The difference is 126,812 l.——With this additional saving, as it fell in and increased from time to time during the course of 12 years, a million more of the public debts bearing 4 *per cent.* might have been redeemed; and this would have made a farther saving of 40,000 l. *per ann.* It appears, therefore, upon the whole, that had the mistakes I have pointed out, in the loans of the last war, been avoided, (all other public measures remaining the same) the nation would *now* have had 13 millions and a half less to pay, in order to redeem its debts; and also an annual charge upon it 166,812 l. less.

(*a*) See the Postscript.

All

All this fuppofes that the capitals of the 5 *per cent.* and 4 *per cent.* annuities in the improved fchemes were redeemable.——But had they been made irredeemable till 1781, as mentioned in page 98, the public would not have been much lefs benefited: For, foon after 1781, thefe 5 and 4 *per cents.* (the former 7.200,000l. and the latter 15.180,000l.) might have been eafily reduced to 3 ½ *per cent.* and this would have occafioned an annual faving of 183,900l. over and above the favings, which would have arifen in that year, from the extinction of the fhort annuities.

I will add, that had thefe annuities been made not only *irredeemable* till 1781; but *irreducible* for fome time beyond that year, in the manner intimated in page 98, the public would ftill have been greatly benefited. For, the annual charge upon it would not at any time have been greater; but its debts would have been 12 millions and a half lefs; and, at the fame time, they would have been capable of being difcharged with more expedition, and at a lefs expence, than a fmaller quantity of its prefent debts. See the note, page 94.

I cannot doubt but that all who will attentively examine thefe obfervations will find them to be juft.——I have confined my enquiries to the loans of the laft war. Had I extended them to all our loans, it would have appeared, that a greater fum than

than moſt perſons can think credible, (a) has been
ſuch a needleſs addition to our debts as I have explained; or, " a pure and uncompenſated loſs,
" which might have been avoided by only framing
" differently the ſchemes of the public loans."

(a) SIXTEEN MILLIONS have been ſpecified. It will come
in my way to mention above FOUR MILLIONS more in the ſecond ſection of the next part. Notes 1, 12, 14.—No notice has
been here taken of the loans of the war before the laſt; but loſſes
of the ſame kind to a great amount were incurred by them.

PART

PART III.

SECT. I.

Abstract of the Exports from and Imports to Great-Britain from 1697 to 1773, with Remarks.

	Imports. £.	Exports. £.	Excess of Exports. £.	
Annual Medium for Four Years ended at 1700 —	4.956,975 —	6.034,724 —	1.077,749	or $\frac{10}{56}$ of the exports.
For Five Years ended at 1710 —	5.321,717 —	6.713,246 —	1.391,529	or $\frac{10}{48}$ of the exports.
at 1715 —	5.304,343 —	7.401,946 —	2.097,603	or $\frac{10}{35}$ of the exports.
at 1725 —	6.628,279 —	9.663,527 —	3.035,248	or $\frac{10}{32}$ of the exports.
at 1735 —	7.470,454 —	11.855,226 —	4.384,772	or $\frac{10}{27}$ of the exports.
at 1745 —	7.363,079 —	11.922,982 —	4.559,903	or $\frac{10}{26}$ of the exports.
at 1750 —	7.429,739 —	12.877,129 —	5.447,390	or $\frac{10}{24}$ of the exports.
at 1755 —	8.264,834 —	13.405,530 —	5.141,696	or $\frac{10}{26}$ of the exports.
at 1760 —	8.877,144 —	14.253,377 —	5.376,233	or $\frac{10}{26}$ of the exports.
For Four Years ended at 1764 —	10.110,870 —	15.793,158 —	5.682,228	or $\frac{10}{28}$ of the exports.
For Nine Years ended at 1773 —	11.996,769 —	14.814,074 —	2.817,305	or $\frac{10}{53}$ of the exports.

I

This

This ABSTRACT has been formed from the accounts delivered annually to the HOUSE OF COMMONS, and lately publifhed by Sir CHARLES WHITWORTH.

In order to draw juft inferences from it, the following particulars fhould be remembered.——— Firft. The EXPORTS in the *Cuftom-Houfe* entries are, for reafons well-known, too high. This excefs has, by fome of the beft judges, been reckoned at a million *per ann.*———Secondly. The IMPORTS are too low, no fmuggled commodities being included in them. This deficiency has been eftimated at another million *per ann.* But, in order to be fure of keeping within bounds, I will take both at a *million and a half per ann.*———Thirdly. The intereft of the national debt paid to foreigners ; the money fpent in foreign countries by *Englifh* travellers ; the bullion confumed in manufactures ; and the wear of the current coin, cannot, perhaps, amount to much lefs than two millions *per ann.* I will, however, take them at no more than the annual fum which has been commonly fuppofed to be due to foreigners from our funds ; or, a *million and a half.*———In order, therefore, to find the GRAND BALANCE OF PAYMENT between *Britain* and the reft of the world *fince* the laft war, all thefe fums (making up THREE MILLIONS) muft be deducted from the excefs of the exports. ———But, in order to find the fame balance *before*

the

the end of the laſt war, leſs muſt be deducted, in proportion as the national debt and the foreign trade were *then* leſs than they are *now*.

If the foregoing Abſtract is examined with a due regard to this rule, it will be found that, from (*a*) 1710 to 1764, the BALANCE OF PAYMENT muſt have been in favour of *Britain*; and that conſequently, there muſt have been, during that period, an influx of money into the kingdom.—— It was this, together with the increaſe of our paper, that produced the rapid fall of intereſt which began a few years before the *Acceſſion.* And it was this alſo that enabled us to bear the great expence of the two laſt wars, and the loſs of thoſe enormous ſums which were ſent out of the kingdom to pay foreign ſubſidies, and to ſupport armies on the continent.

Before 1710 it appears to be doubtful, whether the exceſs of the exports was ſuch as brought any money into the kingdom ; but it ſeems certain, that it could not have been ſuch as in any degree compenſated that drain of the public caſh, which was occaſioned by the continental wars of King

(*a*) In the exports, as delivered to the *Houſe of Commons*, is included bullion exported. If this, as well as the other ſums I have mentioned, is deducted, there will be ſtill a balance left in favour of *Britain* during this period. Since 1764, it does not appear, from the accounts laid before the *Houſe of Commons*, as publiſhed by Sir *Charles Whitworth*, that any bullion has been entered for exportation.

I 2 *William*

William and Queen *Ann.* In confequence of this, the quantity of *fpecie* in the kingdom muft have been greatly diminifhed; and Dr. *Davenant* computes that in 1711 it was nine millions lefs than at the *Revolution.* Hence proceeded the high rate of intereft; the unproductivenefs of the taxes; and the difficulties which government met with in raifing money during thofe two wars: And there is reafon to believe, thefe difficulties would have been infurmountable, had not a fubftitute for *fpecie* been provided by the eftablifhment of the *Bank.*

In the interval of peace between the two laft wars, or from 1748 to 1755, the balance in favour of *Britain* was at the higheft; and this contributed to raife the ftocks (*a*) to fuch a price, as enabled government to reduce the intereft of the public debts from 4 to 3 *per cent.*

But the obfervation I here intended principally to make is, that the *balance*, fince the year 1764, appears, from the preceding abftract, to have been *againft* BRITAIN; and that this accounts for the high price of bullion, the fcarcity of fpecie, and the diftrefs of the *Bank* from that year to 1773.

(*a*) The 3 *per cent.* annuities were then at 105; and, during the firft five years of the war which began in 1755, they were higher than they have generally been *fince* the war.

2

It

It deserves farther to be obſerved that, while the exports were decreaſing from 1764 to 1773, the IMPORTS appear to have increaſed faſter than ever: And thefact is, that ſince 1760, a greater addition has been made to them, than had been made during the whole time from the *Acceſſion* to that year.——This is a ſtriking proof that luxury has been for ſome years increaſing with rapidity among us; and it is worth adding, that the productiveneſs of the taxes has kept pace, as might have been expected, with this increaſe of luxury, both the CUSTOMS and EXCISES having brought in lately, near 250,000l. *per ann.* each, more than they did twelve years ago.——It ſhould be attended to, that this improvement of the revenue muſt be the effect ſolely of an increaſed conſumption occaſioned by luxury; the taxes, ever ſince the end of the laſt war, having been nearly the ſame.

The *exports* from 1710 to 1764 went on increaſing conſtantly. I have obſerved, that from 1764 to 1773 they have decreaſed. One reaſon of this has been, the decline of the PORTUGAL trade; the exports to that country having fallen, ſince 1760, from 1.200,000l. *per ann.* to 600,000l. *per ann.*——Another reaſon has been the check which a wretched policy has been giving, ever ſince 1763, to our trade with the Colonies. This trade had for many years contributed more than any

I 3   other

other trade towards raifing our *exports*; and even
in the period between 1763 and 1774, notwithftanding the checks it received, it went on increafing, and produced a balance in our favour
of a million and a half *per ann.* But fince 1774 it
has been entirely loft. *Before* this lofs, the balance of payment between us and the reft of the
world was, according to the account I have
given, *againft* us. Undoubtedly then, it was
a lofs we could by no means have fuftained, had
it not been for the feafonable interpofition of fome
very particular caufes. Time will fhew whether
thefe caufes are of a permanent nature, or temporary and accidental.

SECT. II.

HISTORICAL DEDUCTION *and* ANALYSIS *of the* PUBLIC DEBTS.

STATE *and* AMOUNT *of the* NATIONAL DEBT, *at Midfummer*, 1775, *with the Charges of Management.*

CAPITALS and ANNUITIES transferrable at the BANK OF ENGLAND.

	Principal. £.	Intereſt. £.
CAPITAL of their original Fund—See Note (1) p. 125 — —	3.200,000	96,000
EXCHEQUER bills, by 3d of *Geo.* I. c. 8th, bearing originally 5 *per cent.* intereſt, but reduced to 4 *per cent.* in 1727, and to 3 *per cent.* by 23d *George* II. 1749. See Note (2) p. 126 -	500,000	15,000
Purchaſed of the SOUTH SEA COMPANY in 1722, —reduced from 6 to 5 *per cent.* intereſt in 1717; from 5 to 4 *per cent.* in 1727; and to 3 *per cent.* by 23d of *George* II. 1749.—See Note (3) — —	4.000,000	120,000
Carried over	7.700,000	231,000

I 4.   Lent

	Principal. £.	Interest. £.
Brought over —	7.700,000	231,000
Lent to government at 4 *per cent.* in 1728, charged on the surplus of the fund for the lottery in 1714, and reduced to 3 *per cent.* by 23d *George* II. 1749	1.250,000	37,500
Lent at 4 *per cent.* in 1727; charged on the duties on coals; and reduced to 3 *per cent.* by 23d of *George* II. 1749 — —	1.750,000	52,500
Lent at 4 *per cent.* in 1746; charged on licences for retailing spirituous liquors; and reduced to 3 *per cent.* by 23d *Geo.* II. 1749 —	986,800	29,604
Amount of Bank capital £.	11.686,800	350,604

See Note (4) p. 126.
Charge of management 5,898 *l. per ann.*

BANK ANNUITIES.

Consolidated 4 *per cent.* annuities due *April* 5, and *October* 10—See Note (5) — —	18,986,300	759,452

Carried over £ 30.673,100 1.110,056

These annuities fall to 3 *per cent.* in *January*, 1781.
Charge of management 10,680 *l. per ann.*

Annuities

	Principal.	Intereſt,
Brought over —£.30.673,100		1.110,056

Annuities at 3¼ *per cent.*
1758, due *Jan.* 5, and
July 5.—Theſe annui-
ties fall to 3 *per cent.*
in 1782 — — 4.500,000 | 157,500
See an account of them
in p. 101.

Charge of management
2,805*l. per ann.* including management on half
a million raiſed at the
ſame time by a lottery,
and made a part of the
conſolidated 3 *per cents.*

CONSOLIDATED 3 *per cent.*
annuities due *Jan.* 5,
and *July* 5. See Note (6) 38.251,696 | 1.147,551
Management 21,087*l. per*
ann.

REDUCED 3 *per cent.* an-
nuities, due *April* 5, and
Oct. 10. See Note (7) 18.353,774 | 550,613
Charge of management
10,324*l. per ann.*

Three *per cent.* 1726, due
Jan. 5, and *July* 5,
charged on the deduc-
tion of 6*d. per* pound
on all penſions from
the civil liſt; and on
all payments from the
crown, except to the
navy and army—See
Note (8) p. 128 — 1.000,000 | 30,000

Carried over £. 92.778,560 | 2.995,720

Management 360*l. per ann.*   Long

	Principal.	Intereſt.
	£.	£.
Brought over —	92.778,560	2.995,720
Long annuity due *Jan.* 5, and *July* 5 — —	6.702,750	248,250

The remaining term from *Jan.* 1776, is 84 years— See Note (9) p. 128. Management 3,491 *l. per ann.*

CAPITALS and ANNUI-TIES transferrable at the SOUTH SEA HOUSE.

	Principal.	Intereſt.
SOUTH SEA STOCK —	3.662,784	109,884

The dividend on this ſtock, at 3¼ *per cent.* is 128,197*l.* 9*s.*—Due *Jan.* 5, and *July* 5.

	Principal.	Intereſt.
SOUTH SEA 3 *per cent.* OLD Annuities due *April* 5, and *Oct.* 10	11.907,470	357,224
Three *per cent.* NEW Annuities due *Jan.* 5, and *July* 5 — —	8.494,830	254,845
Three *per cent.* 1751, due *Jan.* 5, and *July* 5 —	1.919,600	57,588

Charge of management on *South Sea* Stock and Annuities 15,100*l. per ann.*—See Note (10).

Carried over £. 125.465,994 | 4.023,511

CAPITAL

	Principal. £.	Interest. £.
Brought over —	125.465,994	4.023,511

CAPITAL and ANNUITIES transferrable at the INDIA HOUSE.

EAST INDIA STOCK — Interest 3 per cent. Dividend 7 per cent. 224,000l. due Jan. 5, and July 5.——— See Note (11). Charge of management 1.285l. 14s. 4d.	3.200,000	96,000
EAST INDIA Annuity due April 5, and Oct. 10, charged on the surplus of a tax on spirituous liquors. See Note (12) Management 401l. 15s. 8d. per ann.	1.000,000	30,000

ANNUITIES payable at the EXCHEQUER.

ANNUITIES for 96 and 99 years, from various dates, in the time of King William and Queen Anne—See Note (13) — — Salaries to Exchequer officers, and management—5,250l. per ann.	1.836,276	131,203

Annuities for lives, with benefit of survivorship, granted by the 4th of

Carried over £.	131.502,270	4.280,714

William

	Principal. £.	Intereſt. £.
Brought over ——	131.502,270	4.280,714
William and *Mary*, 1693. —— Theſe annuities are not yet extinct, and they are valued at three years purchaſe	22,781	7,567
Annuities for lives, with benefit of ſurvivorſhip, by an Act of the 5th of *Geo.* III. 1765—See Note (14) —— ——	18,000	540
Annuities for two or three lives, granted in 1694. —— Alſo, Annuities on ſingle lives 1745, 1746, and 1757. —— See Note (15) —— Their original amount, taken all together, was very nearly 124,000*l.* but they are now reduced by deaths to near 80,000*l.* and their value is here taken at 10 years purchaſe ——	800,000	80,000
UNFUNDED DEBT, conſiſting of Exchequer bills, (1.250,000*l.*) Navy debt, (1.850,000*l.*) and Civil liſt debt, ſuppoſed 500,000*l.*—The intereſt is reckoned at 2 *per cent.*—See Note (16)	3.600,000	72,000
Salaries to Exchequer bill officers 650*l. per ann.*		
Total of the principal and intereſt of the National Debt at *Midſummer* 1775.	£. 135.943,051	4.440,821

NOTES *containing an* EXPLANATION *and* HISTORY *of the different Articles in the foregoing Account.*

NOTE (1)——BANK OLD CAPITAL. See Page 119.
——The BANK was eſtabliſhed in 1694.. Their original capital was 1.200,000*l.* bearing 8 *per cent.* intereſt, charged on ⅝ths. of 9*d. per* barrel excife, with 4000*l. per ann.* for management.——In 1709, they lent to government 400,000*l.* without intereſt, which increaſed their old capital to 1.600,000*l.* bearing 6 *per cent.* intereſt. In 1742, they again lent to government 1.600,000l. without intereſt; and thereby in-creaſed this capital to its preſent amount, or to 3.200,000 *l.* bearing 3 *per cent.* with the ſame annual ſum for manage-ment.——It is of particular importance to obſerve with reſpect to the ſums of 400,000*l.* and of 1.600,000*l.* juſt mentioned, that they were properly a compenſation from the *Bank* to the public for continuing their excluſive privileges ; and would have been advanced, or at leaſt the greateſt part of them, though government had not bound itſelf to return the purchaſe money, by making it a part of the principal due to the *Bank,* provided the ſame intereſt had been continued for ſome time on their former principal, and the ſame liberty granted to increaſe their *ſtock.*——The like is true of 1.200,000*l.* advanced by the *India* Company without intereſt in 1708.—In theſe inſtances, therefore, a needleſs addition was made to the public debt of 3.200,000*l.* which, had it been avoided, the public would have had not only a principal ſo much leſs to pay ; but it would have ſaved in intereſt at leaſt 96000*l. per ann.* for the old capital of the *Bank* and the capital of the *Eaſt India* Company would have formed, in this caſe, between them, a debt of only 3.200,000*l.* (inſtead of 6.400,000*l.*) the intereſt of which might long ago have been reduced at leaſt one half ; or from 8 *per cent.* the original intereſt, to 4 *per cent.*

NOTE

Note (2)——*Half a million*, part of the Bank Capital.
See Page 119. —— This part of the Bank capital confifted
originally of two millions in *Exchequer* bills, cancelled for government by an act of the 3d of *Geo.* I. But half a million
was difcharged in 1729; and a million in 1738.

Note (3)——Four millions purchafed of the South-
Sea Company; part of the Bank Capital. See Page 119.
——In order to procure this money, the *Bank* fold new ftock
at 18 *per cent.* premium. This produced a faving of 610,169 *l.*
the fale of 3.389,831 *l. ftock* having produced four millions in
money. And, confequently, though by this tranfaction the
capital for which they received intereft was increafed four
millions, yet the *ftock* on which they made their dividends
was increafed only 3.389,831 *l.*

Note (4) —— Bank Stock and Dividend. ——The
ftock on which the *Bank* divides is only 10,780,000 *l.* This
dividend varies as their profits vary; but for feveral years
it has been 5½ *per cent.* payable half-yearly at *Lady-
day* and *Michaelmas.* Their whole annual dividend is, therefore, 592,900 *l.* which fubtracted from 350,604 *l.* the intereft
paid by government, makes their clear annual profit 242,296 *l.*
——Befides intereft, they receive for management of their
capital 4000 *l. per ann.* on account of their old capital, and
1,898 *l. per ann.* on account of four millions purchafed of the
South Sea Company; in all, 5,898 *l. per ann.*——The *Bank*
receives farther the fums fpecified in the foregoing account,
towards bearing the expences of managing the annuities commonly called *Bank Annuities.* All thefe expences, including the
fums granted for managing their capital, amount to 54,645 *l.*
per ann.

Note (5)——Confolidated 4 *per cent.* Bank Annuities. See Page 120.——The capital of thefe Annuities
confifts of two loans, one in 1760, and the other in 1762, confolidated

folidated into one ftock, and charged on the additional duty
of 3 d. per bufhel on malt, the furplus of the duties on fpirituous
liquors, and the additional duties on windows; all which duties
were ordered by 2d Geo. III. to be carried to the Sinking Fund,
and the intereft with which they were charged to be paid out of
that fund.——I have made fome remarks on thefe loans in
page 96, and page 99. They amounted to 20.240,000l. But
1.253,700l. of this capital was changed in 1770, from an
intereft of 4 to 3 per cent. and the capital reduced to the
prefent fum.——A more full account of thefe annuities may
be found in Mr. *Afhmore's* Analyfis of the feveral Bank
Annuities, p. 17.

NOTE (6)——CONSOLIDATED 3 *per cent*. BANK ANNUI-
TIES. See page 121.—The capital of thefe annuities is made
a diftnct ftock from that of the annuities called *Reduced*, becaufe
it never bore a higher intereft than 3 *per cent*.—It confifted originally of the following loans—37,821l. remaining in 1727, of
3 *per cent*. annuities, granted in lieu of St. *Chriftopher's* and
Nevis debentures—800,000l. borrowed in 1731—600,000l.
borrowed in 1736——300,000l. in 1738——6.400,000l. in
1742, 1743, 1744 and 1745, and charged on additional duties
on fpirituous liquors, wines, vinegar, &c.——1.000,000l.
borrowed in 1750——24.490,000l. borrowed in the courfe of
the laft war, and funded on the additional duties on beer,
houfes, ftamps, &c.——4.900,000l. borrowed in 1766, 1767
and 1768——And 1.253,700l. of the 4 *per cent*. annuities,
fubfcribed into the 3 *per cent*. annuities in 1770.

All thefe loans were by 25 Geo. II. 1751, and feveral fubfequent Acts of Parliament, confolidated into one joint ftock;
and carried, with the duties for paying the intereft, to the
Sinking Fund. And in 1770, they formed a capital of
39.781,521l. which has been fince reduced, by the payments
mentioned in the *Poftfcript* at the end of this tract, to the fum
fpecified in the account to which this note refers.—See a more
full

full account in Mr. Afhmore's Analyfis, &c. from page 5 to page 11.

NOTE (7)——REDUCED 3 *per cent.* BANK ANNUITIES. See page 121.—The capital of thefe annuities confifted, in 1749, of loans in 1746, 1747, and 1748, and navy, ordnance and tranfport debts funded in 1749, amounting to 18.402,472*l.* and all bearing 4 *per cent.* interest.——By the 23d of Geo. II. 1749, thefe loans were reduced to an interest of 3 *per cent.* and by the great confolidating Act in 1751, they were converted into one stock, and carried into the Sinking Fund with the duties on carriages, and the additional duties on glafs, fpirituous liquors, houfes, windows, stamps, merchandize imported, &c. which had been granted for paying the interest.—In 1751, certain exchequer tallies and orders, amounting to 129,750*l.* were fubfcribed into this stock; and in 1765, navy bills to the amount of 1,482,000*l.* were fubfcribed into it, which made its whole original amount 20.014.222*l.*——In 1751, there was paid off 830,893*l.* being stock which had not been fubfcribed agreeably to the Act in 1749 for reducing interest; and in 1772, 1774, and 1775, fo much more of this stock was paid off as reduced it to its prefent amount.—See Mr. Afhmore's Analyfis, p. 12—16.

NOTE (8)——CIVIL LIST MILLION. See page 121.—The income fettled upon King George I. for his civil list, was 700,000*l.*——In 1720, there had been granted him befides, from the *Royal Exchange* and *London* Affurance companies, 300,000*l.* And in 1726, this million was farther granted towards paying off his debts.

NOTE (9) —— BANK LONG ANNUITY. See page 122. —— This annuity confifts of 128,250*l. per ann.* for 99 years, given in 1761, as a *premium* to the fubfcribers of 11.400,000*l.* at 3 *per cent*; and of 120,000*l. per ann.* for 98 years, given in 1762, as a premium to the lenders of twelve millions at 4 *per cent.*

cent. See page 95 and 100. It is charged, together with the loans to which it was annexed, on the *Sinking Fund.* ———— Its value in the Alley is about 25 years purchase; but the remaining term is really worth 27 years purchase, reckoning interest at 3½, (or the 3 *per cents.* being at 85¾.) But when interest is at 4 *per cent.* or the 3 *per cents.* are at 75, it is worth only 24 years purchase.——When this annuity is called a *premium,* it must not be imagined, that no compensation was given for it. Government received the value of it; but, at the same time, made itself a debtor for that value. And, what is very surprizing, this has been uniformly practised with respect to all the premiums or douceurs granted by government; and the consequence has been, that great and needless increase of the public debt explained in the 3d section of the 2d Part.

NOTE (10).—SOUTH-SEA STOCK AND ANNUITIES. See page 122.—These four capitals amounting to 25.984,684*l.* 13*s.* consist almost entirely of the remainder of debts contracted in the reigns of *King William* and Queen *Anne.* The following account will probably give sufficient information concerning them.

In 1711, Lord Oxford being minister, the proprietors of certain navy, army, ordnance and transport debts, to the amount of 9.177,968*l.* including arrears of interest, and half a million for the current supplies, were incorporated into a company for trading to the *South-seas.* They were allowed 6 *per cent.* interest for this debt, with 8000*l. per ann.* for management; and the duties on wine, tobacco, *East-India* goods, candles, &c. were made perpetual, and granted as a *Fund* (ever since called the *South-sea Company's Fund)* for paying the interest. This kept up public credit at the time, and has been called the *Earl of Oxford's* master-piece.——By the 1st of Geo. I. 822,032*l.* consisting chiefly of interest payable on the Company's capital, was added to the capital, in consequence of which it was increased to TEN MILLIONS, **(ever since called** their *original capital)* bearing 6 *per cent.*

K   interest.

intereſt.——In 1717, they agreed to take 5 *per cent*; and this
was the firſt great reduction of intereſt, which in conjunction
with the ſame reduction of the other redeemable debts almoſt
all carrying 6 *per cent.* laid the foundation of the SINKING
FUND eſtabliſhed in this year. But it is remarkable, that ſo
faſt did intereſt fall at this time, that the price of *South-ſea
ſtock*, notwithſtanding this reduction, roſe from 101 to 111.——
In 1719, the *South-ſea* capital was increaſed to 11.746,844*l.*
bearing 5 *per cent.* intereſt (with an addition of 1,397*l.* 9*s.*
to their former allowance for management) by advancing to
government 544,142*l.* and by the proprietors of 94,329*l.* 12*s.*
lottery annuities for 32 years granted in 1710, accepting in
lieu of them 1.202,702*l. South Sea ſtock.*——In 1720, the
agreement was made by government with the South Sea Company, which produced the great SOUTH SEA BUBBLE.——
There exiſted at that time *long* annuities to the amount of
666,821*l.* 8*s.* and *ſhort* annuities, for 32 years from 1710, to
the amount of 127,260*l.* 6*s.* The proprietors of theſe
annuities were allowed to ſubſcribe them into the *South Sea*
trading ſtock; and the Company, for every 100*l.* of the *long*
annuity which ſhould be ſubſcribed, were to receive from government an addition to their capital of 2000*l.* bearing 5 *per cent.*
intereſt till 1727, and afterwards 4 *per cent.* till redeemed :
and for every 100*l.* of the *ſhort* annuities, they were to
receive an addition to their capital of 1400*l.* bearing the ſame
intereſts.——They were beſides to take in the redeemable debts
to the amount of 16.546,482*l.* and to receive an addition to
their capital of 100*l.* for every 100*l.* ſubſcribed.——By the
ſubſcription of the *long* and *ſhort* annuities which followed this
agreement, a capital due from government to the Company
was created, which was greater by 3.034,769*l.* than the original ſum advanced for the annuities ſubſcribed. And as
much of theſe annuities and of the redeemable debts were
ſubſcribed, as increaſed the *South Sea* trading capital to
37.802,203*l.*——In 1722, four millions of this capital was

3 purchaſed

purchafed by the BANK, (See Note 3.) which reduced it to 33.802,203*l*.——By 9 Geo. I. 1723, this remaining capital was divided into two equal parts, one of which alone (or 16.901,101*l*.) was ordered to be the trading capital of the Company, and the other part was directed to be called *South Sea Annuities*.——In 1733, the *South Sea* trading capital had been reduced by payments at different times to 14.651,137*l*. 12*s*. By an Act of Parliament in that year, this remaining ftock received a farther divifion ; and only a fourth part, or 3.662,784*l*. was allowed to be the Company's ftock ; and the other three parts, or 10.988,353*l*. were directed to be called NEW South Sea Annuities, in order to diftinguifh them from the former annuities, which have ever fince gone under the name of OLD South Sea annuities.——From 1733, to the prefent time, SOUTH SEA STOCK has continued the fame ; but the capital of the OLD South Sea annuities has been reduced, by redemptions, to 11.907.470*l*. and of the NEW South Sea annuities, to 8.494,830*l*. And of the whole *South Sea* debt, which in 1722 was 33.802,203*l*. there has, fince that year, been paid off in all 9.737,119*l*. This fhould have reduced it to 24.065,081*l*. but it is in reality 25.984,685*l*. The reafon of this is, that the diminution juft mentioned of the *South Sea* debt was made in part with money borrowed in 1751, to pay off fuch proprietors of South Sea annuities as had refufed to confent to the reduction of intereft propofed to them in 1749. The fum borrowed for this purpofe was 2.100,000*l*. bearing 3 *per cent.* with 1181*l*. 5*s*. for management. This debt is now reduced by redemptions to the fum fpecified in the preceding account; or to 1.919,600*l*.

NOTE (11).——EAST-INDIA STOCK.   See page 123. ——In 1698, a company of merchants, in confideration of two millions lent to government at 8 *per cent.* were incorporated, and entitled to the fole privilege of trading to the *Eaft-Indies*.——Thefe two millions formed the firft capital of the prefent *Eaft-India* Company.——In 1702, an old company of traders to the *Eaft-Indies* was united to this company ; and in

1708,

1708, these united companies lent to government 1.200,000*l.* without additional interest, which made their capital 3.200,000*l.* bearing 5 *per cent.*——In 1730, this interest was reduced to 4 *per cent.* and by the 23d Geo. II. 1749, to 3 *per cent.*—— The salt duties, and some additional stamp duties, were at first charged with the annuity due on this capital ; but at present the duties constituting the aggregate fund are charged with it.

NOTE (12).—EAST-INDIA ANNUITY. See page 123.— The capital of this annuity was advanced to government in 1744, at 3 *per cent.* and, in consideration of this loan, the exclu- sive charter of the Company was continued to Lady-day 1783, at which time it is to cease, provided three years notice has been given, and the debt due from government discharged.

An observation here forces itself upon me, which I have often had occasion to make.——Part of this loan was a com- pensation from the *East-India* Company for prolonging the term of its charter ; and, therefore, ought not to have been included in the loan. The Company would have lent 750,000*l.* on the interest common at the time, or 4 *per cent.* and the remainder would have been advanced as a gratuity.— It is a pity those who managed these contracts for the public, did not attend to the absurdity and extravagance of making a *debt* of purchase money, and *borrowing* in the very act of *selling*.

NOTE (13).——EXCHEQUER LONG ANNUITIES. See page 123.——These are the *long* annuities which, in 1720, remained unsubscribed to the South Sea Company. See Note 10.——They consist first of annuities to the amount of 54,900*l.* 14*s.* 6*d.* purchased by the 4th, 5th, and 6th of *William* and *Mary*, for 96 years, from January 1695, with the addition of 1350*l. per ann.* for salaries to exchequer officers. These annuities were originally 14 *per cent.* life- annuities. By the 6th and 7th of *William* and *Mary*, in order to raise more money, these annuitants, or any other
persons

perfons for them, were offered a reverfionary intereft in the
annuities after the failure of the lives, till the end of 96 years
from January 1695, on paying 4¼ years purchafe, (that is 63 l.)
for every annuity of 14 l. —— The predeceffors of the prefent
company of the MILLION BANK (fo called from the MILLION
lottery 1694, in which they were fome of the principal
adventurers) purchafed 30,669 l. 4 s. of thefe reverfionary
annuities. The life annuitants being now reduced to a very
fmall number, almoft the whole of this annuity is lapfed to
the *company*; and though they have divided for feveral years
5 *per cent.* on a capital of half a million, yet their growing
favings, from the falling in of lives, have been fuch, that,
when their annuity ceafes in 1791, they will, I am informed, have accumulated a fund confiderably larger, than the
capital on which they have made their dividends. But to
return.

Thefe EXCHEQUER Annuities confift farther of

£.	s.	d.	
30,400	6	8	purchafed for 99 years from *Chriftmas* 1705, by 2d and 3d of *Anne*, with 1450 l. for management.
23,234	16	6	purchafed for 99 years from *Lady-day*, 1706, by 4 *Anne*, with 1470 l. *per ann.* for management.
7,776	10	0	purchafed for 99 years from *Lady-day*, 1707, by 5 *Anne*, with 375 l. 12 s. *per ann.* for management.
4,710	0	0	purchafed for 99 years from *Lady-day*, 1703, by 6th of *Anne*, with 208 l. 2 s. *per ann.* for management.
10,181	0	0	purchafed for 99 years from *Lady-day*, 1707, by a 2d Act of 5th of *Anne*, with 416 l. *per ann.* for management.

Add 54,900 14 6

131,203 7 8 Total.

K 3   The

The original fum contributed for thefe annuities was 1,836,276*l.* They are even now worth more than this fum. The public has already paid above TEN MILLIONS; and by the time they are all extinct, it will have paid above THIRTEEN MILLIONS, on their account. This is great extravagance; but it is nothing to the extravagance conftantly practifed of borrowing on perpetual annuities, without putting them into a fixed courfe of redemption.

NOTE (14).—TONTINE by an act of 6 Geo. III. See page 124.—The intention of this Act was to raife 300,000*l.* towards paying off navy bills, by offering to fubfcribers for every 100*l.* advanced, an annuity of 3*l.* for their lives, with benefit of furvivorfhip. But the fcheme did not fucceed; and only 18000*l.* was fubfcribed.

NOTE (15).——LIFE ANNUITIES. See page 124.—— The annuities on *two* lives in 1694, were fold at 12*l. per ann.* during *two* lives, of any ages, and the annuities on *three* lives, at 10*l. per ann.* during *three* lives, for every 100*l.* advanced.——This was very extravagant; for, fuppofing the annuitants in general, about the age of 20 or 30, it was the fame, in the cafe of *two* lives, with giving above 10 *per cent.* for money, and in the cafe of three lives, 9 *per cent.*—— It is, likewife, extremely abfurd in thefe cafes to pay no regard to difference of ages. A *fingle* life at the age of 60, fuppofing money improved at 4 *per cent.* is intitled to 11 *per cent.* but at the age of 10, fcarcely to 6 *per cent.* *Two* lives at 60, are entitled, on the fame fuppofition, to 8 ½ *per cent.* but at 10, not to 5 *per cent.*——The original amount of thefe annuities was 22,700*l.* nearly. In 1762, that is, in 68 years, they were reduced by deaths no lower than 9,215*l.*

The other life-annuities mentioned in the preceding account were *douceurs* granted for loans in 1745, 1746, and 1757. An account of the annuities granted in the laft of thefe years may be feen in page 101.

The life-annuities in 1745, amounted to 22,500*l.* and were granted, together with the profits of a lottery, for a loan of two millions at 4 *per cent.*

The

The life-annuities in 1746, amounted to 45,000*l.* and were granted, with the profits of another lottery, for a loan of three millions, at the fame intereft.——The remarks made in the 3d fection of the laft part, and particularly in the note, p. 101, are applicable to thefe two loans. The value of the life-annuities, and the profits of the lotteries, were made a part of the public debt. And, fuppofing the life-annuities worth, one with another, only 14 years purchafe, and the profits of the two lotteries worth 300,000 *l.* it will follow, that the capital created by thefe loans, inftead of being 5.000,000*l.* fhould have been only 3.755,000*l.*

But there is another remark, which it is proper to mention here. The life-annuities granted in 1757, amounting to 33,750*l.* were, in January 1775, that is in 18 years, reduced by deaths to 28,732*l.* or but a little more than a feventh part. But, fuppofing the annuitants all in the firmeft ftage of life, or between the age of 10 and 30, they ought, according to fome of the beft tables of obfervations, to have been reduced a *quarter*. Thefe life-annuities have, therefore, fallen in much more flowly than could have been expected ; and I have found the fame to be true of all the other life-annuities.——The reafon, undoubtedly, is, that the tables exhibit the rate of mortality among all forts and orders of men taken together ; whereas, the lives on which annuities are bought, are a felection of the better fort of lives from the general mafs, and therefore muft be of greater value. —— Indeed I am not acquainted with any table of obfervations which gives the probabilities of the duration of life high enough to be a guide in this cafe ; except that which was formed by Mr. *De Parcieux,* from the French *Tontines.*——A calculation, therefore, of the values of lives, agreeably to this table, would be of confiderable ufe.

Note (16).——Unfunded Debt. See page 124.—— I have given the navy debt, as it was in January, 1775.—— The civil lift debt in 1775, was probably more than the fum at which I have reckoned it. Lord Stair, in his account of the national debt, income, and expenditure, reckons it at 800,000*l.*

Much

Much the greateſt part of the foregoing debts, with the taxes for paying the intereſt, including the duties compoſing the *Aggregate*, *South-Sea*, and *General* Funds, have, by the 25th of *George* the Second, 1751, and ſeveral ſubſequent acts of Parliament, been thrown into one general account; and the *ſurplus* of the whole, after deducting the intereſt, 800,000l. *per ann.* to the civil liſt, and a few other payments, forms the SINKING FUND.——The debts not brought to this account are about ſeven millions and a half in the *South-Sea* Houſe; 11.186,800l. of the *Bank* capital; the Civil Liſt million; four millions and a half borrowed at $3\frac{1}{2}$ *per cent.* in 1758; the capital of the Eaſt-India annuity; and the Exchequer long and life annuities, except thoſe granted in 1758. But the *ſurpluſſes* of the duties which pay the intereſt of theſe debts are either carried *immediately* into the *Sinking Fund* account; or brought *firſt* to the *Aggregate* Fund, and from thence carried into that account.——On the contrary. Deficiencies in theſe duties when they happen, are made good out of the Sinking Fund; and afterwards replaced from the ſupplies.

For example. Three old nine-penny exciſes on beer, with an additional three-pence per barrel, producing above half a million annually; alſo, 3,700 l. *per* week out of the hereditary exciſe on

beer,

beer, together with some duties on paper, coals,
&c. and $\frac{1}{3}$ additional subsidy of tonnage and
poundage, are appropriated to the payment of
the Banker's Annuity; the Life Annuities granted
in 1693 and 1694; the Exchequer Long Annuities; and annuities on various sums subscribed
to the South-Sea Company in 1720. The surplusses make a part of the *Aggregate Fund*; and
after contributing to satisfy the charge on that
fund, are carried into the *Sinking Fund.*——
Again. Certain additional duties on soap, parch-
ment, coals, &c. are appropriated to pay the
interest of 1.250,000l. and of 1.750,000l. parts
of the Bank capital.——The surplusses are carried *directly* to the *Sinking Fund.*——In like manner. The duties on houses and windows imposed by an act of the 20th of *George* the Second,
1747, (*a*) after deducting from them 91,485l.
per ann. to satisfy certain charges on old house-
duties in the *Aggregate Fund*; and, also, other
duties on houses and windows imposed by the
2d and 6th of *George* the Third, amounting in
all to about 205,000l. *per ann.* are carried into the
Sinking Fund, together with the capitals, the in-

(*a*) These duties were appropriated to the payment of the
interest at 4 *per cent.* of a capital of 4.400,000l. created in
1747, for which four millions only had been advanced. It
is now a part of the capital of the reduced 3 *per cent.* annuities.   7

terest

tereſt of which has been charged upon them. But the addition to theſe duties (with a tax on penſions) granted in 1758, and charged with the intereſt (at 3 ½ *per cent.*) of the loan in that year, having not been carried into the *Sinking Fund,* and proving deficient ; the deficiency is conſtantly made good out of this fund, and afterwards re-placed from the ſupplies.

State and Amount of the NATIONAL DEBT *at Chriſtmas* 1753 ; *with the Charges of Management.*

BANK OF ENGLAND.

	Principal. £.	Intereſt. £.
BANK capital —	11.686,800	393,038
Of this capital 3.200,000l. bore at this time 3 *per cent.* intereſt ; and the remainder bore 3 ½ *per cent.* till 1757, by 23d Geo. II. 1749.——See note (1) p. 125.		
Management 5,898l. *per ann.*		
Three *per cent.* BANK An-nuities conſolidated by 25 Geo. II. 1751.—See note (6) p. 127. —	9.137,821	274,135
Management 4,450l. *per ann.*		
Total £20.824,621		667,173

BANK

	Principal. £.	Interest. £.
Brought over	20.824,621	667,173
BANK Annuities consolidated by 25 Geo. II. 2.713,618l. carrying 3¼ *per cent.* interest till 1755; and 14.857,956l. carrying the same interest till 1757. See note (7) p. 128. —	17,7401,32	619,546
Management 9,884l. *per ann.*		
Civil List million, 1726	1.000,000	30,000
Management 360l. *per ann.* Whole charge of Management at the Bank in 1753—20,592l. *per ann.*		
SOUTH-SEA COMPANY.		
SOUTH-SEA Stock carrying 4 *per cent.* till 1757 —	3.662,784	146,511
Old and New SOUTH-SEA Annuities carrying 3¼ *per cent.* till 1757 —	21.362,525	747,688
Three *per cent.* 1751— See note (10) p. 131.	2.100,000	63,000
Whole charge of management at the *South-Sea-House* on stock and annuities, 15,748l. *per ann.*		
EAST-INDIA HOUSE.		
EAST-INDIA STOCK, redued to 3¼ till 1757	3.200,000	112,000
	£.69.851,254	2.385,918

EAST

	Principal.	Intereſt.
	£.	£.
Brought over	69.851,254	2.385,918
EAST-INDIA annuity 1744	1.000,000	30,000
Management 1,687l. 10s. per ann.		
Total (a)	£.70,851,254	2.415,918

(a) The whole of this ſum, (except 16.437,821l. conſiſting of the old Bank capital, the conſolidated 3 per cents, the South-Sea 3 per cent. annuities 1751, the Civil Liſt million, and the Eaſt-India annuity) that is, 54.413,433l. was reduced by 23 Geo. II. 1749, from an intereſt of 4 per cent. to 3 ½ till 1757, and afterwards to 3 per cent.——The proprietors of a capital of 3.290,042l. refuſed to conſent to this reduction, which, therefore, was paid off; 1.190,042l. with Exchequer Bills (afterwards cancelled) ; and 2.100,000l. with money borrowed at 3 per cent. and added to the capital of the South-Sea annuities. The whole ſum, therefore, reduced and paid off, was 57.703,475l. which produced a ſaving to the public, and an addition to the Sinking Fund after 1757, of 612,735l. per ann.

The SALT DUTIES in 1753 had been for ſome time mortgaged to pay the principal and intereſt of a million borrowed in 1745. In 1757, after clearing the mortgage, they became free, and were carried into the Sinking Fund, of which they have ever ſince formed a part. This produced a farther addition to the Sinking Fund, after 1757, of about 220,000l. per ann.

I have not included the million now mentioned in the account given above of the public debts in 1753, becauſe it was in a fixed courſe of redemption ; nor have I included 499,600l. in Exchequer Bills charged on the duty on ſweets, becauſe theſe Exchequer Bills were paid off in 1754.

EXCHEQUER

	Principal. £.	Intereſt. £.
Brought over £70.851,254	70.851,254	2.415,918

EXCHEQUER.

ANNUITIES for 96 and 99 years from various dates in King *William*'s and Queen *Anne*'s times being the original ſum contributed. See note (13) page 132. — 1.836,276 / 131,203

Management 5,230l. *per ann.* incluſive of management for the two next articles.

ANNUITIES for lives with benefit of ſurvivorſhip, being the original ſum contributed — 108,100 / 7,567

ANNUITIES for two and three lives, being the remainder after deduct-ing the annuities fallen in by deaths, and reck-oned worth 10 years purchaſe — — 106,650 / 10,665

ANNUITIES for ſingle lives 1745, being the re-mainder after deducting the annuities fallen in by deaths; and reckon-ed worth 14 years pur-chaſe — . — 296,142 / 21,153

£.73.198,422 | 2.586,506

ANNUITIES

	Principal. £.	Intereſt. £.
Brought over	73.198,422	2.586,506
ANNUITIES for ſingle lives 1746, being the remainder after the lives fallen in ——	582,274	41,591
Navy debt in 1754—Intereſt reckoned at 2 per cent. ——	1.296,568	25,931
Total of the principal and intereſt of the public debts in 1753 ——	£.75.077,264	2.654,028

STATE *and* AMOUNT *of the* NATIONAL DEBT *in* 1739.

BANK OF ENGLAND.

	Principal. £.	Intereſt. £.
BANK CAPITAL, conſiſting of 1.600,000l. old capital carrying 6 per cent; and 7.500,000 l. carrying 4 per cent. See note 1, p. 123. —— ——	9.100,000	396,000
BANK ANNUITIES at 3 per cent. for the lottery in 1731. —— ——	800,000	24,000
	£.9.900,000	420,000

SOUTH-

	Principal. £.	Interest. £.
Brought over	623,312	2.321,215
SOUTH-SEA COMPANY. Stock and annuities bearing 4 *per cent.* — —	27.302,203	1.092,088
EAST-INDIA COMPANY. EAST-INDIA stock carrying 4 *per cent.* —	3.200,000	128,000
EXCHEQUER ANNUITIES. Annuities at 3 ½ by 4 Geo. II. paid off in 1752	400,000	14,000
ANNUITIES at 4 *per cent.* charged on the duty on wrought plate by 6 Geo. I. 1720 — —	312,000	12,480
182,250 l. of this capital was paid off in 1750. The remainder is now included in the capital of the reduced 3 *per cent.* annuities.		
ANNUITIES at 3 *per cent.* charged on the Sinking-Fund by 9 and 10 Geo. II. Now included in the consolidated 3 *per cent.* annuities —	900,000	27,000
ANNUITIES on *Nevis* and St. *Christopher* Debentures at 3 *per cent.* Now included in the consolidated 3 *per cents.* —	37,821	1,135
	£.42,052,024	1.694,703

EXCHEQUER

	Principal.	Interest.
	£.	£.
Brought over	42.052,024	1.694,703
EXCHEQUER BILLS charged on a duty upon victuallers by 12 Geo. I. 1726—Carrying 3 *per cent.* — —	480,000	14,400
EXCHEQUER BILLS charged on a duty on sweets by 10 of Geo. II. 1737— Carrying 3 *per cent.* and paid off in 1754—See the note p. 140. —	499,600	14,988
ANNUITIES for long terms from various dates —	1.836,276	131,203
ANNUITIES for lives with *benefit* of *Survivorship* granted in 1693 —	108,100	7,567
ANNUITIES for two and three lives, 1694 —	106,650	15,000
Navy debt (*a*) —	1.300,000	26,000
Total of the *Principal* and *Interest* of the National Debt in 1739 (*b*) £.46.382,650		1.903,861

(*a*) Having met with no account of the Navy Debt at this time, I have chosen, rather than omit it, to suppose it nearly the same that it was at the commencement of the last war; which, probably, is reckoning it too high.

(*b*) In this account I have omitted a million borrowed in 1734, because the redemption of it was near being completed by the Salt Duties. I have also omitted *Short Annuities* amounting to 24,334l. being the remainder of 9 *per cent.* annuities for 32 years created in 1710, because the term for which they were created was near expiring.

From

From the account in the POSTSCRIPT, at the end of this tract, it will appear, that 10.639,793l. of the public debt was difcharged between the years 1763 and 1775; and alfo that the *funded* debt was, in 1775, 1,400,000l. greater than it was at the end of the laft war. From hence, and from the amount of the public debt in 1775, as ftated in page 124, it follows, that the funded debt at the end of the war was 130.943,051 l. and the whole debt 146.582,844l. and, confequently, that the war left upon the nation an *unfunded debt* amounting to (a) 15.639,793l. This unfunded debt confifted of the following particulars—Of 3,500,000l. borrowed after the peace in 1763, and applied towards bearing fuch expences of the war as could not immediately ceafe with its operations. ——Of near *eight millions* in navy, victualling, ordnance, and tranfport debts.——Of 1.800,000l.

(a) The author of the *Confiderations on the Trade and Finances of this Kingdom* makes this debt 1.318,000 l. more than the fum at which I have here ftated it. See page 22; and *State of the Nation* by the fame auther, page 15, quarto editions.———The reafon of this difference is, that this writer has included in the unfunded debt left by the war the deficiencies of grants and funds in 1763 and 1764, and the *whole* army debt not provided for in thofe years; whereas I have excluded the former entirely; and admitted only as much of the latter as exceeded the army debts common in fubfequent years. See the Poftfcript.

Exchequer bills; and the remainder, of subsidies to foreign princes, extraordinaries of the army, and German demands.

In the interval of peace between 1748 and 1755 the following debts were paid off.

	£.
Bank Annuities bearing 4 *per cent.* —	1.013,148
SOUTH-SEA Annuities bearing 4 *per cent.* —	176,893
Annuities bearing 3 ½ *per cent.* charged by 4 Geo. II. on additional Stamp-duties —	400,000
EXCHEQUER Bills bearing 3 *per cent.* charged by 10 Geo. II. 1737 on the duties on sweets —	499,600
Borrowed in 1745 at 3 ½ *per cent.* on the credit of the Salt duties —	1.000,000
See note, page 140.	

(*a*) Total £.3.089,641

(*b*) In 1751 there was applied to the payment of Navy debts 200,000l. and in 1752, the sum of 900,000l. But I have not reckoned these sums, because they did little more than make up the constant deficiency in the *Peace Establishment* for the Navy.

From

From the whole, the following account of the progreſs of the National Debt, from 1739 to 1775, may be deduced.

	Principal £.	Intereſt £.
Amount of the principal and intereſt of the national debt before the war which begun in 1740 — —	46.382,650	1.903,861
Amount in 1749 immediately after the war	78.166,906	2.765,608
Increaſed by the war —	31.784,256	861,747
Diminiſhed by the Peace from 1748 to 1755	3.089,641	111,590
Amount at the commencement of the laſt war — —	75.077,264	2.654,018
Amount at the end of the war in 1763 —	146.582,844	4.840,821
Increaſed by the laſt war	71.505,580	2.186,803
Diminiſhed by the Peace, in twelve years from 1763 to 1775 —	10.639,793	(a) 400,000
Amount at Midſummer, 1775 — —	135.943,051	4.440,821

We are now involved in another war, and the public debts are increaſing again faſt. *Exchequer* Bills have been increaſed from 1.250,000l. to 1.500,000l. A new capital of 2.150,000l. has been added to the 3 *per cent.* Conſolidated An-

(a) See the Poſtſcript.

L 2

nuities,

nuities. And a vote of credit was given in the
laſt ſeſſion of Parliament for a million. The laſt
year, therefore, has added 3.400,000l. to our
debts, beſides a vaſt ſum not yet provided for,
conſiſting of navy, ordnance, victualling, tranſport
and army debts.———The preſent year (1777) muſt
make another great addition to them; and what
they will be at the end of theſe troubles, no one
can tell.———The union of a *foreign* war to the
preſent *civil* war might perhaps raiſe them to
Two Hundred Millions; but, more probably,
it would ſink them to———Nothing.

S E C T. III.

Of the Debts *and* Resources *of* France.

MINISTERS have of late ſought to remove the public apprehenſions by general
accounts of the weakneſs of powers, which, from
the circumſtances of former wars as well as national prejudices, have been felt by the people as
jealous rivals or formidable enemies.———I wiſh it
was poſſible for me to confirm theſe accounts; and
by contraſting the preceding ſtate of our own
debts with a ſimilar one of thoſe of France, to
ſhew, that from this power in particular we have
nothing to fear. The following particulars, on
the

the correctnefs of which I can rely, may give fome affiftance in judging of this fubject.

The whole expence of the laft war to FRANCE was 1.118.307,047 livres; that is, 49.702,000 l. fterling. of which 23.152,000 l. (520.926,000 livres) confifted of money procured by the fale of taxes, by free-gifts, and extra-impofitions during the war, which left behind them no debts: And 26.550,000 l. (597.380,100 livres) confifted of LOANS, or money raifed on perpetual annuities, life-annuities, and lotteries.—At the beginning of 1769 the whole amount of the debts of *France*, including all arrears and capitals advanced on an-nuities and lotteries, was 128.622,000 l. fterling, or 2.894.053,616 livres. The annual charge de-rived from this debt was 6.707,500 l. fterling (150.919,284 livres)——All the appropriations amounted to 8.218,500 l. fterling (184.919,284 livres).——The expences of the army, navy, king's houfhold, prince's houfhold, foreign affairs, &c. amounted to 8.947,000 l. or 201.307,312 livres. So that the whole annual expence was 17.165,000 l. (386.226,596 livres).--The whole re-venue had amounted, before 1769, to 13.484,500 l. fterling (303.401,696 livres).———The public ex-pence, therefore, had exceeded the revenue 3.681,000 l. (82.860,000 livres) *per ann.*

L 3   From

From the year 1769 to the prefent King's Acceffion, by forced reductions of intereft, and by
new taxes, the public revenue was carried to
16.289,000l. fterling (366.508,000 livres) and
the public expence was reduced fo as not to exceed the revenue above 766,800l. *per annum*
(17.253,000 livres).——The anticipations alfo of
the revenue, which before 1769 had extended to
feventeen months, were reduced to *five* months.——
Such was the progrefs of reformation; namely,
an increafe of revenue amounting to little lefs
than THREE MILLIONS fterling *per ann.* in a few
years, under an unpopular minifter, in the latter
days of a reign never characterized by an attention
to oeconomy, or a regard to the public intereft;
and at this time particularly ftamped by unpre-
cedented profufion and a general relaxation.

A new reign produced a new minifter of
finance whofe name will be refpected by pofterity
for a fet of meafures as new to the *political* world,
as any late difcoveries in the fyftem of nature
have been to the *philofophical* world.——Doubtful in
their operation, as all unproved meafures muft be,
but diftinguifhed by their tendency to lay a folid
foundation for endlefs peace, induftry, and a general
enjoyment of the gifts of nature, arts, and commerce.——The edicts iffued during his adminiftration exhibit indeed a phænomenon of the
moft extraordinary kind. An abfolute king rendering

dering a voluntary account to his fubjects, and
inciting his people to *think*; a right which it has
been the bufinefs of all abfolute princes and their
minifters to extinguifh in the minds of men.——
In thefe edicts the king declared in the moft
diftinct terms againft a bankruptcy, an augmentation of taxes, and new loans; while the minifter
applied himfelf to increafe every public refource
by principles more liberal than *France*, or any
part of *Europe*, ever had in ferious contempla-
tion.——It is much to be regretted, that the oppofition he met with, and the intrigues of a
court, fhould have deprived the world of thofe
lights which muft have refulted from the example
of fuch an adminiftration.

After a fhort interval, a nomination, in fome
refpects ftill more extraordinary, has taken place in
the court of FRANCE. A court which a few years
fince was diftinguifhed by its bigotry and into-
lerance, has raifed a *Proteftant*, the fubject of a
fmall but virtuous republic, to a decifive lead in
the regulation of its finances. It is to be pre-
fumed, that fo fingular a preference will produce
an equally fingular exertion of integrity and ta-
lents. Though differing from Monfieur TURGOT
in feveral principles, which regard the larger
lines of government, he appears by his firft fteps,
and, particularly, the preamble to a late edict

for raifing 24 millions of livres by a lottery, to put his foot on the fame great bafis of general juftice, and a ftrict confervation of the faith of the king; and points more particularly at the fureft of all refources in any modern ftates, a fimplification of taxes and a reformation in the collection of them. This adminiftration, making improvements in the Revenue its immediate ob-ject, is more capable of prefent exertion; and, as fuch, is more formidable.

From thefe facts and obfervations it is impof-fible not to conclude, that if we truft our fafety to the difficulties of FRANCE, we may find our-felves fatally deceived. I will add, that though (like the 3 s. land-tax and lotteries among our-felves) fome of the extraordinary impofitions of the laft war have been continued in *France*, there are fome which ceafed with the war, and which they can renew. It is, particularly, an advantage of unfpeakable importance to them, that they can carry on a war, as they did the laft, at *half* our ex-pence; and that, having no dependence on the flat-tering delufion of paper, they can, as they did in 1759, bear even a bankruptcy in the middle of a war, and yet carry it on vigoroufly.—Their debts time itfelf is finking faft. Of 3.511,000 l. (feventy mil-lions of livres) in annuities on the *Hotel de Ville* at *Paris*, 1.777,000 l. (forty millions of livres) confifted

in

in 1774 of Life Annuities, which were falling by deaths at the rate of 71,000l. (1.600,000 livres) every year.——Even their lofs of credit, whatever prefent embarraffment attends it, favours them upon the whole. To this they owe the advantages juft mentioned. The facility with which our high credit has enabled us to run in debt enfnares us; and, if a change of meafures does not take place, (a) muft *ruin* us. Experience has given them a juft horror at borrowing on permanent funds; and were they inclined to do it, they are not able to do it to any great amount; and, confequently, they cannot go on mortgaging one refource after another till none is left.——While we lofe fight of the capital in the intereft, they carry their views chiefly to the reimburfement of the capital; and after receiving high intereft, for fome years, can be fatisfied with receiving back a part of their capital.——Their debts, being confined in a great meafure to the *Farmers General* and others at PARIS, are not circulated and diffufed among the body of the people in the manner ours are: And it is well known, that they can make ufe of methods to difcharge them which our government muft never think of. The acts of arbitrary power and unjuft expedients to which, on many occa-

(a) " Either the nation (Mr. Hume fays) muft deftroy " public credit, or public credit will deftroy the nation." Political Effays, page 135.

fions,

fions, they have had recourfe for this purpofe without producing any tumults, are fuch as appear to us almoft incredible ; and fhould the time ever come, when it will be neceffary in this country to make ufe of any violence of the fame kind, all government will probably be at an end.

In point of territory and number of inhabitants, the two countries will bear no comparifon (*a*). We have hitherto oppofed *France* by our free fpirit, and our colonies ; and to them chiefly we owe our profperity and victories. Our colonies once feparated from us, the iflands will foon follow. But fhould they remain ours, our comparative advantages will beft appear from the following authentic account of the imports into *France* from their iflands.

In 1774.

	Weight in Pounds.
Sugar imported into *France* —	147.986,959
Indigo — — —	1.734,206
Rocou — — —	210,187
Coffee — — —	58.247,133
	208.178,485

(*a*) The number of inhabitants in *France* is 26 millions. In *Britain* it cannot exceed fix or feven millions. See p. 66. And *Obfervations on Reverfionary Payments*, page 185, third edition.

In

	Weight in Pounds.
Sugar imported into *France*. —	171.932,972
Indigo ——— ——	2.134,247
Rocou — — — —	169,831
Coffee — —— —	58.545,000
	(*a*) 232.782,050

Value of the above commodities re-exported from *France*, taken upon the average price.

	Livres.	Sterling.
In 1774 —	75.901,373 —	3.373,000
In 1775 —	74.961,318 —	3.331,000

The whole importation from the *West Indies* into *Britain* is about three millions *per ann.*

But I have gone much beyond the views with which I begun this section. The facts which have been stated, and the reflections which they have occasioned, are intended principally to shew that we ought not to suffer ourselves to be drawn into security by any assurances of the weakness of *France.* — May she, however, find herself the weakest of kingdoms whenever, from motives of

(*a*) Near one half of all this importation is made into *Bourdeaux* only; and the rest into *Rochelle, Marseilles, Nantz, Havre,* and *Honfleur.*

interest

intereſt or ambition, ſhe ſhall attempt to injure any of her neighbours.——May *Britain*, hitherto the moſt favoured ſpot under heaven, always preſerve her diſtinguiſhed happineſs, and eſcape the danger which now threatens her. And may the time ſoon come, when all mankind, ſenſible of the value of the bleſſings of peace and equal liberty, ſhall ſuffer one another to enjoy them, and learn war no more.

S E C T. IV.

Containing an Account of the National Income and Expenditure; the Surplus of the Revenue; and the Money drawn from the Public by the Taxes; with Remarks on Lord STAIR'S *Account.*

APPROPRIATED REVENUE *at Midsummer,* 1775.

	£.
Interest of the national debt —	4.440,821
Civil list revenue. See the note in page 163 ————	800,000
Expences of management attending the national debt; of which 71,432 l. is the expence of management at the Bank, South-Sea House, and *India* House; and 5.900 l. salaries to *Exchequer Officers.* See Page 119, &c. —	77,332
Annuities payable out of the Aggregate Fund to the DUKE OF GLOUCESTER, 8000 l.—DUKE OF CUMBERLAND, 8000 l.—the Representatives of ARTHUR ONSLOW, Esq; 3000 l.—And the Sheriffs of ENGLAND and WALES, 4000 l.—In all	23,000

Clerk

Clerk of the Hanaper in Chancery—
Coinage (*a*) expence——Tenths
and firſt-fruits of the Clergy appropriated to the augmentation
of ſmall livings—Extra revenues
of the crown, conſiſting of *American* quit-rents; duty of 4¼ *per
cent.* in the Leeward Iſlands;
revenues of Gibraltar and dutchy
of *Cornwall*, &c.—Fees for warrants and orders, for auditing
and engroſſing accounts of dividend warrants, and other charges
at the EXCHEQUER and TREA-
SURY (*b*) —— 100,000

Total of the Appropriated Revenue £. 5.441,153

(*a*) In order to defray the expence of coinage, a duty of 10 s.
per ton has been laid on wines imported; and, as far as this
duty happens to fall ſhort of 15,000 l. the deficiency is made
good out of the ſupplies.

(*b*) I am not able to give the exact amount of this part of
the appropriated revenue. I have, therefore, reckoned it at
ſuch a round ſum, as, I think, cannot much exceed or fall
ſhort of it.

State of the SURPLUS *of the* REVENUE *for*
11 *years ended at* 1775.

UNAPPROPRIATED REVENUE.

NEAT PRODUCE of the Sinking Fund, for five years, including casual surpluses, reckoning to *Christmas* in every year; being the annual medium, after deducting from it about 45,000 l. always carried to it from the supplies, in order to replace so much taken from it every year to make good a deficiency in a Fund established in 1758. — —	£. 2.610,759
Neat annual produce of Land Tax at 3s. militia deducted; and of the Malt Tax *(a)* — —	1.800,000
(N. B. These two taxes in 1773, brought in only 1.665,475 l.)	
There are some casual Receipts, not included in the Sinking Fund, such as Savings in Pay-Office, duties on Gum Senega, American Revenue, &c. But they are so uncertain and inconsiderable, that it is scarcely proper to give them as a part of the permanent Revenue. Add however on this account —	50,000
Total of unappropriated Revenue	£. 4.460,759

(a) The Land-tax at 3 s. is given by Parliament for 1.500,000 l.; and the Malt-tax for 750,000 l. but they are always greatly deficient.—Both these taxes (and also sometimes the income of the Sinking Fund) are borrowed of the *Bank*, and spent long before they come into the Exchequer; and therefore, are debts constantly due to the Bank, for which interest is paid.

Produce

Produce of the SINKING FUND, *reckoned to* Christmas *in every Year.*

1770 ———	£.2.486,836
1771 ———	2.553,505
1772 ———	2.683,831
1773 ———	2.823,150
1774 ———	2.731,476

The average of thefe five years is 2.655,759 l. or, deducting 45,000 l. (as directed in the laft page), 2.610,759 l.

In 1775, the Sinking Fund was taken for 2.900,000 l. including an extraordinary charge of 100,000 l. on the *Aggregate* Fund ; but it produced 2.917,869 l. The average of fix years, including 1775, was 2.654,443 l. The average of five years before 1770, was 2.234,780 l.

ANNUAL EXPENDITURE.

	£.
Peace Eftablifhment, for the Navy and Army, including all mifcellaneous and incidental expences	3.700,000
Annual increafe of the Navy and Civil Lift debts — —	350,000
Intereft at 2 *per cent.* of 3.600,000 l. unfunded debt, which muft be paid out of the unappropriated Revenue — — —	72,000
Total	4.122,000
ANNUAL SURPLUS of the Revenue	338,759
Annual income £.	4.460,759

The

The eftimate for the peace eftablifhment, including mifcellaneous expences, amounted, in
1775, to 3.703,476 l.—But the extraordinary expences, occafioned by the war with America,
made it fall very fhort.—In 1774 it amounted to
3.784,452 l. exclufive of 250,000 l. raifed by Exchequer Bills, towards defraying the expence of
calling in the gold coin. And the medium for e-
leven years, from 1765, has been nearly 3.700,000l.
— According to the accounts which I have collected, the expence of the peace eftablifhment (including mifcellaneous expences) was in 1765,
1766, and 1767, 3.540,000 l. *per ann.*—In 1768,
1769, and 1770, it was 3.354,000l. *per ann.*——
In 1771, 1772, 1773, 1774, and 1775, the average has been nearly four millions *per ann.* exclufive of the expence of calling in the coin.

The parliament votes for the fea fervice 4 l.
per month *per* man, including wages, wear and
tear, victuals and ordnance. This allowance is
infufficient, and falls fhort every year more or lefs,
in proportion to the number of men voted. From
hence, in a great meafure, arifes that annual increafe of the navy debt, mentioned in the fecond
article of the *National Expenditure.* This increafe
in 1772 and 1773 was 669,996 l. or 335,000l. *per
ann.* The number of men voted in thofe two
years, was 20,000. I have fuppofed them reduced to 16,000, and the annual increafe of the Navy

M   Debt

Debt to be only 250,000 l.——Add 100,000 l. for the annual increafe of the Civil Lift Debt, and the total will be 350,000 l.

Soon after the publication of the preceding account in *February* laft year, the EARL OF STAIR obliged the public with another account of the fame kind, which brings out a conclufion much more unfavourable. According to this account, were lotteries abolifhed, and the land-tax at 3 s. in the pound only, there would be a *deficiency* in the revenue, inftead of fuch a *furplus* as I have ftated. The following remarks will fhew the reafon of this difference.

The EARL OF STAIR has taken the annual produce of the *Sinking* Fund at 2.506,400 l. being the average produce of EIGHT years ended at *Lady day* 1775.——I have taken it at 2.610,759 l. being the average of FIVE years ended at *Chriftmas* 1775.——The neat produce of the land and malt taxes has been alfo taken near 50,000 l. higher in my account; and I have befides admitted 50,000 l. *per ann.* for cafual fupplies, which his Lordfhip has not charged.

The annual increafe of the Navy Debt, LORD STAIR ftates at 300,000 l. and of the Civil Lift at 200,000 l. I have ftated the former at 250,000 l. and the latter at 100,000 l.——In order alfo to avoid, as much as poffible, all exaggeration, I have thrown out the expence of the new coinage. Lord Stair has admitted it, and given an yearly

expence

expence derived from hence of 100,000 l.——
He has alfo taken the Peace Eftablifhment for
1774, as a fair medium for common years of
peace, becaufe it was lower in that year than in
the three years preceding 1775. I have taken
the average of *eleven* years of peace, which is
75,000 l. lefs.

In confequence of thefe differences, the national
PEACE expenditure in *Lord Stair*'s account comes
out 325,000 l. *per ann. higher* than in mine; and
the national income comes out 204,359 l. *lower*;
from whence it follows, that without lotteries,
and the land being at 3s. in the pound, the kingdom muft, according to his Lordfhip's calculation,
run out at the rate of about 200,000l. every year.

In fome of the particulars I have mentioned,
this account is probably neareft to the truth; but,
I hope, it will be confidered, that I have ftudied
to give moderate accounts, and aimed at erring
always rather on the favourable than the unfavourable fide.

Second Method of deducing the SURPLUS *of
the* REVENUE.

From the year 1763 to the year 1775, or during
a period of 12 years, 10.639,793 l. of the public
(*a*) debt was paid off.——The money employed for

(*a*) The account given by Lord North at opening the
Budget in 1775, was, that the public debt had been diminifhed
fince 1763, near nine millions and a half. The grounds on
which I have ftated this diminution at 10.639,793 l. may be
feen in the POSTSCRIPT, p. 171.

this

this purpose muft have been derived from the furplus of the *ordinary* revenue, added to the *extraordinary* receipts. Thefe receipts have confifted of the following articles.——1ft. The land-tax at 4s. in the pound in 1764, 1765, 1766, and 1771 ; or 1s. in the pound extraordinary for four years, making 1.750,000 l.——2. The profits of ten lotteries (*a*) making (at 150,000l. each lottery) 1.500,000 l.——3. A contribution of 400,000 l. *per ann.* for five years from the EAST INDIA Company, making 2.000,000 l.——4. Savings by debts difcharged at a difcount, (*b*) making at leaft 400,000 l.——5. Paid by the Bank in 1764 for the renewal of their charter, 110,000l.—6. Savings on high grants during the war ; produce of *French* prizes taken before the declaration of war; fale of lands in the ceded iflands ; and compofition for maintaining *French* prifoners, (*c*) making 2.520,000 l.

(*a*) Four of thefe lotteries have been annexed to annuities ; but it would be a great miftake to think that they have not been equally profitable with the other lotteries. For inftance ; in 1767, a million and a half was borrowed on an annuity of 45,000l. with a lottery of 60,000 tickets annexed. In the fame year, 2.616,777 l. was paid off; but, had it not been for the lottery, only 1.350,000l. could have been raifed on the annuity ; and 150,000l. lefs muft have been paid off.

(*b*) The difcounts on a million and a half paid off in 1772, and two millions paid off in 1774 and 1775, amounted nearly to this fum.

(*c*) The particular fums may be found in a pamphlet, entitled, *The Prefent State of the Nation*, p. 28, quarto edition.

2.520,000 l. ———— All these sums amount to 8.280,000l. There remains to make up 10.639,793l. (the whole debt discharged) 2.359,793 l. and this, therefore, is the amount of the whole surplus of the *ordinary* revenue for twelve years; or 196,000l. *per ann. (b)*

The Earl of STAIR has also, in this method, calculated the *surplus* of the Revenue; and makes the total, for eleven years, to be no more than 2.557,378 l. even with the assistance of lotteries, and the land-tax at 4 s. in the pound for five years; from whence it follows, that *without* these assistances, there would have been a deficiency of near 60,000 l. *per ann.*—The reason is, that his Lordship has taken the whole debt paid since 1763, at no more than 7.053,855 l. or three millions and a half less than I have made it; and he has taken it so much less, chiefly in consequence of including in the amount of the public debt in 1775, the excess of the expences of that year above the common peace expences. This excess is to be charged to the present war; and, in determining the ordinary peace *surplus*, which is my

tion. But I have not included all the sums there enumerated; nor have I admitted the Army savings in 1772, and some other smaller sums.

(b) This surplus, being the medium for the whole 12 years of peace, is less than that in p. 160, which is the medium at the end of this period, when the Sinking-Fund produced above a quarter more than it did at the beginning of it.

M 3   object,

object, it was proper to exclude it, and to terminate
the account at the commencement of the war.——
I will only add, that Lord STAIR has alfo included
more in the extraordinary receipts than I have;
and, particularly, 700,000 l. which he fuppofes
the public gained by the TEA INDEMNITY.——
But this was only a compenfation made by the
Eaſt-India Company for the loſs which the public
fuſtained by taking off, in 1766, a part (or 1 s. *per*
pound) of the duty on tea. In 1772 it was re-
ſtored; and the excife upon tea has fince, if I am
rightly informed, produced as much as ever.
Before 1766, it produced annually 474,091 l. Immediately (*a*) after 1766, it produced 341,284 l.——
But in 1775, it produced near half a million.

*Sketch of an Account of the Money drawn from
the Public by the Taxes, before the Year* 1776.

CUSTOMS in ENGLAND, being the
medium of the payments into the
Exchequer, for 3 years ending in   *£.*
1773 (*b*)   ——   ——   ——   2.528,275
Amount of the EXCISES in ENG-
LAND, including the malt tax,

being

(*a*) I have here taken the average of two years before and
after 1766.

(*b*) The annual medium of the payments into the Exchequer
from the CUSTOMS in ENGLAND, for the laſt five years, has
been

being the medium of 3 years   £.

ending in 1773   — —   4.649,892

Land Tax at 3 s.   — —   1.300,000

been 2.521,769l.—In 1774 the payment into the Exchequer was 2.547,717 l.—In 1775, it was 2.476,302l.—The produce of the CUSTOMS, therefore, has been given rather too high.

The produce of the EXCISES in England has been higher, in 1772 and 1775, than in any two years before 1776; but the average of any three succeffive years, or of all the five years fince 1770, will not differ much from the fum I have given.— In 1754, or the year before the laſt war, the CUSTOMS produced only 1.558,254l.——The Excifes, exclufive of the Malt-tax, produced 2.819,702 l,——And the whole revenue, exclufive of the Malt-tax and Land-tax at 2s. was 5.097,617l. —In 1753 the whole revenue was 5.189,745 l. And the appropriation or annual charge upon it, (confifting of the Civil Lift, 834,443l. intereft of the national debt, exclufive of navy debt, 2.628,087l. expences of management, 43,691l. 4¼ per cent. from the Leeward Iſlands 27,378l. annuity to the late Duke of Cumberland 25,000l. firſt-fruits and tenths of the Clergy 13,597l. &c. &c.) was 3.733,713l. The Sinking-Fund, therefore, produced 1.456,000l.; which, added to 1.500,000l. (the neat produce, at that time, of Land at 2s. and Malt-tax) made the unappropriated revenue 2.956,032l.— The expence of the peace eftablifhment, confifting of 10,000 feamen, and 18,857 landmen, was, in 1753 and 1754, (including an allowance for the increafe of the Navy-debt) 2.400,000l. nearly; which left an annual furplus in the national income of 556,000l. without lotteries, and land at 2s. This furplus (with land at 3s.) has of late fcarcely exceeded 300,000l.; and, therefore, has not been a THIRD of what it was in the laſt peace, and before the reduction of intereft to 3 per cent. was compleated.

M 4   and

Land Tax at 1 s. in the pound —	£. 450,000
Salt Duties, being the medium of the years 1765 and 1766 —	218,739
Duties on Stamps, Cards, Dice, Advertisements, Bonds, Leases, Indentures, News-papers, Almanacks, &c. — —	280,788
Duties on houses and windows, being the medium of 3 years ending in 1771 — —	385,369
Post Office, Seizures, Wine Licences, Hackney Coaches, Tenths of the Clergy, &c. — —	250,000
Excises in Scotland, being the medium of 3 years ending in 1773	95,229.
Customs in Scotland, being the medium of 3 years ending in 1773 — — —	68,369
Annual profit from Lotteries —	150,000
Inland taxes in Scotland, coinage duties, casual revenues, such as the duties on Gum-Senega, American revenue, &c. — —	150,000
Expence of collecting the Excises in England, being the average of the years 1767 and 1768, when their produce was 4.531,075 l. *per ann.*	
6 *per cent.* of the gross produce --	297,887
Expence of collecting the Excises in Scotland, being the medium	

of

of the years 1772 and 1773, and
the difference between the grofs
and nett produce——31 *per cent.*   £.
of the grofs produce   —   43,254
EXPENCE of collecting the CUSTOMS
in ENGLAND, being the average
of 1771 and 1772, bounties included, and 15 *per cent.* of the grofs
produce, exclufive of drawbacks
and over-entries   —   —   468,703
N. B. The bounties for 1771 were
202,840 l.—for 1772, 172,468 l.
The charges of management for
1771, were 276,434 l.
For 1772, 285,764 l. or 10 *per
cent.* nearly.
Intereft of loans on the land tax at
4 s. expences of collection, mi-
litia, &c.   —   —   250,000
PERQUISITES, &c. to Cuftom-houfe
officers, &c. fuppofed   —   —   250,000
EXPENCE of collecting the Salt-du-
ties in ENGLAND, 10¼ *per cent.* —   27,000
Bounties on fifh exported   —   —   18,000
EXPENCE of collecting the duties on
Stamps, Cards, Advertifements,
&c. 5¼ *per cent.*   —   —   18,000
                                       ————————
                        Total £. 11.900,505
                                       ————————

It

It muft be feen, that this account is imperfect and defective. It is, however, fufficient to prove, that the whole money raifed DIRECTLY by the taxes, (exclufive of tithes, county rates, and the taxes which fupport the poor,) cannot be much lefs than TWELVE MILLIONS. The *Earl of Stair* has in his papers made it to be above 400,000 l. more, by including in his eftimate feveral articles which I have omitted; particularly, the intereft and management on the equivalent to *Scotland*, the Scotch crown Revenues, Dutchy of *Cornwall* and *Lancafter* Fines, &c. He has alfo given an eftimate of the fees and perquifites of office of every kind, and reckoned them at half a million; whereas, I have only reckoned the perquifites of office at the *Cuftom-houfe*.

I fhould be inexcufable were I to quit this fubject, without taking notice of the particular gratitude due from the public to *Lord Stair*, for publifhing his papers; and for ftepping forth at this time to draw attention, by the weight of his name and character, to calculations, which, as he juftly fays, " it be- " comes every man of property among us to " underftand; to awaken the nation from the " lethargy into which the mockery of paper " wealth has plunged it; and to bear his teftimony " againft the prefent unnatural war."

POST-

POSTSCRIPT.

THE following POSTSCRIPT has been published only in a few of the last Editions of
the *Observations on Civil Liberty*. It has been often
referred to in the preceding work ; and, therefore,
it is necessary to give it a place here.

ACCOUNT *of Public Debts discharged, Money
borrowed, and Annual Interest saved from*
1763 *to* 1775.

Debts paid off since 1763.	Annuity decreased.	
£.	£.	s.
1765— 870,888 funded, bearing in-terest at 4 *per cent.*	34,835	10
1.500,000 unfunded, 4 *per cent.*	60,000	00
1766—0.870,888 funded, 4 *per cent.*	34,835	10
1.200,000 unfunded, 4 —	48,000	00
1767—2.616,777 funded, 4 —	104,671	0
1768—2.625,000 funded, 4 —	105,000	0
1771—1.500,000 funded, 3 *per cent.*	45,000	0
1772—1.500,000 funded, 3 *per cent.*	45,000	0
1773— 800,000 unfunded, 3 —	24,000	0
1774—1.000,000 funded, 3 —	30,000	0
1775—1.000,000 funded, 3 —	30,000	0
Total 15.483,553	Total 561,342	0

In

In 1764, there was paid off 650,000 *l.* navy-debt; but this I have not charged, becaufe fcarcely equal to that annual increafe of the navy-debt for 1764, 1765, and 1766, which forms a part of the ordinary peace eftablifhment. The fame is true of 300,000 *l.* navy-debt, paid in 1767; of 400,000 *l.* paid in 1769; of 100,200 *l.* paid in 1770; 200,000 *l.* in 1771; 215,883 *l.* in 1772; and 200,000 *l.* in 1774.

Account of money borrowed and debts con-tracted fince 1763.

		£.	Annual inte-reft increafed.
Borrowed and funded, at 3 *per cent.* - in	1765 —	1.500,000 —	45,000
	in 1766 —	1.500,000 —	45,000
	in 1767 —	1.500,000 —	45,000
	in 1768 —	1.900,000 —	57,000
Unfunded in	1774 —	250,000 —	7,500
Civil lift debt in	1775 (a)	500,000	
	Total	7.150,000 —	199,500

(a) This article was omitted in the former editions of this *Poftfcript*; and its infertion here makes the diminution of the public debts, fince 1763, half a million lefs than the fum at which it is taken in p. 104 and 108.——It might have been proper alfo to add, the excefs of Navy debts *contracted* above the Navy debts *difcharged*, from 1763 to 1775; and had this been done, the furplus in p. 165, would have been reduced to 150,000 l.

From

From 15.483,553 *l.* the total of debts difcharged, fubftract 7.150,000 *l.* the total of debts contracted; and the remainder, or 8.333,553 *l.* will be the diminution of the public debts fince 1763. Alfo, from 561,342 *l.* the total of the decreafe of the annual intereft, fubtract 199,500 *l.* (the total of its increafe), and the remainder, or 361,842 *l.* will be the intereft or annuity faved fince 1763.—To this muft be added 12,537 *l. per ann.* faved by changing a capital of 1.253,700 *l.* (part of 20.240,000 *l.*) from an intereft of 4 to 3 *per cent.* purfuant to an act of the 10th of George III. ; alfo the life-annuities that have fallen in; and 7,500 *l. per ann.* gained by the falling (in 1771) of 1.500,000 *l.* from an intereft of 3 ½ to 3 *per cent.*; which will make a faving in the whole of near 400,000 *l. per annum :* And it is to this faving, together with the increafe of luxury, that the increafe of the *Sinking-Fund* for the laft ten years has been owing.

To the debts difcharged the following additions muft be made.

In 1764 there was paid towards difcharging the extraordinary expences of the army, 987,434 *l.*: In 1765, thefe expences amounted to 404,496 *l.*: In 1766, to 479,088 *l.*—Total 1.871,018 *l.*—— This fum is at leaft a million higher than the extraordinary expences of the army for three years in a time of peace. This excefs, being derived from the preceding war, muft be reckoned a debt left

3 by

by the war. And the fame is true of 1.106,000*l.*
applied, in 1764, 1765, and 1766, towards fatis-
fying *German* demands.——There are likewife
fome fmaller fums of the fame kind; fuch as fub-
fidies to *Heffe-Caffel, Brunfwick,* &c. And they
may be taken at 200,000*l.*——The total of all
thefe fums is 2.306,240 *l.* ; which, added to
8.333,553*l.* makes the whole diminution of the
public debt fince 1763, to be 10.639,793*l.*

Soon after the peace in 1763, an unfunded debt,
amounting to 6.983,553*l.* was funded on the
Sinking Fund, and on new duties on wine and cyder, at 4 *per cent.* There has been fince borrowed
and funded on coals exported, window-lights, &c.
6.400,000*l.* The funded debt, therefore, has increafed fince the war 13.383,553*l.* It has decreafed (as appears from page 171) 11.983,553*l.* ;
and, confequently, there has been on the whole an
addition to it of 1.400,000*l.*——During feven
years, from 1767 to 1774, 1.415,883*l.* navy-debt
was paid off. See page 172. But, as this is a
debt arifing from conftant deficiencies in the peace
eftimates for the navy, it is a part of the current
peace expences.—In 1768 this debt was (*a*)
1.226,915*l.*—In 1774 it was 1.850,000*l.* ; and
confequently, though 1.415,883*l.* was paid off, an
addition was made to it, in feven years, of
623,085*l.* It increafed, therefore, at the rate of
291,000*l. per ann.*

(*a*) See *The Prefent State of the Nation,* page 26.

THE

THE paper from which I have taken the following account, came into my hands after almost the whole of this work had been printed off. It contains a fact of so much importance, that I cannot satisfy myself without laying it before the public. ———— In a Committee of CONGRESS in *June* 1775, a declaration was drawn up containing an offer to GREAT BRITAIN, " that " the Colonies would not only continue to grant " extraordinary aids in time of war, but also, if " allowed a free commerce, pay into the SINK- " ING-FUND such a sum annually for ONE HUN- " DRED YEARS, as should be *more* than sufficient " in that time, if faithfully applied, to extinguish " all the present debts of BRITAIN. Or, provided " this was not accepted, that, to remove the " groundless jealousy of *Britain* that the Colonies " aimed at Independence and an abolition of the " Navigation Act, which, in truth, they had never " intended ; and also, to avoid all future disputes " about the right of making that and other Acts " for regulating their commerce for the general " benefit, they would enter into a covenant with " *Britain*, that she should fully possess and exercise " that right for *one hundred years* to come."

At the end of the *Observations on Civil Liberty*, I had the honor of laying before the public the Earl of *Shelburne*'s plan of Pacification with the Colonies.

Colonies. In that plan, it is particularly propofed, that the Colonies fhould grant an annual
fupply to be carried to the Sinking Fund, and
unalienably appropriated to the difcharge of the
public debt.—It muft give this excellent Peer
great pleafure to learn, from this refolution, that
even this part of his plan, as well as all the other
parts, would, moft probably, have been accepted
by the Colonies. For though the refolution only
offers the alternative of either a *free* trade, with
extraordinary aids and an annual fupply, or an
exclufive trade confirmed and extended ; yet there
can be little reafon to doubt, but that to avoid
the calamities of the prefent conteft, BOTH would
have been confented to ; particularly, if, on our
part, fuch a revifal of the laws of trade had been
offered as was propofed in Lord Shelburne's plan.

The preceding refolution was, I have faid,
drawn up in a Committee of the Congrefs. But
it was not entered in their minutes ; a fevere Act
of Parliament happening to arrive at that time,
which determined them not to give the fum propofed in it.

F I N I S.

POSTSCRIPT.

THE following POSTSCRIPT was publifhed only in a few of the laft Editions of the *Obfervations on Civil Liberty*. It has been often referred to in the preceding work; and therefore, it is neceffary to give it a place here.

ACCOUNT *of Public Debts difcharged, Money borrowed, and Annual Intereft faved from* 1763 *to* 1775.

Debts paid off fince 1763.		Annuity decreafed.	
	£.	£.	s.
1765— 876,888 funded, bearing intereft at 4 *per cent.*		34,835	10
1.500,000 unfunded, 4 *per cent.*		60,000	00
1766—0.870,888 funded, 4 *per cent.*		34,835	10
1.200,000 unfunded, 4 —		48,000	00
1767—2.616,777 funded, 4 —		104,671	0
1768—2.625,000 funded, 4 —		105,000	0
1771—1.500,000 funded, 3½ *per cent.*		52,500	0
1772—1.500,000 funded, 3 *per cent.*		45,000	0
1773— 800,000 unfunded, 3 —		24,000	0
1774—1.000,000 funded, 3 —		30,000	0
1775—1.000,000 funded, 3 —		30,000	0
Total 15.483,553		Total 568,842	0

N

In 1764, there was paid off 650,000 l. navy-debt; but this I have not charged, becaufe fcarcely equal to that annual increafe of the navy-debt for 1764, 1765, and 1766, which forms a part of the ordinary peace eftablifhment. The fame is true of 300,000 l. navy debt, paid in 1767; of 400,000l. paid in 1769; of 100,200 l. paid in 1770; 200,000 l. in 1771; 215,883 l. in 1772; and 200,000 l. in 1774.

Account of money borrowed and debts contracted fince 1763.

		£	Annual intereft increafed.
Borrowed and funded, at 3 per cent. - in	1765	1.500,000	45,000
in	1766	1.500,000	45,000
in	1767	1.500,000	45,000
in	1768	1.900,000	57,000
Unfunded in	1774	250,000	7,500
Civil lift debt in	1775 (a)	500,000	
	Total	7.150,000	199,500

(a) This article was omitted in the firft editions of this *Poftfcript*.——It might have been proper to add, the excefs of Navy debts *contracted* above the Navy debts *difcharged*, from 1763 to 1775; and had this been done, the furplus in p. 166, would have been reduced to 150,000 l. *per ann.*

5   From

From 15.483,553l. the total of debts difcharged, fubftract 7.150,000l. the total of debts contracted ; and the remainder, or 8.333,553l. will be the diminution of the public debts fince 1763. Alfo, from 568,842l. the total of the decreafe of the annual intereft, fubtract 199,500l. (the total of its increafe), and the remainder, or 369,342l. will be the intereft or annuity faved fince 1763.— To this muft be added 12,537l. *per ann.* faved by changing a capital of 1.253,700l. (part of 20.240,000l.) from an intereft of 4 to 3 *per cent.* purfuant to an act of the 10th of George III.; alfo the life-annuities that have fallen in ; which will make a faving in the whole of near 400,000l. *per annum:* And it is to this faving, together with the increafe of luxury, that the increafe of the *Sinking Fund* for the laft ten years has been owing.

To the debts difcharged the following additions muft be made.

In 1764 there was paid towards difcharging the extraordinary expences of the army, 987.434l. In 1765, thefe expences amounted to 404,496l. In 1766, to 479,088l.—Total 1.871,018l.—— This fum is 1.100,000l. higher than the extraordinary expences of the army for three years in a time of peace. This excefs, being derived from the preceding war, muft be reckoned a debt left by the war. And the fame is true of 1.106,000l. applied, in 1764, 1765, and 1766, towards fatis-

fying

fying *German* demands.——There are likewife fome fmaller fums of the fame kind; fuch as fub-fidies to *Heffe-Caffel*, *Brunfwick*, &c. And they may be taken at 200,000l.——The total of all thefe fums is 2.406,240 l. which, added to 8.333,553l. makes the whole diminution of the public debts, or the whole faving of the kingdom, fince 1763, to be 10.739,793l.

Soon after the peace in 1763, an unfunded debt, amounting to 6.983,553l. was funded on the *Sinking Fund*, and on new duties on wine and cyder, at 4 *per cent*. There has been fince borrowed and funded on coals exported, window-lights, &c. 6.400,000l. The funded debt, therefore, has increafed fince the war 13.383,553l. It has decreafed (as may appear from page 177) 11.983,553l. and, confequently, there has been on the whole an addition to it of 1.400,000l.——During feven years, from 1768 to 1774, 1.115,883l. navy-debt was paid off. See page 178. But, as this is a debt arifing from conftant deficiencies in the peace eftimates for the navy, it is a part of the current peace expences.——On the 31ft of December, 1767, this debt was 1.213,072l.—On the 31ft of December, 1774, it was 1.850,000l. and confequently, though 1.115,883l. was paid off, an addition was made to it, in feven years, of 673,028l. It increafed, therefore, at the rate of 255,558l. *per ann.*

SUPPLE-

SUPPLEMENT
TO
SECTION III. PART II.

Containing additional Observations on Schemes for raising Money by Public Loans.

IT is impoffible, that any attentive perfon can reflect without concern, on that monftrous accumulation of artificial debt for which no value has been received, which has been pointed out in different parts of the preceding Tract ; and, particularly in the third Section of the fecond Part. This being a fubject which, in the prefent ftate of our finances, is highly interefting ; I have been induced to return to it in this place ; and to offer fome further obfervations and propofals which have occurred to me in re-confidering it, and which I think neceffary to explain and confirm thofe which nave been already offered.

There are two methods in which money is capable of being borrowed for public fervices. The firft is, by offering fuch *high* intereft as may or itfelf be fufficient to induce lenders to advance the fums that are wanted : And the fecond is, by of-

O

fering

fering a *low* interest, with a *gratuity* or *doceur* to produce the acceptance of it.—The last has been the method in which our government has most commonly borrowed money; and the gratuity offered has been either a right to a greater capital than the sum advanced, or a *long* or *short* or *life* annuity, or the profits of a lottery, or some advantages of trade.——The first without doubt, is the most rational method of borrowing; and the latter is so absurd and extravagant as to be incapable of being adopted in the common transactions of life. —In order to give a just and full idea of this, I shall instance in the last loan; specifying the manner in which it *would* have been made if the usual method of borrowing had been followed; and comparing this with the manner in which it *was* made; and the manner in which, I think, it *might* have been made to the greatest advantage.

FIVE MILLIONS, it is well known, were borrowed last year; and, had the old plan of borrowing been adopted, this sum would have been borrowed by some such scheme as one of the *two* following.

First. Interest in the public funds being then near 4 *per cent. per ann.* an interest of only 3 *per cent.* would have been offered; or, in other words, for every 100l. in *money*, 100l. *stock* carrying 3 *per cent.* (worth then 78l.) would have been given; but at the same time, as a *premium* or *compensation* for accepting such low interest, a life-annuity, or

4   a short.

a fhort annuity would have been offered worth
fomewhat more than the difference between
100l. and 78l. or about 24l. The whole premium, therefore, in raifing *five millions*, would
have been equal in value to about 1.200,000l.
and, fuppofing it to have been either a life-annuity,
or a fhort annuity for 17 years of 2l. worth 12
years purchafe, annexed to every 100l. ftock, the
whole annual charge incurred by the loan would
have been 250,000l. for a term of years, and
150,000l. for ever till the capital is redeemed.

It is manifeft that the capital including in it according to this account almoft the whole *premium*,
the public makes itfelf, by this mode of borrowing, a *debtor* for the very thing it *gives*; and,
befides paying the annuity, obliges itfelf to advance
at redemption the whole value of it.—It is proper
to add, that this is done *unneceffarily*, becaufe
1.200,000 might have been procured by felling
the annuity, and the remaining 3.800,000l. neceffary to make up five millions, might have been
procured, as will be fhewn prefently, without
any *doceur* by giving higher intereft.

But there is another method of borrowing
which has been practifed by government on former
occafions, and which might have been adopted in
the laft loan.

For every 100l. advanced a new capital in the
3 *per cent.* funds worth that fum would have been

fold,

fold, including a funded 10l. lottery ticket. This
new capital would have been nearly 127l. three
per cent. ftock for every 100l. in *money*, or
6.343,954l. ftock for FIVE MILLIONS in money;
of which ftock 5.718,954l. would have been fold,
to encourage fubfcriptions, at 2 *per cent.* below the
market price, that is, at 76l. ½; and the remaining ftock, having a lottery annexed, would have
been fold at *par*. A fictitious or artificial capital,
therefore, would have been created, or a debt incurred more than the value received, of 1,343,954l.
befides relinquifhing about 150,000l. which might
have been obtained by the profits of the lottery.

I have been feldom more furprized than at the
preference of this fcheme, which, at the time of
fettling the laft loan, was expreffed by fome very
refpectable members of the Houfe of Commons;
nor can this preference be eafily accounted for on
any other fuppofition than that they confider the
public debts as incumbrances, never to be removed, and, therefore, think it of no confequence with what difficulties the redemption of
them is loaded by an increafe of capitals bearing
low intereft. It muft be acknowledged indeed that
this method of borrowing would have been attended with a fmall prefent advantage; for the
intereft of 6.343,954l. at 3 *per cent.* is 190,318l.
and this, together with the intereft of 150,000l.

4   or

or 6000l. *per ann.* loft by giving up the profits of a lottery, would have been the whole prefent annual charge it would have brought on the public. But if this be a fufficient reafon for preferring fuch a fcheme, it would perhaps be beft to create capitals bearing 2 *per cent.* or even 1 *per cent.* intereft; for probably fuch capitals would bear a better price, in proportion to the rates of intereft, than any 3 *per cent.* capitals, and confequently, a greater prefent faving might be made by felling them. No other objection can be made to this than that by lowering intereft, and laying the public under an obligation to return *double* or *triple* every fum it receives; the redemption of the public debts might be rendered fo expenfive and difficult as to be entirely impracticable. But this would be of no confequence if indeed their redemption is already become impracticable; and if, therefore, every new charge they bring on the public is to be confidered as laid on for eternity.

With thefe fchemes let us now compare the fcheme actually adopted for the laft loan.

Inftead of a 3 *per cent.* capital, a new capital bearing 4 *per cent.* intereft, irredeemable for ten years, was offered at 95l. for every 100l. *ftock,* with two *douceurs* to raife the value of the ftock above 100l. in money; namely, a fhort annuity

of

of a HALF *per cent.* for ten years, (reckoned worth 4l. 2s.) and the profit (reckoned at 3l.) of one ticket in a money lottery confifting of 50,000 tickets.

The chief difference between this fcheme and the firft I have defcribed is, that the new ftock created is a FOUR *per cent.* inftead of a THREE *per cent.* ftock. But this is a difference of particular importance, and brings it near to fuch plans of borrowing as appear to me the beft.——In the *firft* fcheme, the artificial capital is 1.200,000l. In the *fecond,* 1.343,954l. In this *third* fcheme it is only 250,000l. This fcheme, therefore, has evidently great merit ; and perhaps, in the prefent ftate of the public debts, it does not admit of any great improvement. There is, however, an eafy alteration which, I think, would have been an improvement, and which I fhall take the liberty to mention.

According to a preceding obfervation, the two *douceurs* being included in the capital, are granted, and muft be paid twice over. This is fo abfurd and extravagant that it ought to be avoided as far as poffible ; and it might have been avoided, in a great meafure, by offering for every 100l. advanced 95l. ftock, carrying 4 *and a quarter* intereft irredeemable for ten years, with the fame

fhort

fhort annuity and a lottery ticket annexed.(*a*) In this cafe, the new capital would have been 4.750,000l. carrying (at 4¼ *per cent.*) 201,875l. *per ann.* intereſt. There would, therefore, have been a faving of 250,000l. in the capital; and the annual charge would have been nearly the fame.

It muſt be obſerved that this fcheme fuppoſes that a ſtock bearing 4¼ *per cent.* intereſt would have been valued nearly at *par*; and, according to the principles on which the fcheme was calcu-lated, it could not have been valued at much leſs; or, fuppoſing it valued at 1 or 2 *per cent.* leſs, the difference might have been made up by only add-ing two or three years to the duration of the fhort annuity and the term of irredeemableneſs.—Had a *ſtock* been offered bearing 4½ *per cent.* intereſt ir-redeemable for ten years, one *half* at leaſt of the fhort annuity might have been faved. The annual charge for ten years would have been fomewhat leſs; (*b*) and the exceſs afterwards would have been

(*a*) Or, for every 105l. contributed, 100l. STOCK irre-deemable for 10 years might have been given, carrying 4¼ *per cent.* intereſt, with the fame fhort annuity and a lottery ticket annexed; and then the new capital would have been 4.762,000l. carrying (at 4¼ *per cent.*) 202,385l. *per ann.* in-tereſt. The amount of the fhort annuity would have been 23,810l. and the number of lottery tickets 47,620.

(*b*) 211,375l. the intereſt at 4½ of 4.750,000l. and 12,500l. a fhort annuity of a QUARTER *per cent.* annexed to every 100l.

contributed.

been much more than compensated by the advantages at redemption attending a higher interest and a smaller capital.

But, perhaps, such a scheme as the following would have been preferable to any of those now proposed.

For every 100l. in *money* 75l. stock irredeemable for 10 years and carrying $4\frac{1}{4}$ *per cent.* interest, might have been offered, together with an annuity for 27 years of $1\frac{1}{2}$ *per cent.* (valued cheap at 16 years purchase, or 24l.) and the advantage of a lottery ticket. This scheme would have been as likely to be attended with a profit as that which was adopted. The new capital would have been only 3.750,000l. bearing 159,375l. interest. The short annuity would have been 75,000l. and the whole annual charge (supposing no redemptions of the capital to take place after ten years) 234,375l. for 27 years, and afterwards 159,375l. It appears, therefore, that 1.250,000l. or a *quarter* of the capital that was actually created, would have been saved; and also a rent charge on the public after 27 years of 40,750l. *per ann.* for ever.—The additional expence to balance these advantages would have been 9.650l. *per ann.* for ten years, and 34,375l. *per ann.* for 17 years. In other

contributed, make 223,875l. This last sum, therefore, would have been the annual charge for 10 years; and the first sum the annual charge after ten years till redemption.

words ;

words; the public would have abfolutely fecured the redemption of a *quarter* of the loan, (or of 1.250,000l.) befides an eafier redemption of the remainder, at the expence of 680,875l. in the whole, (*a*) to be paid annually in fmall fums during the courfe of 27 years.

All that has been now faid has gone on the fuppofition that, agreeably to the calculations on which the laft loan was formed, 100l. *ftock* irredeemable for ten years and bearing 4 *per cent.* intereft, would fell at 17l. more than 100l. ftock bearing 3 *per cent.* intereft; (or at 95l. when the latter ftock is at 78l.) and alfo, that a fhort annuity for ten years would fell at $8\frac{1}{10}$ years purchafe.—— But events have fhewn that thefe valuations were too high. The new fubfcription (including 100l. four *per cent.* ftock, a half *per cent.* fhort annuity, and the profit of a lottery ticket) fhould have fold, according to thefe valuations, at about $102\frac{1}{2}$. But it never bore fo high a price; and in a little time it fell to *par*, and at laft to *3 per cent.* difcount.—— Various reafons have been affigned for this; but the true reafons were the following.

Firft. A general fall of near 2 *per cent.* which took place in the ftocks foon after the loan was fettled.

(*a*) Ten payments of 9,650l. and feventeen payments of 34,375l. make 680,875l.

Secondly,

Secondly. A lower valuation of the new 4 *per cent.* ſtock and the ſhort annuity which took place in the ALLEY.—This was the principal reaſon ; and it will be proper particularly to explain it. In doing this, it will be neceſſary to look back a little to the hiſtory of the public funds.

In 1717 the public debts were reduced from an intereſt of *6 per cent.* to *5 per cent.* and in 1727, from *5 per cent* to *4 per cent.* In 1737 a bill was brought into the HOUSE of COMMONS by Sir *John Barnard,* for a farther reduction from 4 to *3 per cent.* At this time the *3 per cents.* were above *par ;* and even, during the three firſt years of the war which began in 1740, they continued ſo high that government was able to raiſe the neceſſary ſupplies by borrowing at *3 per cent.*——In ſuch circumſtances, it was impoſſible the public creditors ſhould avoid expecting a *third* reduction ; and this expectation would neceſſarily ſink the value of the FOUR PER CENTS. by leading the public to conſider them as no more than a THREE *per cent.* ſtock having a ſhort annuity of ONE *per·cent.* annexed. Accordingly ; *before* the war the difference of price between the THREE and the FOUR *per cent.* ſtocks was about 10 or 11 *per cent.* After the commencement of the war, a reduction becoming more doubtful and more diſtant, this difference became greater, and generally kept be-

tween

tween 14 and 17 *per cent.* At the approach of
the PEACE in 1748, it funk to 11 *per cent.* and foon
after the PEACE, the 3 *per cents.* having rifen confiderably above *par,* (*a*) and an univerfal expectation of a fpeedy reduction taking place, it funk to
6 *per cent.*————It is evident, therefore, that the
price of the FOUR *per cents.* has been governed by
the expectation of their reduction, (*b*) and that,
had there been no fuch expectation, their price,
compared with the 3 *per cents.* would have been
much higher. It will appear prefently to be moft
probable, that had it not been for this expectation,
the prices of thefe ftocks would not have differed
much from the proportion of the rates of intereft.

In taking this account, I have only compared
the THREE *per cents.* with the SOUTH-SEA FOUR *per*

(*a*) It may be worth obferving, that during this whole war
they never fell below 82, except for a few months during the
rebellion in 1745; that after the PEACE in 1748 they rofe to
105, and in the fucceeding war never fell fo low as they are
now, except in the two laft years; that after the PEACE in 1763
it was expected they would again rife above *par*; but that, inftead of this, they have in general during the whole peace kept
12 or 13 *per cent.* below *par*, and 15 or 16 *per cent.* below the
price they bore before the two laft wars.———One of the reafons of the great alteration which has taken place fince the
laft war is, I think, pointed out in the 3d Section of the 3d
Part of this Tract.

(*b*) Since the reduction in 1749 there has been no FOUR
per cent. capital created except that of the laft year.

cent.

cent. capitals before their reduction in 1749, at which time they amounted to above 27 millions, and were (as the confolidated three *per cent.* annuities are now) the grand ftaple ftock of the kingdom. In 1746 and 1747, two new FOUR *per cent.* capitals were created redeemable at any time, and transferrable at the BANK. The price of thefe new capitals kept for fome time after their creation, confiderably below the price of the old SOUTH-SEA four *per cents.* the reafons of which were, I fuppofe, the general reafons which make new funds bear a lower price than old ones ; and, particularly, their having lefs traffic in them, and being fmall and detached parcels likely to be firft felected for the operations of finance.

Were the caufe now affigned, or the expectation of a reduction of intereft, the only caufe that governed the comparative prices of 3 *per cent.* and 4 *per cent.* capitals, the excefs of one above the other would never be more than the fuppofed value of a fhort annuity of 1l. till *reduction.* ———But there is another caufe which may operate in this inftance, and which ought not to be overlooked; I mean, the expectation of a greater payment at *redemption.* The effect of the former is to *diminifh,* and of the latter to *increafe* the value of FOUR *per cent.* capitals.——In order to underftand this it muft be remembered, that when the 3 *per cents.* are at any
confiderable

confiderable difcount, it becomes practicable to redeem them under *par*, while debts bearing 4 *per cent*. intereft muft be redeemed at *par*. This will make a difference in favour of the latter, which will be greater or lefs in proportion to the greater or lefs difcount at which the *three per cents*. are fold, the greater or lefs quantity of ftock bearing 4 *per cent*. intereft, and the greater or lefs probability that the whole or a confiderable part of it will be foon redeemed (*a*)——Let us fuppofe, for inftance, that all the public debts bearing 4 *per cent*.

(*a*) What is here faid has been verified, in the particular inftance of a *million and a half* borrowed in 1756, which was to carry 3½ *per cent*. intereft till 1771, and then to become redeemable.——During the laft war, and for about three years after the commencement of peace, there was a general expectation that the THREE *per cents*. would rife above *par* as they had done in the former peace; and while this expectation continued, this ftock was reckoned no better than a THREE *per cent*. ftock with a fhort annuity of a *half per cent*. annexed; and for this reafon it bore, during that period, a lower price than another ftock of 4 millions and a half which was to bear the fame intereft till 1782, and then to become redeemable, and to fink to an intereft of 3 *per cent*.——In the latter end of 1767 and beginning of 1768 the price of the former ftock rofe above that of the latter, and continued not far from *par* from that time to the time of its redemption in 1771. The reafon muft have been, that being a fmall ftock bearing a higher intereft than the other ftocks, it was expected, that it would be paid off at *par*, and therefore with a confiderable profit, as foon as it became redeemable; which accordingly happened. See Poftfcript, page 177.

See Poftfcript, page 177.

intereft,

intereſt, conſiſt of a ſingle capital of FIVE MIL-
LIONS redeemable at any time; and that all the
reſt of the public debts are THREE *per cent.* capitals ſold at a diſcount of 12 *per cent.* or at 88l. for
every 100l. ſtock.   In theſe circumſtances, there
would be a certainty that the ſmall ſtock bearing
4 *per cent.* intereſt would be ſelected for redemption as ſoon as poſſible; and, as a ſtock carrying
ſuch high intereſt could not be expected, when the
3 *per cents.* are at 88, to be redeemed under *par*,
its real value would on this account exceed that of
the THREE *per cents.* more or leſs in proportion as
its redemption was more or leſs diſtant.   And its
whole exceſs of value in theſe circumſtances is to be
computed in the following manner.—It would conſiſt of a 3 *per cent.* capital, for every 100l. of
which 100l. in money is to be received; and of
an additional annuity of 1 *per cent.* till redemption.
Its exceſs of value, therefore, if the whole capital
was to be redeemed immediately, would be the
ſame with the diſcount of the 3 *per cents.* or 12
per cent.   If the capital was not to be redeemed
till the end of 7 years, its exceſs of value would
conſiſt of 12 *per cent.* payable ſeven years hence,
and the preſent worth of an annuity of 1 *per cent.*
for the intermediate term of ſeven years.   12l.
payable at the end of 7 years is worth in preſent
money (allowing compound intereſt at 4 *per cent.*)
9l. 2s. 6d.   An annuity of 1l. for ſeven years is
worth

worth (reckoning the fame intereſt) 6l. The whole exceſs of value, therefore, will be 15l. 2s. 6d. for every 100l. ſtock. If the redemption of the capital is to be delayed 15 years, the exceſs of value computed in the fame manner will be 17l. 15s. 6d. —if 20 years, 19l. 1s.—if 30 years, 21l.

If the 3 *per cents.* had been ſuppoſed at a greater diſcount, it is evident, that theſe ſeveral values would have been likewiſe greater; and had the quantity of 4 *per cent.* ſtock been ſuppoſed *double* or *triple,* the effect would have been the fame with a delay of redemption ; and had it been ſuppoſed thirty or forty millions, the effect (in conſequence of our flow progreſs in redeeming our debts) would not have fallen very ſhort of an eternal delay of redemption.

Before 1749, the amount of the public debts carrying 4 *per cent.* intereſt was near 58 millions. The expectation, therefore, of the advantage now explained could not *then* have any effect ; and the only cauſe which could have influenced, in any conſiderable degree, the comparative prices of theſe ſtocks muſt have been the firſt I have aſſigned, or the expectation of their *reduction* ; that is, in other words, the expectation of a *ſudden redemption* of them, as ſoon as the 3 *per cents.* got above *par,* by borrowing money at that intereſt. Had not this been foreſeen, or had there been an act of parliament rendering it impracticable,

ble, there is no reafon to doubt but the price of the FOUR *per cents.* compared with the THREE *per cents.* would have approached nearly to the proportion of the rates of intereft, agreeably to what is faid in page 191.

The ftate of the public funds has been much changed fince the two laft wars; but it is an alteration that has increafed the comparative value of 4 *per cent.* capitals.

I have already obferved, that during the laft war there was reafon to expect, that, as foon as peace came, the THREE *per cents.* would rife above *par.* No one can now entertain any fuch expectation. On the contrary; it is moft probable, that they will never again rife to that which has been their average price during the laft peace from 1763 to 1775, and which, I think, may be ftated at 87 or 88.——My reafon for this affertion is,

Firft, that after the prefent war, fhould we be fo happy as to efcape the ruin with which it threatens us, our taxes and expences will be fo much increafed, and at the fame time our refources fo much diminifhed, as neceffarily to leave the credit and value of our public fecurities lower than ever.

Secondly. Though our credit and refources fhould continue undiminifhed, yet the great addition which the prefent war will make to the public debts, is alone likely to fink their value; because becaufe every increafe of a faleable commodity has always a tendency to lower its price.——It follows from hence, that the purchafers of four *per cent.* capitals have now a profpect of an advantage of 12 or 14 *per cent.* at redemption, which they could not have had before the laft peace.

In connexion with this it muft be confidered, that it is now highly probable, that it will never be again practicable to reduce the intereft of any 4 *per cent.* capitals. In order to fuch a reduction, government muft be able to offer to the proprietors of thefe capitals their *principal*, fhould they not chufe to take lower intereft, and confequently to borrow at an intereft of 3½ or 3¾ *per cent.* But no fums will be lent on fuch lower intereft, unlefs it can be depended upon that capitals bearing that intereft, when brought to market, will bear a premium of 1 or 2 *per cent.* ; and this, when the *three per cents.* are not higher than 87 or 88, would require the excefs of value of fuch capitals to be eftimated at 14 or 15 *per cent.* whereas it has been lately found, that even FOUR *per cent.* capitals irredeemable for ten years, will not bear fuch an excefs of value.—A *reduction*, therefore, of the intereft of FOUR *per cent.* capitals, or a *redemption* of them by borrowed money, cannot now be reckoned upon ; and the only caufe that can REASONABLY fink their value compared with the THREE *per cents.* below the ratio of the rates of intereft, is

P   the

the probability of a redemption of them by the
furplus of the national revenue. I need not fay
how little is to be expected from hence. Suppofing, however, that much may be expected,
I have fhewn what effect it ought to have; and
from the obfervations I have made, and particularly the computation in page 194, &c. it
appears, I think, that the price of the capital of
five millions four *per cent.* annuities lately created
ought to have been near 18 *per cent.* more than
the price of the THREE *per cents.* This appears
to be true on the fuppofition that this capital will
be redeemed in fifteen years; (that is, in five years
after the expiration of the term for which it is made
irredeemable) that the 3 *per cents.* will rife to as
high a price as they bore during the laft peace;
and that purchafers are allowed to make FOUR *per
cent.* compound intereft of their money.———Were
we to fuppofe this capital difcharged even in two
years after it becomes redeemable, the value, made
out in the fame way, would be nearly 17l.

He who will confider all this, and alfo recollect
the general price of the 4 *per cents.* before their reduction in 1749, (fee page 190) muft be convinced
that the TREASURY, at the time the laft loan was
fettled, had good reafon for taking the price of the
new *four per cent.* capitals 17 *per cent.* higher than
the price of the three *per cents.*———It has, however, been found that this was too high a valuation. Inftead of being fold at 17l. more for

4   every

every 100l. ftock than the 3 *per cents*. they have been fold at only 13l. or 14l. more ; and this has been the chief reafon of the difcount to which the laft fubfcription fell.——It is hard to fay, by what principles the money'd men who traffic in the funds have governed themfelves in this inftance ; but certain it is, that they have not been guided by any of the rules of juft calculation : And the fame muft be faid of the value at which they have reckoned the fhort annuity of a half *per cent*. for ten years annexed to the new 4 *per cents*. In forming the fcheme for the laft loan this annuity was, I have faid, eftimated at $8\frac{1}{10}$ years purchafe, agreeably to its real value, fuppofing the payments yearly, the firft payment to be made at the diftance of a year, and money improved at 4 *per cent*. compound intereft. But it has in general been fold at about $7\frac{1}{2}$ years purchafe ; which is *lefs* than its value, fuppofing money improved at $5\frac{1}{4}$ *per cent*. compound intereft. (*a*)

(*a*) Nothing has been more undervalued in the ALLEY than *Annuities on lives*. They have been always granted, very unreafonably, without any limitation of age ; and their value has been taken at no more than 12 or 13 years purchafe ; tho' really worth one with another 16 or 17 years purchafe. This is a ftrong reafon for preferring fhort annuities to them in all fchemes for raifing money. Short annuities for 21 years will be taken for as much as life-annuities ; and yet experience has proved that in this time not a *quarter* of the life-annuities will drop ; and the whole expence brought by them on the public will not be removed in lefs than 70 or 80 years. See Note 15, Page 134.

From

From this account it appears, that could the caprice of the public have been forefeen, the price of the new four *per cents.* fhould not have been reckoned at more than 91l.; (the 3 *per cents.* being at 78l.) and that, confequently, to make up a value which would have produced 102l. for every 100l. advanced, either the term of irredeem-ablenefs and of the fhort annuity fhould have been lengthened ; or, fuppofing this term the fame, the fhort annuity fhould have been more than doubled. An artificial capital, indeed, of near half a million would in this cafe have been created. But this difadvantage might have been avoided, without bringing any additional expence on the public, by fuch alterations as I have before propofed ; and by increafing in the correfted fchemes, page 186, &c. either the term of irredeem-ablenefs, or the fhort annuity, or the rate of in-tereft, or all of them together.

The preceding account will, I fancy, help to fhew what is practicable, *taking things as they are,* in borrowing money for public ufes. It proves, that the nation lofes greatly by the low price of all capitals bearing a higher intereft than 3 *per cent.* and that could their value be raifed, it would be greatly benefited.——For example. Could the new FOUR *per cents.* have been taken at 99l. for every 100l. ftock, inftead of 95l. the whole expence

pence of the ſhort annuity in the ſcheme of the laſt loan, and of a *quarter per cent.* perpetual inter-eſt, in the corrected ſchemes, page 186, &c. might have been ſaved. But had the value of the 4 *per cents.* been raiſed in proportion to the rate of in-tereſt, or *nearly* in that proportion, a farther ſaving might have been made, in all the ſchemes, of the profits of the lottery, and, conſequently, of 6000l. *per annum* in the annual charge.——My next en-quiry, therefore, ſhall be, in what manner and by what regulations this may be done. I have written in the ſection on loans, on the ſuppoſition that ſuch regulations are practicable; and I have pro-poſed one of them; but I will here be more explicit.

It has been ſhewn, that before 1749 the cauſe which depreſſed the value of the 4 *per cents.* was the expectation of their being reduced; and that *now* this cauſe is the expectation of their being ſoon *redeemed.* Remove, therefore, theſe cauſes in any degree, and their value muſt riſe in the ſame degree.——With reſpect to the firſt, it is in my opinion certain that it would be doing great ſervice to the public to exclude it entirely. Our reductions of intereſt have proceeded from a policy too narrow; and the nation is likely to

P 3   ſuffer

suffer by them much more than it has gained. (*a*)
The savings they produce, being expended on
current services, tempt to extravagance; give a
fallacious appearance of opulence; and, by
making our debts sit lighter, render us less
anxious about redeeming them, and less appre-
hensive of . danger from the increase of them.
At the same time they render their redemption a
work of more difficulty, and oblige government,
when under a necessity of contracting new debts,
either to give extravagant interest, or to offer
extravagant premiums. That accumulation of
artificial debts which I have pointed out has
been owing principally to this cause; and had
it not been, in particular, for the reduction in
1749, the public debts would now have been
near 14 millions less; and a debt of above a hundred millions, instead of consisting of capitals
bearing interest at 3 *per cent.* would have consisted
of capitals bearing some of them 3½, some 4, and
some 4½ and 5 *per cent.* interest, which (supposing
them all at a medium to bear 4 *per cent.*) a million
per ann. would have redeemed in six years less

(*a*) I would except here the first reduction in 1717. This
was then necessary to gain a fund for sinking the public
debts; and had the fund thus gained been applied, as the
laws required, invariably to this purpose, and all farther reductions been avoided, we should now have been burthened
with no debts.

time,

time, and at twenty-one millions lefs expence.——
In fhort; reducing of intereft is one of thofe unhappy TEMPORARY EXPEDIENTS to which ftatefmen are apt to betake themfelves; and by which
prefent relief is gained at the expence of *future*
fafety, and diftrefs poftponed by rendering it in the
end more unavoidable and dreadful.——There
cannot, therefore, be any fufficient reafon againft
making the intereft of the new capitals which may
be created by any future loans, IRREDUCIBLE. (*a*)
Should this raife the price of capitals bearing high
intereft in proportion to the increafe of intereft,
government would be enabled to borrow to equal
advantage whatever intereft it offered; the new
loans would not bring any greater annual charge
on the nation than would have been neceffary had
the fame fums been obtained by felling 3 *per cent.*
capitals; and, at the fame time, all the immenfe
expence of *douceurs* and *fictitious capitals* would be
faved, and all the advantages in redeeming the
public debts obtained, arifing from fmaller capitals
bearing higher intereft.

Such a regulation as that now propofed would
be alone fufficient for thefe purpofes, when the
amount of the debts bearing high intereft and declared irreducible, is confiderable, as appears

(*a*) That is; never capable of being redeemed by fubfti-
tuting one debt for another; or of being faved from redemption by accepting lower intereft.

from

from what is faid in page 195. But when a debt happens to bear a higher intereſt than any other, and is at the ſame time ſmall, the probability of a *quick redemption* will operate in the ſame manner on its price with the expectation of a *reduction*; and in this caſe, therefore, it will become neceſ-ſary, in order to avoid the inconveniences I have deſcribed, TO POSTPONE REDEMPTION; and one of the beſt methods of doing this will be, by order-ing, that ſuch a debt ſhall be redeemed *after* ſome other given part of the funded public debts.—So ſlow has been our progreſs in redeeming debts, that this (ſuppoſing the part to be firſt redeemed conſiderable) would be reckoned, in the preſent circumſtances of the funds, the ſame with making the debt to be laſt redeemed, irredeemable for ever. And ſhould ſuch an apprehenſion prove right, the public would loſe nothing, becauſe the debt whoſe redemption was poſtponed, would bring no greater annual charge on the public, than if the ſame ſum had been obtained by ſelling a capital bearing any lower intereſt. But ſhould it prove falſe, or ſhould our debts be ever put into a fixed courſe of redemption, the public would gain greatly by being able, after diſcharging one part of its debts, to diſcharge the remainder more expeditiouſly and eaſily.

I ſhall beg leave to illuſtrate what has been now ſaid by having recourſe again to the laſt loan of

FIVE MILLIONS.——During the laft 60 years, or from the firft eftablifhment of the finking fund to the year 1777, no more than about FIFTEEN MILLIONS of the public funded debts have been paid. An order, therefore, that the capital of five millions bearing 4 *per cent.* created by the laft loan, fhould not be difcharged unlefs a capital of twenty-five or thirty millions in the three *per cents.* fhall have been *firft* difcharged, would have carried its redemption to fo diftant a period, as might probably have raifed it to the fame comparative value with any 3 *per cent.* capitals.

Let it, however, be fuppofed to advance its price only to 102l. when the 3 *per cents.* are at 78; that is, when the ratio of the rates of intereft required the price to be at 104. In thefe circumftances, 4.850,000l. of the five millions would have been advanced for an equal capital carrying 194,000l. intereft at 4 *per cent.*; and the remaining 150,000l. would have been advanced for the lottery: And thus the whole expence of the fhort annuity, and 150,000l. capital, would have been faved. ——And had the fame fum been obtained by felling a 3 *per cent.* capital, the amount of intereft, though the leaft poffible, would not have been much lefs;(*a*)

(*a*) Suppofing the 3 *per cents.* fold at 76½, the capital neceffary to produce 4.850,000l. in money would be 6.339,869l. the intereft of which at 3 *per cent.* is 190,195l.

but,

but, at redemption, there would have been a neceffity of paying above a MILLION AND A QUARTER
for which no value had been received.——When
fuch advantages, uncompenfated by any lofs, can
be obtained by fo eafy and fimple a regulation as
only changing the ORDER of paying the public
debts, (a) what poffible reafon can there be
againft adopting it?

There is another method by which the value of
any ftocks bearing high intereft might be raifed,
which would probably be no lefs effectual; I
mean, by ordering that no part of fuch ftocks
fhall be redeemed, without at the fame time
redeeming an *equal*, or any *larger* fum, in other
capitals. This is the regulation propofed in the
fection on public loans, page 98; and it will not
be amifs here to give an illuftration of it, by
fuppofing, that EIGHT MILLIONS will be wanted
for the neceffary fupplies of this year; and that
this fum will be procured by felling, as was done
in the laft loan, a capital equal to the fum advanced, bearing 4 *per cent.* intereft. Were the

(a) When the amount of intereft, payable for a fum obtained by felling a 4 *per cent.* capital, is the fame with the
amount of intereft, payable for an equal fum obtained by felling a 3 *per cent.* capital, which is nearly the prefent cafe,
poftponing, in the manner I have propofed, the redemption of
the former, becomes as indifferent as it would be to poftpone
in the fame manner the redemption of any 3 *per cents.*

interest

intereſt in this caſe made irreducible, and the capital incapable of being redeemed without at the ſame time redeeming four times as much of the 3 *per ct.* or ſome other ſtocks, an increaſe of value would be communicated to it which would render all DOUCEURS unneceſſary. For it would be a capital, the redemption of which could not be completed without diſcharging in all FORTY (*a*) MILLIONS of the public debts.———I cannot doubt but that, in theſe circumſtances (ſuppoſing the price of the 3 *per cents.* to continue near 78) a 100 l. in money would be given for 100 l. in ſuch a ſtock, and the whole extravagant expence of ſhort annuities, lotteries, and artificial capitals would be ſaved.

(*a*) In this caſe only a FIFTH of the *ſurplus* to be at any time employed in redeeming debts could be applied to the redemption of this *particular* loan. The reſt after nine years might be employed in redeeming the 4 *per cent.* ſtock created laſt year; or jointly with it, ſuch parts of future loans bearing high intereſt, as, in borrowing on the ſame plan, might be left redeemable. And thus no obligation would ariſe from this mode of borrowing to prefer the redemption of 3 *per cents.* to the redemption of capitals bearing higher intereſt. In particular; had this been the plan of borrowing through the laſt war, all ſurplus monies might have been ever ſince employed intirely in paying off 4, 4½ and 5 *per cent.* capitals preferably to any others; and at the ſame time, no *douceurs* would have been granted in order to procure the loans, no artificial debt contracted, or extraordinary charge incurred.

In

In fhort. With the aid of fuch regulations as thofe now propofed, EIGHT MILLIONS might this year be borrowed (fuppofing the 3 *per cents.* not lower than 78 or 77) *probably* at an intereft of 4 *per cent.*, but *certainly* at an intereft an EIGHTH or a QUARTER higher, without offering any *premiums.* Whereas, if no fuch regulations are eftablifhed, either an artificial debt of near (*a*) *two millions and a half* muft be created ; or 5 *per cent.* for 15 or 20 years certain, together with the profits of a lottery, muft be given ; and a new tax laid which will produce 400,000 l. *per ann.*

It may deferve to be added, that an unprofperous ftate of public affairs, and apprehenfions of public danger, would have a tendency, by placing the redemption of our debts at a greater diftance, to promote, rather than obftruct the fuccefs of fchemes attended with fuch regulations.

There remains one propofal more on this fubject which I wifh may be attended to.

(*a*) Should this be difregarded, and a long annuity offered, as a *douceur*, of 1½ *per cent.* for 90 or 100 years, *eight millions* might perhaps be borrowed at an intereft, including the long annuity, of 4½ *per cent.* even though the 3 *per cents.* fhould fall as low as 73.—And this, probably, would be the very fcheme a minifter would prefer, who, minding chiefly prefent eafe, did not care how much he burdened the nation hereafter.

I have

I have obferved, that our reductions of interest have been the effect of too narrow a policy. It feems to me, that one of the beft meafures that could now be adopted, would be to undo what we have done in this inftance, by reftoring the *3 per cent.* capitals to a higher intereft, and making this reftoration, one of the means of raifing the neceffary fupplies. That this is practicable, and that it would be advantageous, will appear from the following fcheme, and obfervations.

For 20 l. in money, let 110 l. ftock bearing $3\frac{1}{2}$ *per cent.* intereft, be offered, in exchange for every 100 l. of the *3 per cent.* ftocks ; and let the new $3\frac{1}{2}$ *per cent.* ftock be capable of being redeemed at any time, but never under *par*, unlefs when the price of the *3 per cents.* happens to be below 85 l.—By this fcheme the public would procure 20 l. from the converfion of every 100 l. *3 per cent.* ftock into 110 l. ftock carrying $3\frac{1}{2}$ *per cent.* ; or FIVE MILLIONS from the converfion of TWENTY-FIVE MILLIONS. The new *additional* capital would be only TWO MILLIONS AND A HALF, (or 10 *per cent.* of the old capital) ; and the *additional* intereft would be 17 s. (that is, a half *per cent.* added to 7 s. the intereft of 10 l. at $3\frac{1}{2}$ *per cent.*) for every 20 l. advanced ; or $4\frac{1}{4}$ *per cent.* for the whole loan.

That fuch a fcheme would afford ample encouragement to fubfcriptions, fuppofing the *3 per cents.*

cents. at or near 78, will appear from considering, that the intereſt offered is above a *quarter per cent.* more than could be made by purchaſing any perpetual annuities, and at the ſame time, in conſequence of forming a part of the intereſt of a THREE AND A HALF *per cent.* capital, is incapable of reduction, and therefore nearly on an equal footing with the intereſt of any 3 *per cent.* capital.——But to be a little more explicit.

The new capital of 110 l. bearing 3½ *per cent.* intereſt would be better than the 100 l. THREE *per cent.* capitals for which it would be ſubſtituted, in the following reſpects.——1ſt. It would carry 17 s. *per ann.* more intereſt; and ſuch an intereſt, when the price of an annuity of 3 l. is 78 l., ought to be worth 22 l. 2 s. The additional intereſt, therefore, would be diſpoſed of at 2 l. 2 s. for every ſum of 22 l. 2 s. (or at 9½ *per cent.*) leſs than its true value, compared with the price of the 3 *per cent.* annuities.

Secondly. The 3 *per cents.* when *peace* comes, will probably be capable of being redeemed at 88 l. (*a*) But this ſtock, in the ſame circumſtances, muſt be redeemed at *par.* It will, therefore, produce 12 l. more in every 100 l. at redemption. Add the 10 l. additional ſtock; and the whole additional ſum to be received at redemption

(*a*) In 1774, a million of the 3 *per cents.* was redeemed at this price; and in 1772, a million and a half at 90.

will

will be 22 l.——There will, therefore, be a profit
at redemption of 10l. *per cent.* of the money advanced ; and this profit deferves the more notice,
becaufe the ftock to which it is annexed, being redeemable at any time, and bearing a higher intereft than the 3 *per cents.* will be felected for redemption before them ; and therefore its price
will be fo much the more likely always to keep
near *par.*—Setting afide, however, this advantage,
and fuppofing only the 20l. advanced likely to
be received at redemption, it may be found by calculating in the manner explained in p. 194, &c.
that the fubftitution of 110l. ftock carrying THREE
AND A HALF *per cent.* for 100 l. carrying THREE
per cent., or, in other words, that 20 l. to be received fome time hereafter, befides an annuity
of 17s. for the intermediate time, is worth in
prefent money more than 20 l., reckoning compound intereft at 4 *per cent.*

Such a fcheme, therefore, in whatever way its
value was rightly calculated, would appear to
offer an advantageous bargain. Should there,
however, be reafon to fear that the public might
judge otherwife ; or fhould the 3 *per cents.* be at
74 or 75, the value might be eafily increafed
near nine *per cent.* by making the fubftituted
ftock 112 l. inftead of 110 l. in which cafe, the
intereft for the 20 l. advanced would become

18 s.

18 s. 5 d. *per ann.*, or a little more than four and a half *per cent.* inſtead of *four and a quarter.*

The advantages to the public which would ariſe from ſuch a ſcheme are——ıſt. That it would be one of the beſt preparations for meaſures that muſt ſome time or other be entered into for putting the public debts into a *fixed* courſe of redemption. (*a*)——In conſequence of being raiſed to a higher intereſt, a conſiderable part of them would be made capable of being redeemed with more eaſe and expedition; and for this reaſon, it is certain that, if there remains a poſſibility of our eſcaping

(*a*) I mean ſuch a courſe of redemption as ſhould not be liable to interruption by a war; or, as would be the effect of the eſtabliſhment of ſuch an unalienable *ſinking* fund as has been deſcribed in the *Appeal to the Public on the Subject of the National Debt,* and the *Obſervations on reverſionary Payments.*——Nothing can ſave us from bankruptcy but ſuch a fund; and were it eſtabliſhed, the 3 *per cents.,* when they came to be redeemed, would ſoon riſe to *par*; and, conſequently, the obligation implied in this ſcheme to pay a part of them at *par* would occaſion no additional expence. It is, however, ſo little to be expected, that ſuch a fund will be ever eſtabliſhed, that it would have been folly to have made the calculation given above, on any ſuppoſition leſs favourable, than that the 3 *per cents.* will bear the ſame price after the preſent war, that they bore after the laſt; and that we ſhall go on as we have hitherto done, paying off a *million,* or a *million and a half,* now and then in a time of peace.

ing a public bankruptcy, the time muſt come when we ſhall wiſh all our debts bore a high intereſt. (*b*)

Secondly. A capital of TWO MILLIONS AND A HALF would be ſaved in raiſing FIVE MILLIONS. That is; the nation in procuring *five millions* would incur a debt of only *half* that ſum; and inſtead of having a QUARTER or a THIRD *more* to pay at redemption than had been received, it would have ONE HALF *leſs* to pay.

Thirdly. Such a ſcheme would keep up public credit; and, by its neceſſary operation, contribute to carry *itſelf* into execution. For the advantages attending it being grounded entirely upon the old 3 *per cent.* ſtocks, few at ſuch a time would chuſe to ſell them, but many would be induced to buy; and, conſequently, their price would be advanced, contrary to the common effect of public loans.——Theſe ſeem to me advantages ſo un-

---

(*b*) The converſion of a 3 *per cent.* ſtock into a 3½ *per cent.* ſtock gives the ſame advantage in redeeming it, that the power of redeeming it at 85¾ for every 100 l. would give.——A million *per ann.* ſurplus would redeem 114 millions and a quarter of the latter ſtock in the ſame time, and therefore at the ſame expence, that it would redeem 100 millions of the former. I ſuppoſe here the 3 *per cents.* paid at *par*; and this I have before obſerved will be found to be neceſſary ſhould a time (ſcarcely the object of hope) ever come when government will ſet itſelf in earneſt and with any effect to pay the public debts.

Q   ſpeakably

fpeakably important, that I cannot but think it
would be right to go to fome extraordinary expence, in making at leaft one experiment of this
kind. If, in confequence of offering high terms
in *one* trial for a fmall fum, fuch an experiment
fhould fucceed, it might be renewed on lower
terms; and the way might be difcovered of managing, in the beft manner, larger loans on the fame
plan.——I cannot help thinking indeed, that it
would be found that in this way great fums might
be raifed without creating *any* new capitals, or
making any addition to the public debts. I fancy,
for inftance, that few, when the 3 *per cents.* are
about 78, would fcruple to pay 25l. for the converfion of 100l. THREE *per cent.* ftock into a 100l.
FOUR *per cent.* ftock, provided this laft ftock was
not to become redeemable till THIRTY or FORTY
MILLIONS of our prefent debts have been difcharged: And fuppofing this true, money for public fervices would be raifed at 4 *per cent.* or at an
intereft nearly as low as poffible; and, at the fame
time, a fum equal to the whole money advanced
would be faved. But were it neceffary to take for
fuch a fubftitution 24l. or even 23l. (that is, to
pay about 4¼ *per cent.* for money) the gain, if our
debts are ever to be redeemed, would abundantly
overbalance the increafed expence of intereft.

CORRECTIONS and ADDITIONS.

IN The Second Tract, page 120, after the words *Lent at 4 per cent. in 1746, charged on licences for retailing spirituous liquors, and reduced to 3 per cent. by 23d of George II. 1749,* add, *and consisting of old Exchequer Bills then cancelled and converted into a debt from Government to the Bank, for which the Bank was allowed to add to its capital an equal sum by 19th George II. Ch. 6.*

In page 128, instead of the words, *In 1751, certain Exchequer tallies and orders, amounting to 129,750l.* read, *In 1751, the remainder of certain Exchequer tallies and orders charged on the duties on wrought plate, and amounting to 129,750l.*

Page 136, line 17, instead of 1758 read 1757.

Page 137, line 2d from the bottom, for 205,000l. read 215,000l.

Page 139, for 17.7401,32l. read 17.701,324l.

Page 144, after *Exchequer Bills charged on a duty upon victuallers by 12th Geo. I. 1726,* add, *and afterwards by 16th Geo. II. 1743, charged on the duties on licences for retailing spirituous liquors. Now included in the Bank Capital by 19th Geo. II. Ch. 6.*

[216]

Page 144, Note (*b*) after the words, *In this account I have omitted a million borrowed in* 1734, add, *and half a million borrowed in* 1736 ; *because these debts had for some time been in a fixed course of redemption by the salt-duties.*

In page 145, line 2d, for 10.639,793l. read 10.739,793l.—Ibid. line 10th, for 146.582,844l. read 146.682,844l.—Ib. line 12th, for 15.639,793l. read 15.739,793l.——Ibid. note, line 2d, for 1.118,000l. read 1.218,000l.

P. 147. For 146.582,844l. read 146.682,844l. —For 71.505,580l. read 71.605,580l.—And for 10.639,793l. read 10.739,793.

F I N I S.

N. B. The Sum borrowed is always fuppofed FIVE M₎dated to any other
Price of the 3 *per*

	OLD SCHEME₎f loans by changing the · ſtocks to ſtocks bearing ereſt.		
	I.	II.	
	Scheme defcrib-ed Page 182.	Scheme def₂c9. ed Page 18:	See Page 214.
	£.	£. I.	IX. £.
SUM ADVANCED - -	5.000,000	5.000,C000	5.000,000
NEW CAPITAL, or fum } payable at redemption }	5.000,000	6.343,9000	— 0 —
Intereſt offered - - -	3 *per cent.*	3 *per cent.*	4 *per cent.*
ARTIFICIAL CAPITAL, or } fum payable at redemp- tion more than the value received - - - }	1.200,000	1.343,C—	— 0 —
DOUCEURS confiſting of ad- } ditional capitals - - }	— 0 —	1.343,C—	— 0 —
Short Annuity worth -	1.200,000	— 0 —	— 0 —
Lottery worth - - -	— 0 —	150,C—	— 0 —
ANNUAL CHARGE. Perpetual - - - - -	150,000	190,500	200,000
Temporary - - - -	100,000 For lives or 17 yrs.	— 0 —	— 0 —
Total of Annual Charge	250,000	190,500	200,000

This Scheme may be altered to avoid the artificial Capital .e 4th or 5th Scheme.

Page 144, Note (*b*) after the words, *In this account I have omitted a million borrowed in* 1734, add, *and half a million borrowed in* 1736 ; *because these debts had for some time been in a fixed course of redemption by the salt-duties.*

In page 145, line 2d, for 10.639,793l. read 10.739,793l.—Ibid. line 10th, for 146.582,844l. read 146.682,844l.—Ib. line 12th, for 15.639,793l. read 15.739,793l.——Ibid. note, line 2d, for 1.118,000l. read 1.218,000l.

P. 147. For 146.582,844l. read 146.682,844l. —For 71.505,580l. read 71.605,580l.—And for 10.639,793l. read 10.739,793.

F I N I S.

www.ingramcontent.com/pod-product-compliance
Lightning Source LLC
Chambersburg PA
CBHW030904270326
41929CB00008B/566